Reciprocity in English

Routledge Studies in Germanic Linguistics

Series Editors: Ekkehard König, *Free University Berlin, Germany*
Johan van der Auwera, *Antwerp University, Belgium*

Reciprocity in English

Historical Development and
Synchronic Structure

Florian Haas

Routledge
Taylor & Francis Group
New York   London

First published 2010
by Routledge
711 Third Avenue, New York, NY 10017

Simultaneously published in the UK
by Routledge
2 Park Square, Milton Park, Abingdon, Oxfordshire OX14 4RN

First issued in paperback 2014

Routledge is an imprint of the Taylor and Francis Group, an informa business

© 2010 Taylor & Francis

Typeset in Sabon by IBT Global.

Library of Congress Cataloging in Publication Data
Haas, Florian, 1978-
    Reciprocity in English : historical development and synchronic structure / by Florian Haas.
        p. cm. — (Routledge studies in Germanic linguistics ; 15)
    Includes bibliographical references and index.
    1. English language—Reciprocals. 2. Grammar, Comparative and general—Reciprocals. I. Title.
    PE1398.R43H33 2009
    425—dc22
    2009032555

ISBN 978-0-415-80435-6 (hbk)
ISBN 978-1-138-86850-2 (pbk)
ISBN 978-0-203-85817-2 (ebk)

Contents

Acknowledgments

This book is a heavily revised and shortened version of my PhD thesis, which I submitted to the Faculty of Humanities at the Freie Universität Berlin in 2007 and defended in 2008. My gratitude to those who helped me prepare the thesis thus carries over to this book.

First of all I would like to thank my thesis supervisor Ekkehard König. Without his constant support and encouragement it would have been much more difficult for me to write the dissertation on which this book is based. He did not only propose the topic and the structure of the text, but also shared with me lots of original ideas and observations on reciprocity in English and other languages. Moreover, our joint work on reciprocity in pidgins and creoles had an important influence on my description of reciprocity in English. Apart from his help with the contents, Ekkehard König has provided me with a working environment in which the preparation of a thesis is anything but a solitary business. I could interact with him and the other members of our group whenever I wanted and in this way profit from his experience and knowledge. For all this I am extremely grateful.

I would also like to thank three anonymous reviewers for many helpful comments and suggestions. I am indebted to my second advisor Matthias Hüning for the challenging, but helpful, questions and remarks during the defence and beyond. Thanks are also due to the other members of the dissertation committee: Norbert Dittmar, Carola Emkow and Volker Gast. In the context of a joint talk Elisabeth Stark and Matthias Hüning investigated the historical development of reciprocal marking in Romance and Dutch respectively. Their results, as well as our discussions preceding the talk, also found their way into my own work. Bill Croft offered several detailed and helpful comments in the early stages of writing and has had a lasting impact on my understanding of, and interest in, grammar and grammatical variation. David Denison and Letizia Vezzosi commented on diachronic issues. Lucy Hottmann and Beth Martin helped with the English data. Beth Martin and Andrew Davison improved the readability of the text by changing my non-native wording in a large number of instances. Thank you very much! Furthermore, I thank Volker Gast, Elma Kerz and Katerina Stathi for interesting discussions during the work on joint papers; Ferdinand von Mengden for helping me find my way through Old English texts; Dieter Mindt for making the British National Corpus available to me; Volker Gast, Kristoff Köpke and Wulf von Muellern for sharing with me their experience in using LaTeX for the preparation of an earlier version; and my new colleagues at the Friedrich-Schiller-Universität Jena for providing me with a stimulating environment during the last stages of writing. I should not forget to express my gratitude to Thomas Hanke for his never-ending stock of relevant cross-linguistic observations and general ideas. Our discussions have influenced this text a lot. A very special mention has to be made of my colleague and friend Volker Gast. Although he may not agree with everything I have written, his advice has been invaluable for me. Apart from constant encouragement and readiness to read my drafts and to assist me in any other possible way, Volker has repeatedly urged me to question assumptions that I would otherwise have accepted too easily. In the preparation of a joint paper and beyond we have had controversial but productive discussions both on specific issues relating to reciprocity and general theoretical questions. Thanks for everything! The usual disclaimer applies.

Thanks are also due to the *Sonderforschungsbereich* 447 for financial support during the preparation of parts of the chapter on historical development and to the ERASMUS programme (and my tutor Thomas Kotschi) for funding the postgraduate study course 'European Master's Degree in Linguistics'. Preparatory research on the typology of reciprocity was carried out at the University of Manchester and in Berlin during this one-year programme. My thanks to Cambridge University Press for giving me permission to include material in Chapter 3 taken from my paper 'The development of English *each other*: Grammaticalization, lexicalization, or both?' published in *English Language and Linguistics*, 11.1 (Cambridge University Press). I also thank Mira Ariel for permitting me to cite from her unpublished paper, 'The making of a construction: From reflexive marking to lower transitivity'.

Finally, I would like to thank my parents Helga and Willibrord Haas for their loving support and optimism over the years. This book is dedicated to them!

1 Introduction

The linguistic expression of reciprocal situations is a phenomenon that pervades different levels of description, including morphology, syntax, semantics and pragmatics. Furthermore, it provides a challenge for several approaches to language, because the semantics of reciprocal situations is rather complex—two (or more) events which are mirror images of each other—and the fact that the nature of reciprocity is, strictly speaking, not compatible with the linear nature of syntax (Haiman, 1985b) is reflected in different ways. Besides these challenges, there are other properties that place reciprocal sentences in a hybrid position with respect to a number of dichotomies normally taken to be categorical. These include the fact that two (or more) participants each fulfil two roles and also that the subevents making up a reciprocal situation may be regarded by speakers and hearers as a single event.

In fact, the main focus of this volume will be on aspects of reciprocity that have in some way to do with this hybrid position that reciprocity adopts with respect to a number of related parameters: intransitive–transitive, single event–distinct events, collective–distributive. The focus is also on these aspects due to the scarcity of previous research, which has instead concentrated on working out a fine-grained categorization of the situation types compatible with the reciprocal expressions *each other* and *one another* and on explicating all of the interpretative possibilities in a formal language. The expressions *each other* and *one another* have also been much discussed in the framework of Binding Theory, with a clear focus on their locality constraints. In contrast to the rich literature on the aforementioned topics, an analysis of the grammar of reciprocity in English which takes into account the hybridity with respect to transitivity, the collective–distributive contrast and event construal has not yet received more than cursory treatment in the literature.

The same holds for investigations on so-called 'symmetric predicates', Gleitman et al. (1996) being an exception. What is still lacking today is a comprehensive study that brings together different issues, such as the meaning and grammatical behaviour of symmetric predicates, the choice between reciprocal situation types, the competition between reciprocal strategies for the expression of a given state of affairs and the historical development of reciprocal markers. With the present study I want to make a step in this direction.

It will be argued that the constructions that express reciprocity in Present-day English are not distributed randomly, but rather form a system in which different forms compete with each other. (The details of this idea will be laid out in Chapter 5.) In Chapter 3 we will track how this system has developed in the history of English. To be sure, it would of course be misleading to claim that Present-day English has a regular system of expressing reciprocity, whereas the linguistic expression of such situations in older stages of English was unsystematic. At every stage of the language there was *some* kind of system of reciprocal constructions. Yet, from the point of view of grammatical constructions becoming more fixed formally, on the one hand, and the number of different constructions being gradually reduced to a well-organized subset on the other, we can indeed observe a change. This change involves at least the following aspects: what will be called the 'basic reciprocal construction', the construction containing the expression *each other/one another*, emerges as a result of grammaticalization and lexicalization. Furthermore, the basic reciprocal construction does not become too specialized semantically and as a result interacts with the two other main types of reciprocal construction in such a way that in all contexts a functional differentiation is possible.

The phrase 'reciprocity in English' does not restrict us to a particular type of linguistic expression, since the semantic concept of reciprocity may be encoded by various formal expression types, including—among other things—verbs part of whose lexical meaning is a reciprocal relation, specialized markers like *each other* and *one another* and several non-specialized ways of spelling out the reciprocal situation, e.g. clause conjunction. One aspect that has been approached mainly in the context of typological research is the relation between reciprocity and other semantic concepts such as collectivity and reflexivity. It has been observed that in many languages reciprocity, on the one hand, and one of the latter two concepts on the other, are expressed by the same marker (see, for instance, Lichtenberk, 1985; Dench, 1987; Seidl and Dimitriadis, 2003; Maslova and Nedjalkov, 2005; Bril, 2005). Given that in English there is no inflectional affix expressing collectivity and given that reflexive pronouns do not serve as markers of reciprocity, studies on reciprocity specialized on English have not normally been concerned with the relation between these domains. The relationship between reciprocity and collectivity in particular will be a major focus of my study.

RECIPROCITY AND SYMMETRIC PREDICATES: A VERY BRIEF INTRODUCTION

Reciprocal situations may be linguistically expressed by a variety of grammatical as well as lexical means, both across languages and within a single

language (for overviews of cross-linguistic variation, see König and Kokutani, 2006; Evans, 2008).[1] In English the expression of reciprocity is not
restricted to a single strategy either. We will see, however, that in the course
of the history of the language some strategies became impossible (e.g. the
reciprocal use of reflexive pronouns) and others have received a specialized
meaning that the default strategy—the 'reciprocals' *each other* and *one
another*—is not able to convey. The latter point concerns, for example, the
adverb *together* and strategies of the type *each . . . the other.*

What we seem to find in every language is a limited set of predicates
which contain a reciprocal component within their lexical meaning ('symmetric predicates') and often do not (have to) combine with a grammatical
reciprocal marker. These predicates denote concepts such as social interaction ('meet'), similarity ('be similar'), local relations ('intersect', 'be next
to') and kinship ('cousin'). Predicates which are prototypically used for
reciprocal situations (hence 'prototypically reciprocal predicates') without
entailing symmetry in their meaning often behave similarly. These include
verbs like English *kiss* and *embrace.*

In English, symmetric and prototypically reciprocal predicates are
characterized by their special syntactic behaviour: they alternate between
different argument realization patterns and do not require the reciprocal (*each other/one another*) as an object argument. It depends on one's
perspective whether the use of symmetric and prototypically reciprocal
predicates counts as an independent reciprocal strategy or not (see Evans,
2008), but in any case they interact and compete with the unquestionable
reciprocal strategies and should therefore be included in a comprehensive
analysis.

THEORETICAL BACKGROUND

Introduction

In my view, theories should be evaluated both in terms of their fundamental principles (and the conceptual and empirical justification of the latter)
and the way in which they cope with specific phenomena. Although these
two ways of evaluating a theoretical framework are clearly related in that
for a theory to be successful it should be necessary for both of them to
be convincing, it is nevertheless helpful to examine them one by one. In
this way I will make clear in the following why from a general theoretical point of view this book should be guided by the assumptions of the
usage-based model. In the remainder of the book, the focus will rather
be on specific analyses and facts, abstracting away from more general
theoretical issues.

Symmetric predicates and reciprocal constructions have received a
great deal of attention from linguists working in the generative grammar

tradition and those working in the field of formal semantics. In fact, most of the studies dealing with English display these points of view. Formal semantic treatments of symmetric predicates and reciprocal sentences are numerous and often very informative. The fact that my own use of formal meaning representations is rather modest is not meant to suggest that the relevant studies are useless. Very often, however, the relevant semantic distinctions can be described equally well in a more informal manner and a formal semantic representation would arguably not add insights into the issues that I will be dealing with in this study.[2] As far as the generatively oriented literature is concerned, a number of generalizations presented in this book will take issue with generative analyses of reciprocal constructions. In order to get the basic issues out of the way, let me point out in the following why I consider this framework problematic from a more general point of view.

Language Acquisition and 'Plato's Problem'

Many of the principles and much of the machinery of Mainstream Generative Grammar (MGG)[3] rest on the conjecture that the linguistic input that children get is not sufficient for acquiring the complexities of syntax. The supposition is commonly called 'poverty of the stimulus' or 'Plato's problem'. On the basis of the seemingly axiomatic status of this hypothesis, the innateness of a Universal Grammar (UG), including a number of well-known principles and abstract structures has been postulated (cf. Boas, 1984: 19–22). However, as has repeatedly been pointed out (cf. Pullum and Scholz, 2002; Tomasello, 2003, 2005; Clark, 2009: 394–396) the poverty-of-the-stimulus argument is contradicted by child language research showing that infants actually receive sufficient input in order to construct a grammar. Their language acquisition involves a gradual process of abstracting away from concrete patterns heard in the input and in this way building up a system of more abstract patterns without having to revert to innate structures (cf. Bates, 1998; Tomasello, 2003, 2005; Goldberg, 2005: 69–92).

Underlying Structures and Derivational Operations

Abstract categories and multilevel sentence representations are an essential component of MGG. The need for representations in which a sentence is represented on different levels, the surface form of the sentence being derived from a more basic or 'underlying' structure, rests upon a number of hypotheses concerning the relation (or 'interface') between the form and the meaning of a sentence (cf. Culicover and Jackendoff, 2005: 46–50; Moravcsik, 2006: 180–183). The need for derivations including movement operations and abstract categories as well as the problems arising from this type of analysis vanish if one accepts that the relation between form and meaning is more direct, viz. syntactic structures bear meaning in the same way that words bear meaning, although the meaning is typically less abstract in the latter case.

Linguistics as a Cognitive Science

A major aspect of the so-called 'Chomskyan revolution' (see Koerner, 1994) in linguistics concerned the status of linguistics as a science examining the human language faculty. An important new insight was that language is a psychological phenomenon and had to be treated as such in linguistic investigation. Accordingly, the speakers' linguistic competence has to be characterized with reference to the psychological processes that are responsible for language production and comprehension as well as its mental representation. Interestingly, generative linguistics does not seem to have contributed very much to this research programme. The actual analyses and the design of the grammatical models have become farther and farther removed from a plausible account of the psychological processes and representations involved, including both higher-level mental operations and what we know about the structure of the human brain (this point is made from different perspectives in Bates and Goodman, 1997; Jackendoff, 2002; Ritter, 2005; Lieberman, 2005; Itkonen, 2005: 44–45, 131; Dąbrowska, 2006; Culicover and Jackendoff, 2006: 415). Lieberman (2000), for example, concludes that '[g]iven our current knowledge concerning neural plasticity and phenotypic organization of the details of neural circuitry, it is most unlikely a detailed Chomskyan Universal Grammar is instantiated in the human brain' (69).[4]

The Description and Explanation of Typological Variation

Although it would be incorrect to say that MGG has been worked out on the basis of English exclusively (see Newmeyer, 1980: 48–49; 1983: 67–72; 2005: 28–72), the bulk of work which has led to assumptions concerning the architecture of the human language faculty has been carried out on a rather small number of languages including English, German, Dutch, Italian and French. In this way a large number of fine-grained observations and generalizations have been made. Yet, the problem is that one of the aims of MGG has always been to give a characterization of UG, that is, the human linguistic competence underlying all possible—and thus of course all existing—languages. It has been argued that the architecture of UG would look very different if a more 'exotic' language had been taken as a starting point (Van Valin and LaPolla, 1997; Croft, 2001: 29–47; Van Valin, 2005). Furthermore, if one investigates the structural properties of a large number of languages, representing the variety that exists, the assumption of a small number of innate categories and structures becomes highly problematic, or they would have to be very abstract (see Croft, 2001). Accordingly, proposals for an actual list of parameters in the sense of Principles and Parameters Theory differ markedly (see Newmeyer, 2005: 81–83; Haspelmath, 2008b: 80–86).

The Locus of Language Change

Generative grammar takes child language acquisition to be the only place where languages change: children get triggers from the linguistic input and in conjunction with their innate knowledge build up their grammatical system. From time to time children misanalyze the structures they hear and keep the wrongly analyzed structures in their grammar. In this way the grammar of a speaker undergoes a change. There are serious problems with this view. Firstly, child language research shows that children do misanalyze their input, but do not usually retain these analyses (Clark, 2009: 393–394). Secondly, sociolinguistic investigations into language change have demonstrated that it is adults rather than children who innovate, retain and propagate linguistic changes (e.g. Milroy and Milroy, 1985; see Croft, 1995: 520; 2000: 46–59; Aitchison 2001: 210 for summaries of the relevant studies and discussion).

The Usage-Based Model

My view of the phenomena under discussion—reciprocal constructions—follows the assumptions of the usage-based model (for a concise summary of arguments in favour of this approach, see Bybee and McClelland, 2005) and (usage-based) construction grammar (cf. Goldberg 1995, 2005; Croft, 2001; Michaelis, 2003). Construction grammar takes grammar to be a structured inventory of form-meaning pairings, i.e. constructions.

The principles advocated in these frameworks that will turn out to be relevant to my discussion of symmetric predicates and reciprocal constructions are the following:

(1) Grammar is shaped by language use. Therefore, an adequate explanation of the observed patterns can only be achieved if conditions of use are taken into account.
(2) Linguistic competence involves knowledge of both item-specific information and abstract patterns, whereby there is not a categorical but a gradual difference between the two types of knowledge.[5]
(3) The frequency of complex words and constructions in speech affects the way in which they are represented and processed.
(4) Subtle semantic and pragmatic differences between variant grammatical structures are highly relevant to the analysis of syntax, including their mental representation and processing.

The generalizations that will be made in the remainder of this book will be led by the aforementioned assumptions. Accordingly, issues like the search for semantic contrasts between reciprocal constructions will be more prominent than in many of the previous studies on reciprocity. In turn, some other aspects like conditions on 'binding', i.e. the syntactic relation between the reciprocals *each other/one another* and their antecedent, or the semantics of reciprocal situation types, will be touched on only in passing. The following section outlines the structure of the book.

OUTLINE AND OBJECTIVES

After a descriptive survey of reciprocity in Present-day English (hence-forth PDE) (Chapter 2), including pointers to previous research, I present a synopsis of the historical development of reciprocal strategies (Chapter 3). Here, the focus will be on the changes that are responsible for the situation in PDE: reduction of competing strategies and thus the ongoing grammaticalization of the 'basic reciprocal strategy' involving *each other* and *one another*.

Chapter 4 concentrates on those verbs in English that are able to express reciprocal situations without special formal marking: symmetric and pro-totypically reciprocal predicates. Specifically, I will explore the different factors that determine the use of the different possible argument struc-tures that these verbs may occur in. After critically summarizing previ-ous research on this issue, I will consider corpus data of the verb *meet*. Given a number of observations on the interaction between the meaning of symmetric verbs and the constructions they occur in, I will reconsider the notion of 'symmetric verb' and argue that on closer inspection the class of verb (uses) that can be characterized as 'symmetric' in the logical sense commonly employed is more marginal than one might expect.

Chapter 5 focuses on the status of the reciprocal *each other* and its rela-tion to other reciprocal strategies in the grammar of PDE. It is shown that an adequate analysis of the meaning of the reciprocal can only be achieved if we examine its competition with other reciprocal strategies and the moti-vations for choosing one or the other strategy in a given context. In this regard I will relate the distribution of the English reciprocal to typologi-cal observations on middle marking and event construal. Specifically, it is argued that a major determining factor in the choice between reciprocal strategies is the construal of a reciprocal situation as a single event (typi-cally correlating with a collective interpretation of the participants) or as distinct events (typically going together with a distributive interpretation of the participants).

One of the strategies that are part of this system is the use of symmetric or prototypically reciprocal predicates without dedicated reciprocal mark-ing as discussed in Chapter 4. The conditions on the use of symmetric and prototypically reciprocal verbs and the constructions they occur in will be related to those of the basic reciprocal construction and other strategies of expressing reciprocity.

A summarizing section of the end of Chapter 5 will conclude this book, relating the findings of the preceding discussion to each other and in this way attempting an integrative view of how English grammar deals with the concept of reciprocity.

2 Reciprocity in English

An Overview of the Facts and Previous Research

2.1 INTRODUCTION

This chapter firstly offers a descriptive overview of how reciprocal situations are expressed in PDE and also relates certain phenomena to previous research. The subsequent chapters will then address more specific issues, either by building on the data presented in this chapter or by adding more data. This chapter will thus constitute the descriptive basis on which later generalizations will be made.

As far as the data in this chapter and the remainder of the study are concerned, I will for the most part avoid using constructed examples and employ authentic data instead. These come from a number of contemporary British and American novels, as well as PDE corpora, mainly the British National Corpus (BNC),[1] and the Internet.[2] If I carry out frequency counts in order to support a point, I will mainly use the BNC and the Corpus of Contemporary American English (COCA)[3] for PDE data and the Helsinki Corpus as well as the Lampeter Corpus for older stages of English (see the respective chapters for details). If not marked otherwise, references are to the BNC.

2.2 TERMINOLOGY

The Expression of Reciprocal Situations

In this study, the means of expressing a reciprocal situation are generally termed CONSTRUCTIONS. Thus it is acknowledged that, strictly speaking, reciprocity is never expressed by a single, isolated expression, but by a syntactic configuration of which a RECIPROCAL MARKER is only a part. In this way, 'reciprocal marker' is merely shorthand for the most salient part of a reciprocal construction.

Again abstracting away from the fact that their reciprocal meaning only arises when they are part of a larger syntactic configuration, I call the reciprocal markers *each other* and *one another* RECIPROCALS. Sentences that—by whatever means—express a RECIPROCAL SITUATION are referred to as RECIPROCAL SENTENCES. Defining the semantics of a 'reciprocal situation' is not at all a trivial task, especially if situations with more than two participants are taken into account. For the time being let us follow the preliminary definition in (1), which is restricted to two-participant situations:

> (1) A reciprocal situation is defined as a situation with at least two participants (A, B) in which the relation between A and B is the same as the one between B and A.

The individuals that are involved in the reciprocal situation as expressed by a reciprocal sentence will be called PARTICIPANTS. Since it is mainly reciprocal sentences that are discussed here anyway, I will not make use of the more specialized term 'reciprocant' (cf. also the term 'mutuant' in Haspelmath, 2007).

Symmetric and Prototypically Reciprocal Predicates

Coming to the realm of symmetric predicates and related phenomena, there is no agreement on a standard terminology in the literature. The verbs at issue have been variously termed 'symmetric', 'inherently symmetric', 'irreducibly symmetric', 'inherently reciprocal', 'reciprocal' and 'lexical reciprocal', to name just some terms that one comes across. On the one hand, I follow the classical approach of viewing symmetry as a property of predicates, as opposed to considering it a property of reciprocal sentences and situations (see, for instance, Lakoff and Peters, 1969). On the other hand, I will use the terms SYMMETRIC and ASYMMETRIC also in relation to the situations expressed by the relevant verbs in Chapter 4. Apart from this, I distinguish two different verb classes: SYMMETRIC verbs and PROTYPICALLY RECIPROCAL verbs (cf. König and Kokutani, 2006: 273 on the need for drawing a distinction here). Although I will argue in Chapter 4 that it would be misleading to assume the strict mathematical property of symmetry for 'symmetric predicates', the two classes are still crucially different. Symmetric verbs such as *marry* and *intersect* have a lexical meaning part of which is the bidirectional relation characteristic of reciprocal situations. Prototypically reciprocal verbs, by contrast, do not have such a meaning component. What makes them special with respect to ordinary transitive verbs is the fact that they are very frequently (and thus prototypically) used in reciprocal contexts. Examples of the latter type are *embrace* and *kiss*.[4]

2.3 A BRIEF SURVEY OF RECIPROCAL STRATEGIES

Clause Coordination

English, like probably any other language, can spell out a reciprocal situation in different non-grammaticalized ways. In (2), the characteristic bidirectionality of a reciprocal situation is spelled out by asserting both directions individually, each in a clause on its own.

(2) You help us, we help you. [McEwan, Saturday, 105]

A more thorough discussion of this strategy is given in section 2.5.

Noun Phrase Repetition

It is also possible to repeat not the whole clause with reversed roles, but rather the antecedent and thus end up with identical noun phrases in the relevant argument slots. This is illustrated in (3).

(3) a. Human beings did it to human beings, [. . .] [Auster, Oracle Night, 78]
b. Men understand men, [. . .] [Updike, Villages, 212]
c. For the most part Great Russians were fighting Great Russians, [. . .] [A64 120]

This type of noun phrase repetition is mainly used in generic contexts. Note that a reciprocal reading is actually easier to arrive at in (3) if the repeated noun phrases have generic reference. Generic noun phrases refer to the whole class of individuals that belong to the relevant category and thus the two noun phrases cannot denote two distinct sets of the same type. For this reason, the first and the second noun phrases need to be interpreted as co-referential.

Noun phrase repetition with non-generic reference is different. Consider example (3) a. Since the verb (*do*) is in the simple past, thus describing a specific and completed event in the past, non-generic reference of the two instances of *human beings* is strongly suggested. It now becomes possible for the sentence to be interpreted in such a way that one group of human beings did something to a distinct, second set of human beings, a non-reciprocal reading of (3) a. Such a reading is much harder to get for a sentence like (3) b., in which the present tense of the verb *understand* favours a generic interpretation. Summing up, the noun repetition strategy is quite marginal in the grammar of reciprocity, being mainly restricted to generic statements.

The [N Prep N] Construction

A slightly different reciprocal strategy, which also involves the repetition of a noun, is illustrated by the following examples:

(4) a. [. . .] they sat face to face in the restaurant car [. . .] [Lodge, Small World, 220]

b. Arm in arm the girls walked towards Westminster Bridge. [McEwan, Atonement, 290]

In (4) a local configuration in which two body parts stand in a reciprocal relation with each other is expressed via the structure [N Prep N] in an adjunct position, the two nouns being identical (see König and Moyse-Faurie, 2009 for examples from other languages). Jackendoff (2008) notes that the construction [N *to* N], which he describes as having to do with 'close contact or juxtaposition of similar parts of similar objects, particularly body parts' (16), is idiosyncratic in usage and restricted in productivity (see also Hurst and Nordlinger, forthcoming). Thus, on the one hand it cannot be extended to any body part: ?*foot to foot*, ?*finger to finger*, *wrist to wrist, ?*arm to arm*, ?*lip to lip* (Jackendoff's judgments). On the other hand, the structure becomes even less acceptable or takes on a different meaning if it is extended to nouns that are not human body parts. The examples in (5) do not seem to be possible with the meaning just described:

(5) a. ?*The two envelopes lay on the table flap to flap.
    b. ?*The cars sat in the parking lot trunk to trunk.
    c. ?*The houses are facing each other, porch to porch.

Besides, a phrase like *side to side* cannot express juxtaposition of two objects, but rather denotes oscillatory motion (Jackendoff, 2008: 12).

Collective Adverbs

As will be seen in Chapter 3 (section 3.2), it was quite common in earlier stages of English to indicate the reciprocal nature of a situation via adverbs like *together*. In PDE such a strategy is less common and has become restricted to specific verbs, especially *meet* and *fight*. In these cases the employment of the adverb *together* should not be regarded as expressing reciprocity. It rather selects a certain (shade of) meaning of the verb or disambiguates between two or more readings of an ambiguous reciprocal sentence. For example, in (6) a. the use of *together* seems to select the meaning 'come together for a planned meeting'. *Together* in (6) b. disambiguates between the following readings: (a) The meeting relation involves both pairs of older people within the national groups and between them; (b) It involves only pairs of older people within the national groups. The employment of the adverb rules out the (b) reading.

(6) a. Each region has a director and the regional directors meet together as the Branches Committee. [A13 160]
    b. Older people from the Caribbean, China, Asia, and India meet together and have a chance to discuss their culture and their memories. [B3G 269]

c. Night Goblin Netters and Clubbers fight together in order to immobilise and either destroy or capture dangerous creatures. [CMC 1627]

In the case of *fight* in (6) c., the function of *together* is even the selection of a non-reciprocal reading of the sentence: it says that Goblin Netters and Clubbers do not fight among each other, but as a single party against the group of *dangerous creatures*.

Collective Reflexivity

Consider now a structure that at first sight appears to boil down to the reciprocal use of object pronouns or reflexive pronouns.

(7) a. They passed the wine between them [. . .] [McEwan, Atonement, 257]
b. Boldwood was standing near the fire, and he had just noticed that a group of villagers were whispering among themselves. [FRE 2038]

The structure in (7) appears to falsify the widely held claim that neither reflexive pronouns nor simple object pronouns can be used in a reciprocal context in PDE. In view of the following two observations it seems plausible to maintain that reflexives and objective pronouns may not generally be used to express reciprocity, however. Firstly, the seemingly reciprocal uses of *themselves* and *them* (and the corresponding forms in the first and the second person) occur only in a very restricted context, namely when the two expressions follow one of the two prepositions *between* and *among*.[5] Secondly, other languages, including ones for which the reciprocal use of reflexive pronouns is usually said to be excluded, also feature the same phenomenon in the same context, i.e. after semantically similar prepositions. Latin, for instance, is said to have employed this structure as its main reciprocal strategy (cf. Thielmann, 1892: 344–353).

But why is this particular structure compatible with a reciprocal meaning? If we consider the meanings of the prepositions *between* and *among* in combination with a plural pronoun like *themselves*, we can observe that these combinations denote reciprocal relations inside the set of individuals referred to by the pronoun. Crucially, however, it is the preposition and not the pronoun which contributes the reciprocal meaning component. The pronoun retains a reflexive meaning, indicating co-reference between subject and complement. This way of expressing reciprocal situations is called COLLECTIVE REFLEXIVE in Gast and Haas (2008: 321).

Reciprocal 'Pronouns'

The most important way of expressing reciprocity in English is the strategy that employs one of the two expressions *each other* and *one another*:

(8) a. Hadn't they told each other everything? [Eugenides, Middlesex, 27]
    b. [. . .], drivers shouting obscenities at each other, [. . .] [Auster, Oracle Night, 41]

Paradoxically, it is to a large extent unclear whether and, if so, in what way, the two reciprocals differ from each other in use, although this has been a notorious topic in the literature (cf. section 2.4).

The term 'reciprocal pronoun' is the most common one when reference is made to the two expressions in the literature. In fact, *each other* and *one another* seem to behave like other pronouns syntactically, and their meaning, furthermore, does not seem to be too different from reflexive pronouns. In order not to prejudge their meaning and syntactic status, however, I will use the more neutral term 'reciprocal'.

Spell-Out Constructions

The words that make up the two reciprocals *each other* and *one another* can also occur on their own in reciprocal sentences:

(9) a. He felt he was present, as one pleasantry followed another, at a duel. [Updike, Villages, 65]
    b. Stations of the former West Berlin passed one after another. [Eugenides, Middlesex, 40]
    c. Each glanced surreptitiously at the other's reading matter. [Lodge, Small World, 118]

Symmetric and Prototypically Reciprocal Predicates

A limited number of lexical items feature a reciprocal relation either as part of their lexical meaning or as prototypically associated with them. They are usually not combined with a reciprocal:

(10) . . . two air force pilots died when a pair of phantom jets collided, . . . [KRT 4199]

Here also belong most of the nouns that occur in what Hurst and Nordlinger (forthcoming) call 'nominal reciprocal construction' (attested examples from Hurst and Nordlinger, forthcoming):

(11) a. They are having an argument.
    b. Two people in a conversation.
    c. Four girls all having a group hug.
    d. An introduction between people.

Let us now consider these strategies in more detail, beginning with the reciprocals *each other* and *one another*.

2.4 *EACH OTHER* AND *ONE ANOTHER*: THE BASIC RECIPROCAL CONSTRUCTION

The default strategy of expressing reciprocity in PDE employs the expressions *each other* and *one another*. For this reason I will call this the BASIC RECIPROCAL CONSTRUCTION. As will be discussed in more detail in the chapters to come, reciprocal sentences involving verbs that are not of the symmetric or the prototypically reciprocal type mentioned earlier are normally of the basic type and only in certain marked contexts of the spell-out types already discussed. In what follows, the formal and distributional properties of the two reciprocals are described in more detail.

Formal Properties

I consider those expressions to be reciprocals in which the word strings *each other* or *one another* occur in a position that hosts expressions of category noun phrase. This excludes occurrences of the relevant words in sentences where they do not occur adjacent to each other, on the one hand, and those where they do not form a complete noun phrase—e.g. (12)—on the other.

(12) [. . .] although each other place has an interesting story too.[6]

This is not an arbitrary demarcation, but one that filters out exactly those strings *one another* and *each other* that do in fact function as a reciprocal marker, and which can be shown to behave as a lexicalized reciprocal expression.

Perhaps somewhat surprisingly, these complex reciprocal expressions are not subject to reduction or elision processes in any obvious way, something one might expect of a fixed but complex expression. Yet, other properties indicate that the reciprocals are lexemes and not just regular syntagms of two words. Firstly, *each other* and *one another* in the basic reciprocal strategy are formally invariable. It is thus impossible to change their stress pattern or to produce an overtly marked plural form. Similarly, there is no option of adding a determiner to the alterity word *other* in the case of *each other* or to either substitute a definite *the* for the indefinite *an* or simply leave *an* out in the case of *one another*. The formal invariability of the two reciprocals is illustrated in (13)–(14).

(13) a. each óther
  b. *éach other
  c. *each others
  d. *each another
  e. *each the other[7]
  f. *one other

(14) a. one anóther
  b. *óne another

    c. *the one another
    d. *one the other
    e. *one others

The starred forms in these examples are not inconceivable as forms indicating reciprocal situations. In fact, some of the forms were possible earlier in the history of English. For this reason, I take these constraints to indicate that the expressions *each other* and *one another* are in fact invariable and not merely unattested as a result of really being nonsensical.

    A further property of reciprocals that underlines their invariability is the fact that they do not interact with negation in the way the quantifiers *each* and *one* normally do. Compare (15) and (16):

(15) a. Each of the two candidates didn't criticize the other.
     b. Neither of the two candidates criticized the other.
     c. The two candidates didn't criticize each other.
     d. *The two candidates criticized neither other.

(16) a. One of the properties didn't adjoin the other.
     b. None of the properties adjoined the other.
     c. The properties didn't adjoin to one another.
     d. *The properties adjoined to none another.

Although neither *each* nor *one* are positive polarity items in the sense of being incompatible with sentential negation, the alternations between (15) a. and b. and (16) a. and b. show that it is possible for the two words to 'attract' negation. Simplifying slightly,[8] *each* + *not* corresponds to *neither* in (15) a.–b. and *one* + *not* corresponds to *none* in (16) a.–b. Now consider (15) c. with the reciprocal *each other* in object position. It seems that here the invariability of the reciprocal prevents *each* changing its form in accordance with the negation. This is illustrated by the fact that (15) d., where the reciprocal has undergone 'negative attraction', results in ungrammaticality. The same applies to the behaviour of *one* and *one another* in (16).

Distribution

Besides their use as nominal possessors, reciprocals may fill almost every argument position in the clause. Consider the following examples:

(17) a. Then you can all see how each other are doing. [J1C 2286]
     b. While he was at Arista, Charles and I got to know each other well. [A6A 826]
     c. Right, we're going to have an exercise in giving each other positive feedback. [K74 617]

    d. . . . stretching their arms across each other's shoulders so they dance as one . . . [BNU 328]

    e. The gilt-edged market and the foreign exchange market were, and are, influenced by each other, . . . [EC3 1548]

    f. His state of nature is not Hobbes's, for it is not composed of individuals following their natural instincts and living in fear of each other. [ABM 1199]

Some comments concerning the occurrences in subject position are in order. First, it is only the subject position of complement clauses that may host a reciprocal. Second, reciprocals in subject position are often considered to be substandard.[9] Certainly it cannot be denied that reciprocals in subject position do occur. Nevertheless, there is one property of the relevant structure that may indicate that it is not (yet) completely integrated into the system of reciprocal strategies: verb agreement. This point will be taken up further later.

One aspect of their (pro-)noun-like behaviour is the ability of reciprocals to be coordinated with other noun phrases and also to appear in non-canonical positions in the clause, i.e. to be the target of topicalization and focalization operations. The examples in (18) exemplify the first of these points, coordination:

(18) a. [. . .] the moon and the sun, and their distance from us and from each other. [Lodge, Small World, 39]

    b. Newcomers to motherhood and one another, [. . .] [Updike, Villages, 136–137]

Note that the coordinability illustrated in (18) makes English reciprocals distinct from originally reflexive markers like German *sich* or the corresponding items in the Romance and Scandinavian languages, which cannot be coordinated in their reciprocal function (Kemmer, 1993b; Gast and Haas, 2008: 318–319). This is illustrated in (19), the German translations of (18). These sentences are not acceptable if *sich* is taken to mean *each other*:

(19) a. * . . . die Erde und die Sonne, und deren Abstand zu uns und zu sich.

    b. *Anfänger in Bezug auf die Mutterschaft und sich.

The same holds for topicalization and focalization constructions. I use this cover term for all syntactic structures in which, for information-packaging reasons, a noun phrase occurs in a non-canonical position. From the list of structures given in Ward et al. (2002: 1366), preposing (*This one she accepted*), clefts (*It was you who broke it*) and the passive (*The car was taken by Kim*) are conceivable with a reciprocal in the relevant prominent position.[10] It appears that, although relatively rare (the constructions under discussion cannot be found in the BNC), reciprocals in at least cleft and passive structures can be found on the Internet. The two sentences in (20) illustrate cleft constructions involving a reciprocal:

(20) a. It's too bad the script couldn't have ended with the brides realizing that it was each other they truly loved, not their boring boyfriends, ... [11]

   b. As far as each other is concerned they have both been travelling at high speed. [12]

As for passives, we have to distinguish between reciprocals in the subject position of passives, on the one hand, and the optional *by*-phrase (or 'demoted subject'), on the other. While the latter position can host reciprocals—see (17) e. and (21) for random examples and Bolinger (1987: 11) for constructed sentences—passive sentences with a reciprocal in subject position do not occur.

(21) a. Any other consumables (punctures, bulbs etc) are to be paid for by each other [...] [13]

   b. The contestants were less worried by the course than by each other. [14]

Verb Agreement

It is well known and very obvious from the point of view of their meaning that reciprocals require a (semantically) plural antecedent. As a consequence, the verb exhibits plural agreement. There are types of reciprocal sentences, however, where the issue of verb agreement is more complex: reciprocal sentences with collective nouns in subject position and sentences where the reciprocal itself acts as subject and thus as the controller of verb agreement. Reciprocals as subjects and their agreement behaviour will be discussed in the following, while collective nouns in subject position will be one aspect of a more comprehensive section on reciprocal antecedents later.

As mentioned earlier, the reciprocal may function as embedded subject in a complex sentence. What is particularly interesting about this configuration is the variability in verbal number agreement. The data following show that one finds both singular and plural agreement. To be sure, this phenomenon is independent of the issue of how the verb agrees with the antecedent of a reciprocal. Yet, in view of the widespread assumption that *each other* and *one another* are plural anaphors indicating co-reference with their antecedent (e.g. Culicover, 2009: 405), it is revealing to see that they do not always trigger plural agreement of the verb if they are the agreement controller themselves. Consider the following examples:

(22) a. You, you just see what each other are doing. [J1C 2286]
    b. [. . .] saw over 45 on the ground workers from all backgrounds
        come together to meet new faces, as well as old and find out more
        about what each other does.[15]

The examples in (22) show that *each other* in subject position can control both singular and plural agreement of the verb. There are a number of questions that one might ask in relation to this variability. For example, does the choice between singular as opposed to plural inflection correspond to a meaning difference? If not, is there a motivation for choosing one or the other form, or are we dealing with a case of completely free variation? The data I have looked at (WebCorp results to searches containing the reciprocal *each other* preceded by *wh*-words such as *why* and *what*) do not seem to suggest any clear meaning distinction corresponding to the singular–plural variation. In any case, such facts demonstrate that assuming reciprocals to be plural anaphors would not account for this kind of variation. In Chapter 5 I will argue that the anaphoric meaning component of reciprocals is only part of their meaning.

Properties of the Antecedent

The reciprocals *each other* and *one another* are in construction with a noun phrase that refers to the individuals participating in the reciprocal situation: the (reciprocal) ANTECEDENT. In this section I will outline properties of the reciprocal antecedent, both from a grammatical and a semantic viewpoint.

The most fundamental constraint on the antecedent is arguably that it must be plural. This should be far from surprising; reciprocal situations are not conceivable for a single individual and therefore sentences predicating a reciprocal situation of one individual are not possible (but see Behrens, 2007).[16] As is often noted in the literature, however, plurality must here be taken to be a semantic property, singular collective nouns being a possible antecedent in reciprocal sentences. It is noteworthy that one does not as easily find a singular collective antecedent in the basic reciprocal strategy as in reciprocal sentences of the intransitive type. The latter option is illustrated in (23):

(23) The committee met for the first time in Edinburgh in October 1979.
    [HTK 1056]

A different type of singular antecedent is the one discussed by Landau (2000: 50). He notes that in control structures such as the ones in (24) certain (American English) speakers do not reject *each other* in interaction with a syntactically singular subject as readily as a plural reflexive pronoun.

(24) a. John told Mary that he wanted to accept their differences together.
　　b. ??John told Mary that he wanted to accept each other with more maturity.
　　c. *John told Mary that he wanted to accept themselves with more maturity.

Importantly, despite the marginal status of collective singular nouns in the basic reciprocal strategy, the aforementioned contrast between reciprocals and reflexives also seems to hold there:

(25) a. ??That couple accepted each other with maturity.
　　b. *That couple accepted themselves with maturity.
　　c. These couples accept each other as he or she is without criticizing, blaming or judging the other person.[17]
　　d. [. . .] all marriage ceremonies to include a declaration that the couple accepts each other as husband and wife, [. . .].[18]

It is well known that collective nouns like *couple* control both singular and plural agreement (with variation across dialects, see Levin, 2006; Bock et al., 2006). This variation obviously carries over to reciprocal sentences. Compare (25) c. to (25) d., the former showing plural and the latter singular agreement.

Note also that syntactically plural antecedents may be single pluralic nouns or complex coordinated noun phrases. This seemingly trivial fact should not be overlooked, given that certain languages are said to exclude the latter option (see Maslova and Nedjalkov, 2005: 430).[19] A further qualification to the statement that reciprocals need a grammatically plural antecedent is represented by cases like (26) a.– c. In these examples the reciprocals are not preceded by any overt antecedent whatsoever. Depending of the syntactic theory one is adhering to one can of course assume various types of non-overt noun phrases (for similar data from Norwegian and discussion in a generative framework see Lødrup, 2007), but if we restrict our attention to the actual surface structure of the sentence, neither *each other* in (26) a. nor *one another* in (26) b. and c. has an antecedent in the usual sense. In (26) c. there is not even a non-finite verb for which an implicit controlled argument (PRO) could be assumed on the syntactic level.

(26) a. I was suddenly filled with great remorse at the thought of having neglected opportunities for touching each other much, [. . .] [Lodge, Thinks, 68]
　　b. The plea to be true to one another [. . .]. [McEwan, Saturday, 222]
　　c. I was once in a ward with nine other people for a year and I know how, except when passed away, I know how that can really get on one another's nerves [. . .] [J43 84]

What these examples demonstrate is that the essential precondition for a reciprocal sentence with *each other* and *one another* to be grammatical is not a structural relation between the latter and a nominal antecedent that is co-referent with the reciprocal, but rather the availability of at least two individuals that can be construed as being in a reciprocal situation. The prototypical means to make these individuals available is a noun phrase preceding the reciprocal, but—as shown by the earlier examples—these individuals may also be made available by the context. Yet, in situations where a reciprocal is preceded by two potential antecedents, i.e. two noun phrases referring to a plural set between the members of which a reciprocal relation would be logically possible, interpretations are not unconstrained. Such restrictions are often described in terms of 'Binding Theory'. It is argued that in such cases only the next c-commanding subject can serve as antecedent.[20] Consider (27) from Haegemann and Gueron (1998: 370):

(27) Patsy and Edina think that Thelma and Louise consider each other the best candidate.

Following the aforementioned principle, the reciprocal can only be bound by *Thelma and Louise*, the first c-commanding subject, and not by *Patsy and Edina*, which is outside the relevant domain.

Let us now consider constraints on the antecedent that do not concern its structural relation with the reciprocal, but rather its meaning. As noted by Givón (1993), many transitive verbs select arguments that 'differ radically in semantic terms, such as concreteness, animacy, humanity, etc.' (85–86). Correspondingly, they do not allow simple transitive clauses with arguments of the same status, as illustrated in (28) c. And importantly, since in reciprocal sentences each argument of the verb expresses both semantic roles specified by the verb, reciprocal antecedents comprising two participants of unequal status are excluded.

(28) a. John built the house.
  b. *The house built John.
  c. *John built Mary.
  d. *John and Mary built each other.

Conversely, it can be stated that the participants in a reciprocal situation have to have an equal status in terms of properties such as concreteness, animacy and humanity, the exact nature of this constraint depends of course on the meaning of the particular verb involved.

Interestingly, the acceptability of reciprocal sentences decreases if the noun in the antecedent is quantified by a distributive quantifier such as *each* or *both*. We will see later that modification of reciprocal antecedents by these quantifiers does occur, and in fact their occurrence can be taken to argue against the assumption that the element *each* in *each other* quantifies the antecedent on some level of derivation. Yet, the fact that such sentences are rare and generally not accepted as standard indicates that a distributively quantified antecedent is less compatible with the semantics of reciprocal sentences than an antecedent that is quantified by, for example, *all*, hence a quantifier that is not strictly distributive. In the following, some quantifiers will be looked at in detail.

The universal quantifier *each* as determiner of a noun that serves as a reciprocal antecedent would be expected to be excluded due to the fact that the relevant noun phrase would be singular alone. We will see later that the reciprocal is not in principle incompatible with a singular antecedent, but *each* in the aforementioned position does not seem to occur in sentences unambiguously involving the reciprocal. In the fifty-six concordance lines generated by WebCorp for the string 'each * * each other', there is none that could not also be analyzed as involving *each* in *each other* as a regular determiner of *other* used nominally. In other words, these data support the assumption that the reciprocal *each other* may very well co-occur with the quantifier *each*, but only if the latter is a floating quantifier and thus interacts with a plural subject (cf. [29]).

(29) The state and city each blame each other for part of the problem.[21]

Let us consider other quantifiers. Sentence (30) contains an antecedent that is determined by *both*:

(30) [. . .], so both men were toasting each other [. . .]. [Lodge, Author Author, 250]

Both appears to be more acceptable than *each* when quantifying a reciprocal antecedent, especially when used adnominally (as against its function as a floating quantifier). This is very probably related to the fact that *both* requires plural verb agreement, while *each* requires singular agreement. Yet, as mentioned earlier, a verb agreeing with its subject in the singular does not strictly exclude the reciprocal. The following data with *every* and *everyone* are a case in point:

(31) a. [. . .], everyone knows each other, we all get on and there's no prima donnas. [CEM 1253]
     b. [. . .] like the Costa Brava: everyone oiling themselves and each other. [A1S 632]

As noted by Huddleston and Pullum (2002: 1501), *everyone* is different from the determiner *every* in this respect. The latter, according to Huddleston and Pullum (2002), cannot appear in the antecedent to a reciprocal. Instead, a plural antecedent such as *all the girls* in (32) a. would have to be used.

(32) a. *Every girl knew each other.
 b. All the girls knew each other.

Negative quantifiers are generally compatible with reciprocals, as shown by the following examples extracted from the Internet via WebCorp:

(33) a. Religion hardly led to no-one killing each other did it?[22]
 b. I don't believe in being in numerous crews where no one knows each other [. . .][23]
 c. [. . .], nobody helping each other out, [. . .][24]

Having looked at the interaction between the reciprocals and their various types of antecedent, let us finally discuss an issue that I have glossed over so far: possible semantic and grammatical differences between *each other* and *one another*.

Differences Between *Each Other* and *One Another*

There is no obvious grammatical difference between *each other* and *one another*. In other words, in all syntactic contexts in which one occurs the other can occur as well. Reputed differences in use between *each other* and *one another* have been a notorious topic in usage guides and older studies on English grammar. Most often the issue has been whether the choice between the two expressions should or should not be determined by the number of participants who are involved in the reciprocal event. The relevant prescriptive rule says that *each other* should be used with two participants and *one another* with more than two (Partridge 1957: 101). Many linguists have argued (and presented support in the form of numerous counterexamples) that speakers do not adhere to the rule if—apart from the attitude of prescriptivists—it has any reality at all (see e.g. Visser, 1963: 447–448).

Contrastingly, Bolinger (1987) notes that by emphatically denying the existence of the aforementioned prescriptive rule over and over again, one may have lost sight of real differences between the two reciprocals. Bolinger's discussion is probably the one that comes closest to what might distinguish *each other* and *one another* apart from register differences.[25] His central argument is the contrast between what he calls 'commutation' and 'mutuality'. This contrast is related to the fact—also discussed later— that events involving reciprocal relations are very similar to and sometimes not distinguishable from collective events, i.e. events in which two or more participants act not as individuals, but as a set of individuals which is in some sense more than the sum of its parts. Indeed, Bolinger (1987: 13–16) shows for a number of examples that *one another* is the form that is more compatible with 'mutuality', whereas *each other* is more compatible with 'commutation', although it remains to be seen whether this generalization would also hold for a larger set of natural data. What is at issue here is not necessarily a truth-conditional difference between sentences, but rather one of construal. Every reciprocal event involves two components; the bidirectional nature of the event ('commutation') on the one hand, and the fact that by carrying out the same action two (or more) participants are jointly involved in the event ('mutuality') on the other (see Chapter 5 for detailed discussion). From the point of view of the reciprocal relation to be expressed, this implies that *each other* achieves a greater degree of precision than *one another*, a contrast which, according to Bolinger (1987: 15), derives from the 'specificity of *each* and the indefiniteness of *one*'.[26] Consider the following pairs of examples (Bolinger, 1987: 15), in which exchanging *each other* and *one another* would result in the loss of the shade of meaning at issue (Bolinger's judgments):

(34) a. The books were carefully stacked on top of each other in a single neat pile.
b. ?The books were carefully stacked on top of one another in a single neat pile.
c. The books were all jumbled on top of one another in total disarray.
d. ?The books were all jumbled on top of each other in total disarray.

(35) a. They abruptly faced each other and squared off.
b. ?They abruptly faced one another and squared off.
c. They could sit and gaze at one another for hours.
d. ?They could sit and gaze at each other for hours.

As factors related to 'precision', Bolinger illustrates the relevance of 'rigidity', 'vividness' and 'muscularity' in (36), (37) and (38) respectively (1987: 15).

(36) a. The two columns leaned precariously towards each other, ready to topple.
b. ?The two columns leaned precariously towards one another, ready to topple.

(37) a. They damned each other to hell.
b. ?They damned one another to hell.

(38) a. They are willing to forgive one another's faults.
b. ?They are willing to forgive each other's faults.

Again, to substitute *one another* for *each other* in (36) a. and (37) a. and to use *each other* instead of *one another* in (38) a. would make the sentences sound less acceptable, according to Bolinger.

Bolinger's (1987) attempt at characterizing the contrast is not too different from earlier analyses. Erades (1950), for instance, proposes that *one another* has a 'general meaning', while *each other* 'suggests a definite group with individual members' (Erades, 1950: 154). It has been shown by Kjellmer (1982: 247–253) on the basis of a questionnaire study, for instance, that Erades (1950) overstates his own intuitions (see also Jørgensen, 1985). Kjellmer concludes that 'there is nothing like a consensus of opinion in these matters. The subjects differ a great deal amongst themselves, and not one of them conforms notably to the "correct" version as set forth by [. . .] Erades' (1982: 250). Potter (1953) makes the weaker claim that '[i]f the speaker is thinking of agents as individuals or single units, he will say *each other*, if he is thinking first of actions as shared or mutual, he will say *one another*' (257). Although Potter's analysis may capture an important intuition about the use of the two expressions, it is even more difficult to test than the one presented by Bolinger (1987). Unfortunately, the latter proposal has never been taken up and tested systematically, neither experimentally nor on the basis of a large amount of corpus data. For this reason, the only conclusion about which one can be certain at this point is that there is a register difference, *each other* being more colloquial than *one another*.[27]

Whatever the exact nature of the difference between the two expressions may be, it seems clear that it is very slight. It is therefore unclear why speakers do not abolish one of these two near-synonymous expressions. A not implausible explanation would be that it is the register difference between the two expressions that prevents the choice from disappearing. More specifically, the fact that *one another* is the standard form in certain more formal text types might prevent it from falling into disuse in the language as a whole. Note, however, that from a cross-linguistic point of view it is not at all a remarkable fact of English that there are two bipartite reciprocal expressions not featuring any obvious semantic or syntactic differences, as Hanke (in prep.) shows in reference to a number of languages.

As for their distribution across registers, Biber et al. (1999: 346–347) find that firstly *each other* is considerably more common than *one another* across the board. *One another*, in turn, is relatively common in fiction and academic prose. As their figures show, this does not mean that *one another* is more frequent than *each other* in these registers. The former is generally less frequent than the latter, but the proportion of *one another* to *each other* differs across registers. It is interesting to note at this point that, whereas synchronically the PDE reciprocals *each other* and *one another* do not happen to display any obvious differences between them, it is far from clear that their historical development has been of the same type. This question will be taken up in Chapter 3.

2.5 OTHER MEANS OF EXPRESSING RECIPROCITY

As has been argued at length earlier, a two-participant reciprocal situation can best be conceptualized as consisting of two subevents each of which

represents one of the two directions that make up the bidirectional relation characteristic of such situations. For this reason it should not come as
a surprise that languages are able to explicitly encode these two relations
one by one. The structure which renders the idea that reciprocal situations
consist of two subevents most directly is the coordination of two syntactically independent clauses.

Clause Coordination

Example (39) is a case in point:

(39) You help us, we help you. [McEwan, Saturday, 105]

Examples of clause coordination with more than two participants are hard
to find and it seems that in such cases a less cumbersome reciprocal strategy
is preferred to a clause coordination consisting of three or more clauses.
Note in this context that a syntactic analysis of reciprocal sentences according to which they are always derived from a coordination of simple transitive clauses has in fact been rejected because—among other things—the
more clauses are conjoined, the less the resulting complex sentence appears
to be a (psychologically) plausible underlying structure for a reciprocal sentence (cf. e.g. Dougherty, 1974: 9).

Example (39) is an instance of how an entire clause is copied, except for
adjusting the personal pronoun forms. Such structures are rare (scanning
through eleven PDE novels I have only come across a handful of examples).
More common are sentences in which one of the conjoined clauses is in
some way reduced with respect to the other clause:

(40) a. Our managers sued us, and we sued them.[28]
    b. [...], she does not immediately turn to him, nor he to her. [Lodge,
       Small World, 239]
    c. They decide that one's hurting the other and the other hurts back,
       [...] [FLD 126]

In (40) a. the pronominalization of one of the arguments makes the second
clause not an exact mirror image of the first clause. Example (40) b. illustrates further reduction of the second clause. Here also the verb is elided.
The type shown in (40) c. can be considered an additional step in the direction of a structure in which the two subevents are not expressed independently, since the verb phrase *hurts back* makes reference to the subevent
expressed first and links the two events causally. Yet, note that there is still
more independence of the two subevents than with a reciprocal sentence
involving the basic reciprocal strategy, since one event is causally and tem-
porally prior to the other and the two events in such sentences typically
take place in a sequence.

Considering the earlier examples from a more general point of view, it can be noted that they differ from ordinary reciprocal sentences of the basic reciprocal type not only in that they are not instances of a grammaticalized reciprocal strategy, but also in that they make two individual statements. The reciprocal situation can thus only be interpreted on the textual level.[29] Going one step further towards a grammaticalized reciprocal strategy, consider the following sentence:

(41) Juliet was a sex object to Romeo, and vice versa. [AE0 2724]

The example in (41) differs from the ones in (40) in that the two component situations constituting the reciprocal situation are not spelled out in the same way. One direction is explicitly asserted and the other expressed by an adverbial phrase designating the converse relation of the one asserted first. Yet, both of the aforementioned types of reciprocal sentences have in common the fact that a reciprocal situation is split up into its component subsituations and that these are asserted individually. What differs is only their respective grammatical independence.

The Split Quantificational Construction

The next type of reciprocal strategy to be discussed is crucially different. What I call the SPLIT QUANTIFICATIONAL CONSTRUCTION does not involve the repetition of the predicate. Instead it is the reference to the participants which is modified in such a way that a reciprocal reading results. This is typically achieved by using elements of those categories that can still be identified as forming the reciprocals *each other* and *one another*; hence a universal quantifier or the numeral *one*, on the one hand, and the alterity word *other*, on the other. The crucial difference between the two types is that in the case of the split quantificational construction the two words are syntactically independent and in fact do not occur adjacent to each other, whereas in the case of the basic reciprocal construction they are parts of a lexicalized nominal expression (see Chapter 3).

The split quantificational construction also includes universal quantifiers other than *each*, for instance *every* and *all*. In this the strategy differs from the basic reciprocal strategy, which exhibits invariability both in terms of its component forms and in terms of their distribution in the sentence. The fact that the split quantificational strategy is not as constrained formally in expressing a reciprocal situation as the reciprocals *each other* and *one another* is naturally explained by the assumption that, whereas the former are not specialized grammatical constructions, the latter are, as will be shown later. Thus, 'split quantificational construction' is strictly speaking a cover term for reciprocal sentences that spell out a reciprocal situation by making use of the independent meanings of those terms that also happen to form part of the reciprocals *each other* and *one another*, including comparable expressions such as *every* and *all*. Some of the other terms suggested in the literature are 'split construction' (Huddleston and Pullum, 2002: 1499), '*each-the-other* construction' (Fiengo and Lasnik, 1973; Hurst and Nordlinger, forthcoming), and '*each . . . the other* construction' (Bolinger, 1987).

As mentioned earlier, we find variation both in the choice of quantifiers and in the determination as well as number inflection of the alterity word. Apart from *every* (see [42] a.), the negative quantifier *neither* also interacts with the alterity word (cf. [42] b.).

(42) a. [. . .], every point is wrestled, bludgeoned from the other. [McEwan, Saturday, 113]
　　b. And so it went on, neither of them hearing the real concern of the other. [CGE 33]

In (43) *one* combines with the alterity word, and as these examples show, it is typically the indefinite form of the alterity word (*another*) that co-occurs with *one* in the analytic strategy.

(43) a. . . . and if this function were to be shared by several characters in the course of a novel, it should be passed from one to another, . . . [Lodge, Author, Author, 230]
　　b. . . . , he keeps wanting to change his place from one chair to another. [Lodge, Author, Author, 25]

The split quantificational construction was loosely defined as a structure in which those elements that make up the reciprocals *each other* and *one another*, as well as semantically comparable expressions, are used in a syntactically independent way. Let us now be more precise as to the latter point. If we consider the most straightforward case of a transitive verb being the predicate in a reciprocal sentence, the alterity word generally occurs in object position. The first element, i.e. the quantifier, may however exhibit different syntactic functions. *Each* can be the subject of the clause, as in (44) a., the head of a complex noun phrase, as in (44) b., or a 'floating quantifier', as in (44) c.:

(44) a. Each glanced surreptitiously at the other's reading matter. [Lodge, Small World, 118]
　　b. So during that stretch each of them would know that the other was there, [. . .] [Swift, The Light of Day, 100]
　　c. You each then provide the others with a copy of the notes, [. . .]. [CBT 2510]

The distribution of *one* in the split quantificational construction is different in that *one* cannot follow the subject as a 'floating quantifier' in a way comparable to (44) c. It is therefore not possible to replace *each* with *one* in this example: *You one then provide the others/another with a copy of the notes.* The other types of distribution exemplified in (44) are also possible for *one*.

A borderline case of the split quantificational construction is the one in which the alterity word is not accompanied by a quantifier in one of the relevant positions:

(45) a. [. . .] it was frustrating, so many balls bopped into the net [. . .] or blooped into the air where the other could not reach them. [Updike, Villages, 310]

   b. The trick was to make the attempt while passing between, say, licking one's lips and smiling broadly, and at the same time catch the other's eye. [McEwan, Atonement, 51]

Before discussing motivations for using a spell-out construction instead of the basic reciprocal strategy, let us now examine functional differences *between* the subtypes of the split quantificational construction.

An important generalization is that in those instances of the split quantificational construction where *one* occupies the subject slot (either by itself or as part of a complex noun phrase) a reciprocal reading is not normally required. If the sentence does turn out to have a reciprocal reading, it is enforced by the context. Consider the following examples:

(46) a. [. . .] and one stockinged leg was supported by the knee of the other, [. . .] [McEwan, Atonement, 161]

   b. [. . .] as one pleasantry followed another, [. . .] [Updike, Villages, 65]

   c. Stations of the former West Berlin passed one after another. [Eugenides, Middlesex, 40]

   d. [. . .] the pressure of deceit deformed one of them beyond what the other could love; [. . .] [Updike, Villages, 209]

As the examples in (46) b.–c. show, it is not a necessarily bidirectional relation, but rather a chaining relation that may be expressed by combining *one* and *(an)other*. In (46) b., pleasantry A follows pleasantry B, pleasantry B follows pleasantry C, etc. B does not follow A, however. The same holds for the stations referred to in (46) c. To be sure, the reciprocal *one another* may also express chaining situations. What it cannot express, however, is a situation such as the one described in (46) a., where each of the expressions *one* and *other* refers to only one of the two participants, respectively. In the example given it is only one of the legs that supports and only one leg that is in turn supported; the roles do not change. Similarly, example (46) d. leaves open whether the deformation of one beyond what the other could love applies in both directions or only in one. If we accept a narrower definition of reciprocal situations and exclude chaining situations, it can be stated that the relevant structure is not able to unambiguously express a reciprocal situation. The situation is crucially different with *each* and *other* as parts of the split quantificational construction. These items express a reciprocal situation in the narrow sense. This is illustrated in example (9) c., repeated here as (47) a.:

(47) a. Each glanced surreptitiously at the other's reading matter.
     b. One glanced surreptitiously at the other's reading matter

If the *each* in (47) a. is replaced by *one*, as illustrated in (47) b., the sentence does not assert a bidirectional relation anymore. The use of *one* leaves open who of the two participants is chosen as actor and undergoer respectively, yet it is only one direction that is asserted. The same holds for (48), a modified version of (46) d.

(48) She and Owen might have gone on longer, meeting never more than once a week and in summers less than that, until the pressure of deceit deformed each of them beyond what the other could love.

As soon as *each* occurs instead of *one*, a universal quantification over the set of participants is achieved and a reading results in which the relation expressed holds in both directions. *One* quantifies existentially and thus picks out only one of the two participants as the first argument of the predicate.

A non-reciprocal reading for sentences involving *each* and *other* as in (47) a. is in fact not totally excluded. It is possible for the alterity word to refer to an individual or a group of individuals that is not coreferent with those introduced by the subject (a fact which shows that the split quantificational construction is different from the basic reciprocal construction not only in terms of the adjacency of *each* and *other*):

(49) a. The youngest three of the women each gave lectures to the others.
     b. The youngest three of the women gave lectures to each other.

Thus, (49) a.[30] allows a reading in which there was no reciprocal lecturing among the youngest three of the women, but rather a situation in which these three women gave a lecture to a distinct set of women, a reading excluded by (49) b. As also noted by Maslova (2008) on the corresponding structures in Russian, however, 'in the absence of overt references to different sets the reciprocal interpretation is most likely in most contexts' (238). In any case, the fact that the analytic strategy allows a non-reciprocal reading does not invalidate the generalization with respect to the difference between *each* and *one* discussed earlier, if we restrict our attention to situations where only a single set of participants is under discussion.

Motivating the Use of Spell-Out Constructions

The contrast between (49) a. and b. now brings us back to the issue of why a speaker would employ the split quantificational construction at the expense of the basic reciprocal construction. If we find that the split quantificational and the basic construction are not in free variation, the choice between them being determined by some semantic difference between the two structures, it would be particularly interesting for the following reason: it would demonstrate that in order to describe the meaning of the basic reciprocal strategy (or the meaning of the reciprocals *each other* and *one another*, for that matter) it will not suffice and will actually be incorrect to paraphrase the relevant sentences by means of a reciprocal sentence involving the split quantificational construction or a logical formula corresponding to the latter.

As will be argued in more detail in Chapter 5, the semantic contrast between split quantificational and basic reciprocal strategy can roughly be characterized as the contrast between expressing a reciprocal situation that is also construed as one event being collectively undergone or carried out by the two or more participants on the one hand, and expressing a reciprocal situation made up of subevents, which lacks this collective component, on the other. The choice between other types of spell-out construction (e.g. clause coordination) and basic reciprocal construction is assumed to be analogously defined by the factors that are here described with regard to the split quantificational subtype. The lack of the collective, single-event interpretation is signalled by the use of the split quantificational construction, although there are some complications to be discussed in Chapter 5. The following examples may serve to illustrate this specific property of the split quantificational construction.

(50) a. [. . .] a half-contentious, half-flirtatious relationship, in which each at different times pretended to be 'experimentally' paying attention to the other [. . .] [Lodge, Author Author, 68]

b. Neither of them smiled, but each knew the other's thoughts. [FPK 2345]

c. At first, communication was something of a problem for the couple, as neither of them could speak the other's native tongue. [HRT 2883]

d. Afterwards he felt it had been as if each of them had been waiting for the other to touch on a delicate subject. [CDE 2303]

Sentence (50) a. focuses on the fact that the two participants are independently paying attention to the other person, without the intention of making the other one aware of this attitude. Sentence (50) b. involves only two participants, but I would hold that the collectivity factor mentioned earlier is also relevant here. The sentence is not about a joint mental experience of the two participants, but rather about the fact that each of them individually knew what the other was thinking. Rendering the situation as *They knew each other's thoughts* would suggest a joint experience, the latter not to be understood as some supernatural way of using the same mind, but rather as a mutual awareness of doing the same thing.[31] A similar analysis can be given of (50) c. The alternative variant . . . *as they could not speak each other's native tongue* is less able to stress the fact that for every one of the two participants the relevant ability is absent and that two different languages are concerned. This becomes more obvious if one takes into account the fact that the negated pronoun *neither* could be stressed in (50) c. and the semantic effect that would be conveyed in this way could not be achieved in the alternative version of the sentence. A stressed *they* in that variant would rather contrast the two participants to (a set of) alternatives, instead of focusing on the corresponding participants individually.

The motivation for using the split quantificational construction in (50) d. may be described in similar terms, but note that a further factor comes in at this point. That is the special status of *each other* in an embedded subject position. It was mentioned earlier that the use of the reciprocal in this position is considered to be substandard by many people. Therefore, it seems plausible that in those cases where replacing a split quantificational structure by the basic reciprocal construction would result in having the reciprocal in subject position, speakers conscious of normative rules may avoid this structure and make use of the more complex strategy instead (see also Chapter 5, section 5.1).

2.6 MEANING COMPOSITION AND THE RELATION BETWEEN BASIC AND SPELL-OUT STRATEGY

Given that the two elements constituting the reciprocal *each other* are highly transparent, it should not be surprising that linguists have in some way tried to derive the reciprocal meaning of sentences involving the expression from the interaction of the meanings of *each* and *other*. The idea is not far-fetched, given that historically the reciprocal is the result of two independent items having been lexicalized (cf. Chapter 3). It is controversial, however, to what extent the single elements still provide independent meaning contributions at the synchronic level. In the following I will sketch Heim, Lasnik and May's (1991) hypothesis as an attempt of this type and also survey the main arguments that have been argued to contradict the analysis. Roughly, the upshot of the discussion will be that although the meaning of a reciprocal sentence can to some extent be paraphrased by using the expressions *each* and *other*, a theory that derives the sentence meaning directly from the meaning contribution of the two words (in combination with the remainder of the sentence) makes false predictions.[32]

The gist of Heim, Lasnik and May's (1991) article is the idea that the 'reciprocal pronoun' *each other* should be seen as a word the two components of which each make a distinct contribution to the meaning of the sentence. Thus, 'reciprocal expressions have no properties peculiarly their own and [. . .] their meaning instead arises from the compositional interactions of the meanings that their constituent parts have in isolation' (Heim et al., 1991: 67). Despite the idiosyncratic position of *each*, the meaning contributions of the two words are therefore those that they would have if the quantifier *each* were in one of its familiar positions, i.e. preceding the subject as a determiner or preceding the main verb as a floated quantifier. Technically, this is implemented as LF ('logical form') movement, i.e. a movement of the 'distributor' *each* (of *each other*) to adjoin the reciprocal antecedent at LF. For the reciprocal sentence in (51) a. the corresponding LF representation is the one in (51) b.

(51) a. The men saw each other.
  b. $[_S[_{NP}[_{NP} \text{the men}_1] \text{ each}_2] [_S \text{e}_2[_{VP}[_{NP} \text{e other}]_3 [_{VP} \text{saw e}_3]]]]$

Hence, the function of *each*, being a distributive quantifier interacting with the subject, is not visible in the surface structure of the sentence. An important part of their argument is scope ambiguities of the type illustrated in the following example:

(52) John and Mary think they like each other.

As extensively discussed in Higginbotham (1985), Dimitriadis (2000) and Büring (2005: 209–211), sentence (52) can refer to two logically distinct situations. In one reading, John thinks that Mary likes him and Mary thinks that John likes her. In the second reading John thinks that there is a mutual liking relation between himself and Mary, and Mary thinks the same.[33] Heim et al. (1991) attribute the scopal ambiguity to the fact that the distributor may move either to the matrix subject (*John and Mary* in [52]) or to the embedded subject (*they* in [52]). In the former case, the second aforementioned reading arises, whereas in the latter case the first reading arises (see Higginbotham, 1985; Dimitriadis, 2000). Despite the fact that the ambiguity in (52) can be represented in the alleged 'logical form', it is obvious that this account is at odds with the assumption that the basic and the split quantificational reciprocal constructions are not only structurally but also semantically distinct. Since the functional difference between the two constructions is a central point in the remaining chapters, I will therefore summarize the main points of criticism that have been directed at Heim et al.'s (1991) theory in the following.

Dalrymple et al. (1994) compare English to Chicheŵa, a language in which reciprocity is not expressed by a bipartite noun phrase such as English *each other*, but rather by a verbal affix. As shown by a number of tests (Mchombo and Ngalande, 1980; Mchombo and Ngunga, 1994), the element in Chicheŵa and the corresponding morphs in other Bantu languages are derivational affixes deriving intransitive verbs and can therefore not be considered incorporated arguments. Consequently, the Bantu reciprocal affix is morphosyntactically different from the English reciprocal, which is a noun phrase filling an argument position. Yet, Dalrymple et al. (1994)

show that reciprocal sentences in Chicheŵa feature exactly the same scope ambiguities as their English counterparts.[34] This observation clearly weakens the hypothesis that the semantic properties of the English reciprocal are a direct consequence of the fact that it consists of the two elements *each* and *other* and their respective semantic contributions.[35] Reciprocal expressions like Danish *hinanden* 'each other' are also a problem for Heim et al.'s (1991) hypothesis. In Danish the reciprocal *hinanden* is even more clearly a word morphologically than English *each other*. Unlike *each*, the Danish counterpart *hin* has lost its status as a free morph and thus cannot occur on its own. For this reason, the argument that there is no reciprocal pronoun as such, but merely the interaction of two independent items, could hardly be applied to Danish and other languages whose reciprocals preserve quantifiers that are not used outside these particular expressions anymore.

Williams (1991) and Brisson (1998) put forward arguments that specifically argue against Heim et al.'s (1991) analysis of the English data. Among other things, these arguments concern facts about the reciprocal that were first observed in Fiengo and Lasnik (1973), namely, the possibility of 'weak distributivity' in sentences involving *each other*.[36] A frequently cited pair of examples in this context is the following (see Fiengo and Lasnik, 1973; Williams, 1991; Brisson, 1998).

(53) a. The men were hitting each other.
b. The men were each hitting the others.

Whereas (53) a. can describe a situation in which not every member of the set denoted by the noun phrase *the men* is a hitter, the variant in (53) b. turns out to be stricter in this respect; in (53) b. no exceptions are allowed. Williams (1991) calls this property of the reciprocal 'weak distributivity' and correctly notes that the property of allowing weak distributivity is shared by both plural noun phrases and reciprocal *each other*, and so the meaning of *each other* is best explained not by compositionally building it up from the meaning of *each* and *other*, but by treating *each other* as an anaphor which must be semantically represented as a plural variable.

Obviously, *each* is a maximally distributing quantifier, its functions thus being firstly the distribution over single individuals and secondly to rule out exceptions (see Dowty, 1987: 102; Brisson, 1998: 23, for further discussion of the notion 'maximality'). If we assume—as Heim et al. (1991) do—that in a reciprocal sentence like (53) a. the element *each* of the reciprocal *each other* functions as an ordinary distributive quantifier, albeit merely at the level of 'logical form', the possibility of exceptions in (53) a. is unexpected. This may seem rather trivial, but note that Heim et al. (1991) do not consider examples with more than two participants. Obviously, in sentences with only two participants the question of maximality does not arise:

(54) a. The ten men were hitting each other.
b. The two men were hitting each other.

Example (54) a. corresponds to (53) a. in that maximality need not hold. Example (54) b., by contrast, involves two participants and since there can be no reciprocal relation if only one participant is involved maximality necessarily holds. If we want to investigate the relation between the parameter of maximality, on the one hand, and the choice between different reciprocal strategies, on the other, we should not confine our attention to reciprocal sentences with two participants. Indeed Heim et al. (1991: 70–71) mention the semantic contrast between *each other* and *each . . . the other*, but do not accept it as a crucial problem for their own analysis. Rather, they openly 'finesse it, by considering just groups of two, where universal or existential force would yield indistinguishable truth conditions' (1991: 70). In a different context they propose that '[f]loated *each* is a genuine universal quantifier, whereas the *each* of *each other* might be more accurately described as signaling the presence of a quantifier, whose force it determines only vaguely or in composition with a cooccurring quantifier' (1991: 95). I take these statements to be retreats from the authors' own hypothesis (see also Brisson, 1998: 42), without acknowledging the import of the problems for their assumption that the meaning of the reciprocal 'arises from the compositional interactions of the meanings that their constituent parts have in isolation' (Heim et al., 1991: 67).

Further arguments against Heim et al.'s (1991) analysis are given in Asudeh (1998: 109–135) and Safir (2004: 200–201). Whereas the former shows with reference to a number of tests that the first part of the reciprocal *each other* does not have the behaviour of a quantifier, the latter points out that the alterity word in the reciprocal does not behave like a pronoun, as assumed by Heim et al. (1991). Instead of going into these arguments in detail, let us finally consider the role of the second reciprocal *one another* in derivational accounts of reciprocal sentences. Although this point has never been explicitly addressed in the relevant literature, I take the null hypothesis to be the following: the (near-) synonymy of *each other* and *one another* implies that a derivation of the meaning of the reciprocal from the independent meanings of its parts should work equally well for both forms. In other words, treating *each other* as making its meaning contribution to the sentence via the allegedly independent meanings of its parts, on the one hand, and regarding *one another* as a fixed unit making its meaning contribution as a whole, on the other, would hardly be convincing. Anyone taking this step would have a hard time justifying why speakers should process the two formally similar and semantically (near-) identical reciprocals in such fundamentally different ways. Heim et al. (1991) do not approach *one another* in any detail. The only statement suggesting that the two reciprocals should be treated equally is the following: '[The logico-semantic translation of reciprocal sentences; cf. (21) in Heim et al. (1991: 71)] captures the logical role of *each* and *other* (or, for that matter, of *one* and *another*) in the interpretation of reciprocals, and the contributions each of them makes to its composition' (1991: 71).

It remains unclear why the independent expression *one* should be regarded as introducing universal quantification effecting a distribution over the individuals in the participant set at issue, other than by analogy with the alleged role of *each* in *each other*. If the element *one* in reciprocal sentences has to be assigned a special semantic function, it would have to be a kind of 'choice function'. Thus the reciprocal reading of a sentence like *One was embracing the other* in a context involving more than two participants would be derived in the following way: *one* picks out an individual from the set of participants and relates it to a different participant from the same set. This procedure is repeated for every individual in the set, as it were (leaving aside the possibility of non-maximality for the time being). Importantly, it is only in reciprocal sentences that—by *repeating* the choice function—*one* seems to behave like a universal quantifier. *Each*, by contrast, is always a universal quantifier (unless it is part of the reciprocal *each other*). The same problems apply to Dougherty's (1970, 1971, 1974) transformational analysis of *each other*, in which *one another* is not even mentioned. Again, it would be theoretically possible, of course, that language users interpret the meaning of *each other* in a completely different way from *one another*. Given the ad hoc flavour of such an approach, as well as the fact that neither of the aforementioned authors explicitly entertains this option, however, it does not appear that they actually intended it (see also Hudson, 1984: 205–206).

Jackendoff's (1972: 170) early discussion of *each other*, in part a reaction to Dougherty's (1970) account, offers an alternative variant of an analysis that takes the reciprocal to be regularly built up from its parts. In contrast to Heim et al. (1991), he claims that the reciprocal is generated in the form that also shows up on the surface, thus being part of the regular paradigm in (55):

(55) a. {one, each} of the {houses, men, others}
     b. {*one, *each} of {houses, men, others}
     c. {one, each} {house, man, other}

As for its external syntax, Jackendoff notes that it behaves in a way very similar, if not identical, to the reflexive *self*-forms; it has to be kept in mind that Jackendoff (1972) predates the advent of Binding Theory and thus also the detailed discussion of distributional differences between reflexives and reciprocals, see Huang (1983: 554); Bouchard (1985); Farmer (1987); Haegemann (1994: 231); Everaert (2000). As a consequence he suggests analyzing *each other* as a reflexive pronoun. As far as the syntactic composition of the reciprocal is concerned, it looks indeed like a simple branching noun phrase of the form $[each_{Det} \ other_N]_{NP}$. I view it as more plausible, however, to analyze *each other* as a conventionalized unit without the internal structure of a regularly composed noun phrase. Apart from the fact that the type of historical development that would have led to the representation envisaged by Jackendoff is not very likely (see Chapter 3), the following arguments support the view adopted here, according to which the reciprocal is processed as a syntactically frozen unit, even though its component elements may still be morphologically transparent.

Firstly, the well-known problem of maximality would also figure in the case of the complex noun phrase analysis. Consider (54) a. again. If *each* were the determiner of *other*, a non-maximal reading would be unexpected. If every individual in the relevant group hit *each other* individual in the group, there are no individuals that are not hit. One may object that in an analysis where *each* distributes over the group designated by *other* (by virtue of being its determiner) non-maximality is to be traced to the subject, in contrast to the analysis in Heim et al. (1991), where *each* 'LF-moves' to the subject of the clause. To put it differently, Jackendoff's analysis would allow a non-maximal group of hitters, whilst the group of 'hittees' excludes exceptions. However, if a non-maximal reading of (54) a. were possible because non-quantified definite plural noun phrases do not necessarily distribute down to each and every member of the set, the non-maximal reading of the sentence would have to be of the following nature: not all men are active hitters, but each of the men would be a 'hittee'. A reading of (54) a. in which there are men who are not being hit would thus be excluded. But the latter reading is possible. If the sentence has a non-maximal reading, this can either mean that there are exceptions to the hitters, that there are exceptions to the 'hittees', or both. Jackendoff (1972: 173) does not expect semantic and syntactic composition to necessarily go together. Therefore, the missing correspondence between the two levels is not a problem in that particular framework. From the point of view followed in this study, however, it is a problem.

Secondly, note that in reciprocal situations with only two participants the meaning of a noun phrase $[each_{Det}\ other_N]_{NP}$ would be unexpected. Consider (56) a. and the semi-formal paraphrase of its meaning in (56) b.:

(56) a. Lynn and Brian are teasing each other.
  b. Each of Lynn and Brian is such that he or she is teasing the other.

If, in two-participant situations, one participant is related to all remaining participants in the relevant set, the cardinality of the remaining participants is always one. The quantifier *each*, however, can only interact with a noun denoting a set larger than a singleton set. In other words, in an interpretation of (56) a. where *each other* is analyzed as $[each_{Det}\ other_N]_{NP}$, the latter phrase would have to refer to a set of at least two individuals. But—adhering to the example—if there are two individuals involved in a teasing relationship in total, only one individual can be the one being teased for any possible direction of teasing. I hold that for these reasons the element *each* as part of the reciprocal *each other* does not function as the determiner of the second element, *other*.

2.7 INTRANSITIVE VERBS

Symmetric vs. Prototypically Reciprocal

As mentioned earlier, we can distinguish two relevant classes among the verbs that can be used intransitively in reciprocal contexts: symmetric verbs and prototypically reciprocal verbs. While in the former class a reciprocal relation is part of the verb meaning, it is only prototypically associated with it in the latter class. To be more specific, in a traditional view of verb meaning and valency a verb such as *meet* is monotransitive (see, for instance, Haegemann, 1994: 41) and an essential part of its lexical meaning is that the relation holding between actor and undergoer holds in two ways. Thus, if we were to paraphrase the meaning of *meet*, or attempt a feature analysis type of meaning description, the bidirectionality of any meeting relation would be an essential part of the paraphrase or an essential feature of the decomposition.

By contrast, a prototypically reciprocal verb like *embrace* is not lexically specified in this way. Again, if we were to paraphrase its lexical meaning, no mention of bidirectionality would need to be made. Whether the possibility of using prototypically reciprocal verbs intransitively with a plural subject goes back to the derivation of a new lexical entry, i.e. an intransitive verb, or some other mechanism, need not concern us here.

Symmetric Adjectives, Nouns and Prepositions

In this study I focus on verbs, yet symmetric relations can also be part of the meaning of words belonging to other word classes, as shown by the following examples:

(57) a. King William IV had a younger brother, the Duke of Kent, who had married Victoire, [...] [ALY 393]
   b. The changes in parking behaviour in St. John's Wood are similar to those observed in the period after wheelclamping was introduced in central London in 1982. [A49 353]
   c. This applies in particular to such features of English High Court procedure as mutual discovery of documents by the parties with or without a court order; [...] [EDL 791]

Thus the relational noun *brother* in (57) a. is symmetric in that both the following statements have to be true in order for the sentence to be true: King William IV is the Duke of Kent's brother and the Duke of Kent is King William's brother. Sentence (57) b. contains the symmetric adjective *similar*. Again we observe a symmetric relation: the changes in parking behaviour in St. John's Wood can only be similar to those in London if the changes in

London are also similar to those in St. John's Wood. *Mutual* in (57) c. is an example of a symmetric adjective used attributively.

Clear examples of nouns that entail a reciprocal relation are *relative, friend, opposite, partner, mirror image* and *counterpart* (cf. König and Kokutani, 2006: 273). Whereas these nouns directly denote a member of a pair for which a symmetric relation holds, there are also nouns which hold symmetrically only in certain syntactic contexts. Hunston and Francis (2000: 191–192) provide a list of symmetric nouns that appear in three specific contexts involving a prepositional phrase. If both or all participants are expressed as a single subject, the prepositional phrase follows the verb alone. It is also possible for the prepositional phrase to be followed by the phrase [*with* X], where X stands for one of the two participants, the other one being realized as the subject.

(58) a. *at . . . with* cross-purposes, loggerheads, odds, variance, war
  b. *in . . . with* accord, agreement, alliance, cahoots, collusion, commu-
    nication, competition, conference, conflict, consultation, contact,
    conversation, disagreement, dispute, harmony, league, negotiation,
    partnership, step, touch
  c. *in/out of . . . with* phase, sync

A list of adjectives is given in (59) (Hunston and Francis, 2000: 191):

(59) agreed, apart, betrothed, close, comparable, compatible, concurrent,
    congruent, deadlocked, different, divided, engaged, equal, friendly
    with, identical, incompatible, inseparable, interchangeable, interde-
    pendent, interlaced, intimate, irreconcilable, locked, married, neck-
    and-neck, opposed, the same, similar, split, suited, synonymous,
    unanimous, unconnected, well-matched

The adjectives in (59) are symmetric in that they are predicated of or attributed to a set of at least two participants and express a symmetric relation
between these participants. Most adjectives are compatible with a noun
referring to a single individual. The adjective *married*, for example, is often
used to characterize a single individual:

(60) "Are you married, Commissioner?" she asked suddenly. [HTT 809]

Yet, such sentences entail that the relation at issue holds between at least
two participants. The question in (60) does not ask for the identity of the
commissioner's wife, who is backgrounded. Nevertheless, if the addressee
is married, he also has to be married *to* someone.

As for prepositions, it has been argued that *with* is the only instance of a
symmetric preposition (König and Kokutani, 2006: 273). Interestingly, it is

in fact *with* that introduces the second participant in most non-intransitive uses of symmetric verbs in English:

(61) [. . .] using evidence of how these people are recruited, where they live and who they meet with. [CS3 187]

In the following, the focus will be on verbs, notwithstanding the fact that the generalizations on symmetric/prototypically reciprocal verbs and their argument structure alternations can probably be extended to the ways in which the relevant items from other word classes are used.

Possible Argument Realizations

As mentioned earlier, the class of prototypically reciprocal predicates such as *embrace* is semantically different from symmetric predicates, but similar in terms of their syntactic behaviour. In English, this concerns first and foremost the occurrence in the structure [NP$_{Pl}$ V]:

(62) a. They met at his flat. [GUU 3249]
     b. They appeared to have their arms around each other, either having just embraced or being just about to embrace. [J54 2189]

Example (63) presents lists of symmetric and prototypically reciprocal verbs that I compiled from Levin (1993) and other studies. The verbs are grouped according to the alternations that they undergo. In (63) a. we see verbs which have a realization pattern (possibly among other realization patterns) that has the two or more participants of the reciprocal situation in a joint subject position. In other words, whereas in the basic reciprocal strategy—and, for that matter, in all the ways of spelling out a reciprocal situation discussed earlier—all argument positions of a verb are filled, in the case of the intransitive argument realization the valency seems to be reduced by one, all participant roles being realized by only one syntactic argument. The group in (63) b., by contrast, contains verbs with a realization pattern (others being again possible) in which the two reciprocal participants are coded as a joint direct object. The verbs in (63) c., which overlap with those in (63) d., undergo what Levin (1993: 61) calls the 'Together Reciprocal Alternation': all participants being realized as the joint direct object of the verb, the adverb *together* may follow the direct object. Example (63) d. represents the same alternation, the only difference to (63) c. is that these verbs require the adverb *apart* instead of *together*. The corresponding meaning contrast between the two classes of verbs is obvious: connecting two entities in some way versus disconnecting two entities in some way.

(63) a. adjoin, affiliate, agree, alliterate, alternate, amalgamate, argue, assemble, banter, bargain, battle, be, bicker, blend, box, brawl,

bump (into), chat, chatter, chitchat, clash, coalesce, coexist, coincide, collaborate, collide, combine, comingle, commiserate, communicate, compare, compete, concatenate, concur, confabulate, confederate, confer, conflict, conjoin, connect, consolidate, consort, consult, contrast, converse, cooperate, copulate, correlate, correspond (via letters), criss-cross, debate, dicker, differ, disagree, dispute, dissent, divorce, duel, elope, embrace, entangle, entwine, feud, fight, flirt, fuse, gab, gather, get in touch, go steady, gossip, greet, haggle, harmonize, hit,[37] hobnob, hug, integrate, interchange, interconnect, interlace, interlink, interlock, intermingle, interrelate, intersect, intertwine, interweave, jest, join with, join in battle, joke, joust, kiss, link, make love, marry, match, mate, meet, merge, mingle, miss, mix, neck, negotiate, pair, play, plot, quarrel, quibble, rap, rendezvous, resemble, rhyme, schmooze, scuffle, skirmish, spar, spat, speak, spoon, squabble, struggle, talk, tilt, tussle, unify, unite, vie, war, wrangle, wrestle, yak

b. affiliate, alternate, amalgamate, associate, blend, coalesce, coincide, combine, commingle, compare, concatenate, confederate, confuse, conjoin, connect, consolidate, contrast, correlate, crisscross, entangle, entwine, fuse, harmonize, incorporate, integrate, interchange, interconnect, interlace, interlink, interlock, intermingle, interrelate, intersperse, intertwine, interweave, join, link, mate, merge, mingle, mix, muddle, ?pair, pool, rhyme, ?team, total, unify, unite, blend, cream, mix, add, connect, engage, introduce, join, link, marry, oppose, network, wed, decouple, differentiate, disconnect, disentangle, dissociate, distinguish, divide, divorce, part, segregate, separate, sever

c. band, beat, blend, bundle, cluster, combine, commingle, concatenate, connect, consolidate, fuse, gather, glom, group, herd, join, link, lump, mass, merge, mingle, mix, package, pair, pool, roll, scramble, shake, shuffle, stir, whip, whisk, add, append, baste, bind, bond, connect, fasten, fuse, graft, join, link, moor, network, sew, splice, stick, weld, anchor, band, be moor, muzzle, nail, padlock, paste, peg, pin, plaster, rivet, rope, screw, shackle, skewer, solder, staple, stitch, strap, string, tack, tape, tether, thumbtack, tie, trammel, wire, yoke, zip, beat, blend, collect, cream, mix, scramble, shake, shuffle, splice, stir, swirl, whip, whisk

d. blow, break, cut, draw, hack, hew, kick, knock, pry, pull, push, rip, roll, saw, shove, slip, split, tear, tug, yank

As mentioned earlier, most of the verbs undergo some kind of argument structure alternation and thus occur in different clause patterns. Some of them, the frequently mentioned verb *resemble*, for instance, occur in only one structure. Let us now consider the different clause patterns in which the relevant verbs occur. I focus on those verbs that are listed in (63) a., i.e. verbs denoting events whose participants are all directly involved in the reciprocal situation, as opposed to the verbs in the remaining groups, where one participant is not directly involved but acts on two or more additional participants such that the latter come to stand in a reciprocal relation to each other.

A number of verbs can be realized transitively, i.e. coding one participant as subject and the other as direct object. If an allegedly symmetric verb occurs in this frame it is commonly argued that the two arguments may be exchanged without changing the truth values of the sentence. In fact, not in all cases in which a given verb alternates between transitive and intransitive realization can the two arguments of the transitive realization be exchanged. Such an exchange is excluded, for instance, if subject and object differ in their animacy status. Example (64) provides instances of symmetric verbs in a transitive construction.

(64) a. The clergyman shook Owen's hand. [Updike, Villages, 267]
　　 b. [. . .] she would marry no man who had not served in the Royal Navy. [McEwan, Atonement, 287]
　　 c. Julia had of course not yet been to Pennsylvania to meet the prickly old woman. [Updike, Villages, 287]
　　 d. [. . .] to help him divorce her, [. . .] [Updike, Villages, 282]
　　 e. This part of Baxter's skull now resembles crazy paving, [. . .] [McEwan, Saturday, 256]

With prototypically reciprocal verbs that undergo the intransitive–transitive alternation it is not possible to exchange the arguments of the transitive realization without either changing the meaning of the sentence or making the sentence unacceptable. As already mentioned, the latter results, for example, if subject and object differ in animacy:

(65) [. . .]; he kisses her hand, puts her on his knee, whispers to her. [A18 992]

Sentences like (65) are basically nothing remarkable at all, the verbs being non-symmetric and the meaning of the sentence as a whole not designating a reciprocal situation. The very fact that symmetric verbs are able to appear in a transitive clause construction, however, is in a sense paradoxical, given that a transitive clause renders its two arguments in an asymmetric way. As will be seen in Chapter 4, there are various motivations for using these verbs transitively, and very often the reciprocal situation to be expressed does not become asymmetric just as a result of employing the transitive construction. Yet it is not always the case that the transitive realization preserves the symmetric event structure of the verb. This becomes obvious if we consider passive sentences involving symmetric verbs. As is well known, passives require a higher degree of semantic transitivity than active transitive clauses (see Rice, 1987). Since one of the central features of transitivity (understood in the sense of Hopper and Thompson, 1980) is an asymmetric relation between the two participants, it is revealing to look at passive clauses with symmetric and prototypically reciprocal verbs.

Forming a passive with a symmetric or prototypically reciprocal verb is not an option for all of the verbs in the two classes. Generally, prototypically reciprocal verbs can be freely used in the passive—see (66) a. With symmetric verbs the situation is more complex. To passivize the verb *meet*, for instance, seems to be much easier if the verb is used in one of the senses that we may roughly describe as 'non-symmetric'. This means that we find many examples of the type in (66) b., where *meet* refers to the event of A reaching a standard B (see Haas, 2008, for a detailed discussion of *meet* and the passive).

(66) a. After the verdict he was hugged by his tearful mother Patricia Bell. [K4W 58]
b. Many plan targets were not met, however, as industrial output fell in the second half of the year. [HKT 3051]

There is a realization type that is similar to the properly transitive realization in that the participants of the reciprocal situation are again coded by distinct syntactic arguments. The two syntactic slots are subject, on the one hand, and the complement of a preposition following the verb, in most cases the comitative preposition *with*, on the other:

(67) [. . .] as the heat of the bodies interfaced with the cold walls. [Updike, Villages, 85]

If there are two participants, they are equally distributed over the two syntactic slots. With more than two participants each of the two arguments must at least relate to one participant, such that different ways of distributing participants over syntactic positions are possible. It hast long been noted that this may affect the meaning of the sentence in the prepositional and the transitive type, even if only truth-conditions are considered the relevant level of semantic distinctions. Compare (68) a. and b.:

(68) a. Willie and Kate argued with Trevor.
b. Willie and Trevor argued with Kate.

In (68) a. Willie and Kate need not argue with each other, whereas in (68) b. it is Willie and Trevor who need not argue with each other.

Distinguishing Symmetric and Collective Events

An essential property of reciprocal situations is the presence of two subevents that are mirror images of each other. In terms of semantic roles we might also say that each participant fulfils the roles of both Actor and Undergoer. Importantly, however, by virtue of both participants having the same roles they are also acting in a similar or even identical way—they do the same thing, as it were. As Evans (forthcoming) puts it: '[A]t least for events denoting human reciprocity, we should also add a further semantic component specifying their mutual intent to cooperate and/or reciprocate, something like "do together (j&m)", which is now a one-place predicate with a plural argument'.[38] Having noticed that languages often code these two meanings in similar or identical ways (cf. Lichtenberk, 1985, 2000), Kemmer (1993a: 87) succinctly characterizes the commonalities and differences between the two types of relation:

> The collective/reciprocal polysemy is motivated by a similarity in the semantic configurations associated with these two categories, as Lichtenberk notes. For one thing, in both the collective and the reciprocal situation types more than one entity is carrying out the same type of action; secondly, each entity plays two roles in the event. In the most basic type of reciprocal situation, there are two participants, and each is at the same time an agent (or other event-initiating participant) and a patient (or other type of affected entity). For example, in a sentence designating the event 'the girls see each other', each girl is both a seer and a 'seen' entity. In the case of collective situations, the acting entities can be seen as participants that each play two roles, although these roles typically do not receive separate grammatical instantiation: Each is at the same time an agent and a 'companion' of the other entities (or a 'co-actant'). The fact of the presence of two roles is a prominent part of the semantics of reciprocality, but not particularly prominent for the collective, for which the dual roles simply follow from the fact that the participants take part in the same action.

Evans (forthcoming) demonstrates how reciprocal constructions in a variety of languages deal with this collective semantic component of reciprocal situations. In his account, reciprocal situations basically involve three propositions: the two subevents making up the bidirectionality mentioned earlier plus the collective component (Evans does not use the term 'collective'). Given the complexity of this 'propositional overlay', reciprocal constructions in different languages do not consistently code all three components overtly (see also Haiman, 1985b). In English, it is the coding of the entire set of participants in a single noun phrase and, in the case of the intransitive structure, the intransitive verb that could be analyzed as being an overt concomitant of the collective component.

Let us call BIDIRECTIONALITY the characteristic component of reciprocal situations that is left if we subtract the collective component. I would hold that those situations expressed by reciprocal sentences do not generally invoke the same proportions of bidirectionality and collectivity respectively. One of the more straightforward factors playing a role here is the dichotomy simultaneous versus sequential. Thus, a situation in which the two relevant subevents take place simultaneously can reasonably be assumed to display a higher degree of collectivity than a situation where first one event occurs, then the other. Furthermore, the proportion of collectivity involved depends both on the verb and the specific reciprocal strategy that is chosen (see Chapter 5). I argue, for instance, that the speaker's choice between basic reciprocal and spell-out construction for expressing a given reciprocal situation depends on whether the relevant subevents are carried out collectively (or construed as a single event by the speaker) or not. Also, the verbs under discussion here exhibit variation with respect to this parameter.

In this way, one can distinguish the general affinity between reciprocity and collectivity mentioned earlier from the relation between the two semantic components in the meaning of verbs on the other. It is on the latter type of affinity that I concentrate in this section (for the relationship in general, see Chapter 5). The predicates that are commonly listed as 'symmetric' involve different degrees of collectivity in the sense described earlier. In fact, in a number of cases the bidirectionality which is normally taken to be the defining feature of these predicates does not play a role at all and therefore it makes little sense to include them in the category 'symmetric predicate', unless one wants to extend the category disproportionately. What makes the relevant predicates (again, I will concentrate on verbs) suspiciously similar to symmetric predicates in the strict sense is the fact that the former class also requires there to be (at least) two participants who have to act together in a certain way. They are thus 'symmetric' in the sense that one subevent is not possible without the other. The verb *discuss* in a sentence like *Bush and Blair discussed in private before they made the announcement,* for instance, requires there to be at least two participants who act in a coordinated way.

Again, Kemmer (1997: 236–239) provides an insightful discussion of the semantic relationship between collective and bidirectional situations. She considers predicates like *dance, play, compete, quarrel* and *talk* intermediate between a 'reciprocal' and a 'collective' prototype and calls them INDIRECT BILATERAL. Recall that it is predicates like these that are often subsumed under the class of symmetric predicates, although their meaning does not involve the type of bidirectionality characteristic of what we take well-behaved symmetric verbs like *meet* and *marry* to have. What distinguishes the indirect bilateral event type from the reciprocal event type, according to Kemmer (1997), is that the energy input from the participants is indirect:

> In the prototypical reciprocal situation (e.g. 'hit each other', 'touched each other'), the energy input directly affects each participant. As such, the level of affectedness is relatively high. In the 'dance with each other' type, on the other hand, the interaction is indirect rather than direct.

This is why we find some oblique preposition or case marking present rather than a simple transitive construction with the affected entity as direct object. The focus of such constructions is not on affectedness of the participants by the verbal action, but on mutual interaction. There is far more input from both sides, for example in the fact that each participant must adjust his/her actions to a considerable extent to those of the partner, or the mutual activity designated cannot be said to take place. The sense of accompaniment in carrying out some overarching event is therefore considerably strengthened compared to the reciprocal. (237)

Regarding the verbs in (63) we might now ask how Levin (1993), on whose classification this list is largely based, has arrived at her categorization, and if she has taken into account the aforementioned continuum between the bidirectional and the collective situation type. Levin (1993) categorizes her verb classes according to the alternations that they do or do not undergo. The propensity to take part in a given alternation is indeed illuminating for the analysis of verb meanings, given that the availability of alternations very often depends on specific features that the meaning of the relevant verb displays. Yet, as Baker and Ruppenhofer (2002) point out: 'Although the whole thesis of Levin's work is that grouping words according to alternations tends to produce semantically coherent word classes, it can also split words that are close in meaning, or lump semantically disparate words' (30).

Interestingly, Baker and Ruppenhofer (2002: 31–32) specifically discuss the type of verbs at issue here and point out that they are a problem for Levin's methodology of establishing verb classes. Levin's classes are too broad, and verbs that fall in one class in Levin's framework are assigned distinct frames in their own classification system FrameNet. Note that the intransitive clause construction with a plural subject allows readings in which the relevant subevents are not directed at each other, and crucially this holds for verbs that occur both in this construction and in the one where one participant is realized as an argument preceded by *with*, hence Levin's (1993) Simple Reciprocal Alternation. The aforementioned tripartite distinction between reciprocal, indirect bilateral and collective thus remains unaccounted for. In order to establish a comprehensive classification of verbs in the functional domains under discussion, we would have to consider, for every verb, which kinds of subevents it denotes and how these subevents are related to each other. Specifically we would have to take into account whether participants are—in Kemmer's terminology— directly affected by the action that the other participant carries out. (Note that the notion of affectedness is not easily applicable to verbs like *intersect*, which denote purely local relations.) The question is, therefore: are the subevents directed at the other participant or are they rather carried out by both (or all) participants collectively and directed elsewhere? Putting Kemmer's discussion in a nutshell and applying it to the verbs in (63), we have symmetric verbs in the former case and collective verbs in the latter. If both components are present to some degree, the 'indirect bilateral' class would apply. In Chapter 5 it will be proposed that the syntactically similar behaviour of reciprocal and collective verbs (and predicates in general) is no coincidence, given that the collective meaning component is always present in the intransitive realization of symmetric verbs. This becomes particularly obvious in those cases where the meaning of a verb changes between intransitive and non-intransitive argument realization.

2.8 RECIPROCAL SITUATION TYPES

Overview

As mentioned earlier, sentences involving one of the reciprocals *each other* and *one another* and a number of participants larger than two allow readings that are not accounted for by the simple definition of reciprocity as requiring bidirectional relations holding between all possible pairs of participants.[39] It appears that languages are strikingly similar in this respect (see Bruening, 2004 on Japanese, Mandarin Chinese, Turkish and Indonesian; and Dalrymple et al., 1994 on Chicheŵa). The most frequently cited typology of situation types is offered in Dalrymple et al. (1998), building on earlier studies such as Fiengo and Lasnik (1973) and Langendoen (1978). Evans et al. (forthcoming) have established (and empirically tested) a more fine-grained typology that includes additional parameters such as the (non-) simultaneity of subevents. The situation types distinguished by Dalrymple et al. (1998) are illustrated by the examples in (69)–(73) (including the terms that Dalrymple et al. assign to these types):

(69) All the people in the house know each other really well. (Strong reciprocity[40])

(70) Five Boston pitchers sat alongside each other: Larry Anderson, Jeff Reardon, Jeff Gray, Dennis Lamp and Tom Bolton. (Intermediate reciprocity)

(71) "The captain!" said the pirates, staring at each other in surprise. (One-way weak reciprocity)

(72) The third-grade students gave each other measles. (Intermediate alternative reciprocity)

(73) Ile and scores of other inmates slept on foot-wide wooden planks stacked atop each other like sardines in a can in garage-sized holes in the ground. (Inclusive alternative ordering)

In the case of strong reciprocity (SR), every member of the relevant set is directly related to every other member of the set. Intermediate reciprocity (IR) is weaker in that it is only possible for every participant to be directly or indirectly related to every other participant via the relation expressed, in the case of (70) *sit alongside*. An even weaker type of reciprocity is expressed by a sentence featuring one-way weak reciprocity (OWR), such as (71). Here, every member participates with some other member in the relation 'as the first argument of the relation' (Dalrymple et al., 1998: 172). Note that in the example under discussion, world knowledge favours the reading in which each pirate stares at every other pirate at the same time. The crucial point in the example of intermediate alternative reciprocity (IAR) (cf. [72]) is that the participants form a single connected structure. Inclusive alternative ordering (IAO), as exemplified in (73), requires that every participant interacts with some other participant as actor or undergoer, but not necessarily in both roles. For formal definitions of these situation types, see Dalrymple et al. (1998: 169–174).

It is obvious that all situation types other than SR differ in an important way from the type of situation that is normally taken to be characteristic of reciprocity: a situation with two participants between which a bidirectional relation holds, or a situation with more participants in which a bidirectional relation holds for every possible pair of participants. Intuitively, the further one goes through the list of situation types the more marginal the type of reciprocity seems to become. This impression corresponds to the analysis in Dalrymple et al. (1998: 186–192), where reciprocity is parameterized, the three parameters FUL, LIN and TOT being relevant:

(i) FUL: each pair of individuals in A may be required to participate in the relation R directly.

(ii) LIN: each pair of individuals in A may be required to participate in the relation R either directly or indirectly.

(iii) TOT: each single individual in A may be required to participate in the relation R with another one.

Combining these parameters yields different degrees of reciprocal strength (Dalrymple et al., 1998: 188), formally expressed as implications from the stronger to the weaker types. It is furthermore assumed that a reciprocal sentence always expresses the strongest reading that is logically compatible with the proposition expressed ('Strongest Meaning Hypothesis'; see also Winter, 2001).

I think it is important to point out that the particular set of situation types under discussion is not derived from some pre-established concept of reciprocity that would cover all of them. Rather it is the fact that sentences involving the reciprocal *each other* are able to express these situations, which keeps them together. Unless one wants to define 'reciprocal' as 'a situation compatible with the expression *each other*', it is thus difficult to tell where the realm of reciprocity as a semantic notion ends.

On the one hand, we can be quite certain that the range of meanings that reciprocal sentences of the basic reciprocal type may express is not related via accidental homonymy. The fact that the same kind or at least similar ranges of meanings can be found in language after language strongly supports the assumption that we are witnessing a set of meanings which are conceptually related (see the contributions in Evans et al., forthcoming, for instance). On the other hand, whether we want to call all or only some of these meanings 'reciprocal' is eventually an arbitrary terminological decision.

How Many Situation Types?

A crucial observation with respect to the situation types that reciprocal sentences express is the one made by Fiengo and Lasnik (1973: 453–454), who examine examples like (74) a. and b.:

(74) a. The people in the room knew each other.
   b. The people in the room helped each other.

Whereas (74) a. suggests an SR relationship, i.e. every individual in the room knew all other individuals in the room, (74) b. is weaker in this respect. The sentence is true in a situation in which every individual in the room helped some other individual and gets help from some other individual. In fact, depending on the number of individuals at issue the reading may even be weaker, but what is important for the moment is just the contrast between (74) a. and b.

Bruening (2004) follows up Fiengo and Lasnik's (1973) observation and claims that the distinction between stative and eventive predicates in reciprocal sentences correlates with a binary opposition between two types of reciprocal strength. Importantly, the generalization also holds for the other languages he investigated in this respect: Japanese, Mandarin Chinese, Turkish and Indonesian. In general, he argues that Dalrymple et al.'s (1998) well-known classification of reciprocal situation types can be reduced to SR for stative predicates and two-way weak reciprocity (henceforth TWR) for eventive predicates (for details and exemplification see Bruening, 2004). TWR says that every participant acts on some other participant and is acted on by some other participant.

How can TWR account for 'chaining' cases (cf. Lichtenberk, 2000), analyzed as IR, IAR and IAO in Dalrymple et al. (1998: 170)?

(75) a. The students followed each other in to the lecture hall.
   b. The campsites sit right alongside each other. [COCA]

Bruening (2004) argues convincingly that, by taking into account non-maximality, Dalrymple et al.'s (1998) additional types can be reduced to TWR. At the same time this expunges certain wrong predictions that Dalrymple et al.'s (1998) definitions make (see Bruening, 2004: 33). If we imagine (75) a. to describe a single line of students walking into the lecture hall, TWR would in principle require every student to follow at least one other student and be followed by at least one other student. On the face of it this situation is not covered by TWR—at the beginning of the line there is one student who does not follow another student and at the end of the line there is one student who is not followed by another student. If we take into account the fact, however, that TWR allows exceptions in situations with a sufficiently large number of participants, the first and the last student in the line would count as exceptions and thus not contradict TWR.

The possibility of exceptions in reciprocal situations is not restricted to chaining situations and has been well known for a long time. As mentioned earlier, Fiengo and Lasnik (1973) and Williams (1991) observe that the sentence *They were hitting each other* would be appropriate in a situation involving a brawling group of people in a bar, with two individuals who are neither hitting anyone nor being hit by anyone else. Beck (2000a) did a recent study that is concerned with exceptions (i.e. non-maximality) and their relevance to relational plurals and reciprocals. As a starting point, note that predications over plural noun phrases do not always require strict universal quantification over all referents of the plural noun phrase. Consider the following example:

(76) The boys are building a tree house.

If the group of boys in (76) is large enough, the sentence does not entail that every single boy is actively engaged in the building of the tree house. This holds for both the collective reading (the boys are building one tree house as a group) and the distributive reading (the boys are building individual tree houses). The possibility of having exceptions is removed by a universal quantifier like *all* or *each*, in both reciprocal and non-reciprocal sentences.[41]

If we assume that non-maximality is a factor which is in principle independent of reciprocal strength, semantic effects which are due to non-maximality should not lead us to posit new types of reciprocal strength. Let us again consider the examples in (75). Sentence (75) a. describes a situation in which there is a queue of students such that the first student in the line does not follow any other student and the last student in the line is not followed by any other student. TWR thus appears to be violated. If we take into account the possibility of non-maximality, however, the two students at the beginning and the end of the line can be regarded as exceptions. By the same token, the two campsites sitting at the left and the right end of the relevant stretch of land in (75) b. do not present a problem for TWR if we consider them to be exceptions to the kind of relation that TWR requires. Given that we need non-maximality for plural predications in general and reciprocal sentences like *They were hitting each other* in particular, it is no ad hoc move to invoke it in chaining situations as well.

Also Dalrymple et al.'s (1998) OWR has been criticized. Beck (2000a) reconsiders (71), repeated here as (77):

(77) "The captain!" said the pirates, staring at each other in surprise.

Recall that OWR requires that every individual in the set denoted by the subject acts on some other member of the set, or in other words: for every x there must be some y such that (xVy), V standing for the verbal predicate. Beck (2000a) now shows that OWR is too weak a reading for the situation referred to in (77). OWR would correctly account for the situation that is schematically rendered in Figure 2.1. What OWR would also admit, however, is the situation in Figure 2.2.

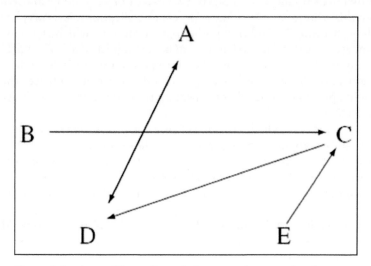

Figure 2.1   A possible reading of *pirates staring at each other*.

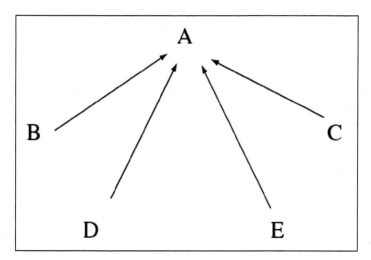

Figure 2.2   An impossible reading of *pirates staring at each other*.

Sentence (77) is not acceptable as a description of the situation in Figure 2.2. Beck (2000a) concludes: 'It seems to be too weak to require that only one member of the pirate group needs to be stared at' (4). If we analyze example (77) as a sentence exhibiting TWR admitting a limited number of exceptions, a situation such as the one in Figure 2.2 is ruled out, because there are too many exceptions. In Figure 2.1 there are two exceptions: pirates B and E are not stared at. Figure 2.2, by contrast, has three exceptions: pirates B, C and D are not stared at.[42] Although no one has yet come up with a theory of how to predict the acceptable number of exceptions for a given number of participants, it is intuitively plausible that in a group of five individuals no more than one or two exceptions should be allowed. To sum up this section, despite some apparent complications, it seems plausible to follow Bruening's (2004) hypothesis, according to which the only two types of reciprocal strength that have to be distinguished are SR and TWR, especially if non-maximality is taken into account as an independent factor. Let us now have a brief look at a class of reciprocal sentences that on first sight appears to contradict the neat division of reciprocal readings into SR and TWR.

In those cases in which the subject of a reciprocal sentence refers to a set of non-overlapping subsets, reciprocal relations may hold either within or between those subsets. In such sentences the domain in which variation between different degrees of reciprocal strength takes place is not necessarily the whole set of individuals introduced by the subject. Consider (78):

(78) a. In reality, adults and children usually ended up furtively edging around each other, anxious trying to detect matching personalities. [BNN 140]

b. They are married to one another. (Langendoen, 1978: 191)

Example (78) a. has at least three readings, the most salient of which is the following: adults were edging around children and children were edging around adults. The second reading is less plausible, but could be made more prominent by an appropriate context: adults were edging around adults and children were edging around children. Only the third reading corresponds to those cases that we have looked at so far: adults and children form an undifferentiated group, and individuals from that group were edging around each other. In the latter type of reading we have the same situation as in (74) a. and (74) b. There is a non-partitioned set of individuals of which a certain reciprocal relation is predicated. But reciprocal sentences with subsets should not be taken to contradict the generalizations under discussion in this chapter. The latter concerns the necessary strength of reciprocity within a non-partitioned set—Bruening (2004: 35–36) comes to the same conclusion. In (74) a. and (74) b. this set consists of all the referents introduced by the subject noun phrase, while in cases like (78) there are two or more sets in which a certain strength of reciprocity holds. The relevant domain is thus any non-partitioned set, irrespective of whether it is a subset of a larger set or not.

Example (78) b. is interesting in this respect, because here it is not the form of the subject noun phrase that suggests a partitioning, but rather the meaning of the predicate (see also Schwarzschild, 1996: 109–110). A 'married-to' relation can only hold between two individuals (in Western societies). As soon as *they* in (78) b. refers to a set of, say, eight individuals, the only logically possible reading would be a subset reading in which there are four married couples.

It should have become clear that by taking into account non-maximality and subset partitioning the logically necessary number of reciprocal situation types posited by Dalrymple et al. (1998) can sensibly be reduced to the ones distinguished in Bruening (2004). It is another issue, however, according to which parameters languages actually differentiate situation types. Since Dalrymple et al. (1998) restrict their attention to reciprocal sentences in English, we do not know whether there are perhaps other semantic parameters according to which languages distinguish situation types. This concerns the temporal dimension, for instance: is it relevant for the applicability of a reciprocal construction whether the two (or more) subevents take place simultaneously or rather one after the other? We will see in Chapter 5 that this is one of the factors that in English determine the choice between the reciprocal constructions available for a given verb. The chapters in Evans et al. (forthcoming) as well as the data in the Berlin-Utrecht Reciprocals Survey (http://reciprocals.eu/) provide evidence from other languages.[43]

2.9 RECIPROCITY AS A GRAMMATICAL CATEGORY

There is an important difference between reciprocal situations and the concepts expressed by many other grammatical markers, especially inflectional morphemes. Whereas the latter cannot normally be left unexpressed inflectionally just because they are spelled out by non-specialized means, this is different for reciprocity. Consider the inflectional categories number and person. The examples in (79) illustrate that the inflectional marking of the value 'third person (singular)' on the verb cannot be dispensed with in favour of spelling out this value in an additional clause.

(79) a. Ellen loves ice cream.
   b. *Ellen love-ø ice cream, Ellen being third person.
   c. *Ellen love-ø ice cream, and Ellen is neither me nor you.

By the same token, the nominal category number is obligatorily coded on the noun in English. A spelling out of the relevant concept in a separate clause is not allowed to replace the inflectional marking. For this reason,

(80) b. and (80) c. are ungrammatical. Note again that, as in the case of (79), the meaning that would be conveyed by the relevant inflectional affix is made clear by the added clause. On top of that, the numeral *three* preceding the noun *guitar(s)* in (80) already selects for a plural interpretation of the noun.

(80) a. I bought three guitars.
   b. *I bought three guitars-ø, and the set of guitars I bought was not a singleton set.
   c. *I bought three guitars-ø, the number of guitars I bought being more than two.

In sum, what these rather obvious facts about inflectional categories are meant to make clear is that grammatical information must normally be expressed in a fixed way and the piece of information at issue cannot be spelled out by the speaker in any manner that might make the semantics of the category and its chosen value clear. I would like to stress this, because reciprocity is crucially different. As illustrated in (81), and (2)–(7) earlier, reciprocal situations are not obligatorily expressed by the basic reciprocal strategy, i.e. the strategy that was characterized as the default way of conveying reciprocity.

(81) a. We love each other.
   b. I love her and she loves me.
   c. Each of us loves the other.

To be sure, speakers do not seem to choose arbitrarily between the different strategies. The basic reciprocal strategy is the most frequent and semantically most general reciprocal strategy with ordinary transitive verbs (thus excluding symmetric and prototypically reciprocal verbs and reciprocal situations expressed by words from other parts of speech). Alternative strategies are usually used if certain aspects of the situation (or the speaker's construal of the situation) to be expressed select for them. In this way, as soon as one moves beyond the semantic level of truth-conditions, the three sentences in (81) are not synonymous. Yet, as long as we call the situations expressed by (81) a., b. and c. 'reciprocal situations' the fact remains that there are various ways of linguistically expressing these situations, something that is excluded for other grammatical categories like person and number. In fact, the observation that the different ways of expressing reciprocal situations also correspond to functional differences underlines the aforementioned contrast between reciprocity and other grammatical categories. With categories such as number or person no subtle modifications of the meanings to be expressed are allowed. In my view, this property of reciprocity as a category is compatible with the fact that even the basic reciprocal strategy, i.e. the reciprocal strategy which seems to be most integrated into the grammatical system of English, is slightly variable in its meaning (see Chapter 5). In this way the basic reciprocal strategy is situated between fully fledged grammatical morphemes like person or number, on the one hand, and a description of a state of affairs without grammatical means, on the other.

3 Historical Development

This chapter deals with the diachronic side of reciprocity in English. Rather than being a fully fledged historical investigation into the available historical data, I will make use of extant studies on the relevant topics and information provided in historical handbooks and other reference works, as well as data extracted from historical corpora and texts. In addition, some more theoretical issues will be brought up and dealt with in greater detail. In general, this chapter is meant to provide the historical background for the characterization of how the expression of reciprocity is organized in PDE. My guiding assumption is that synchronic facts can only be fully explained if they are seen in the light of their diachronic developments.

The structure of Chapter 3 is the following: after a general overview of reciprocal marking in the history of English, I will concentrate on the development of the reciprocal expressions *each other* and *one another*. In this context, we will come across the issue of which types of linguistic change have played a role in the formation of these expressions. The second major part of the chapter will deal with intransitive verbs of the type *meet* and *marry*, and changes that the use of such verbs has undergone.

3.1 GENERAL OVERVIEW

I subscribe to the standard view of dividing the history of English into the following periods: Old English (700–1100; henceforth OE), Middle English (1100–1400, henceforth ME), Early Modern English (1400–1700; henceforth eModE), Modern English (1700–1900; henceforth ModE), PDE (1900–the present). As usual in historical studies on English, it should be noted that the assumption of a straightforward path from a variety called OE to a variety called PDE is an extreme simplification. The major reason is that what I refer to here as 'English' is really a set of dialects which in parts display remarkable differences. The bulk of textual data from OE belongs to the dialect of West Saxon, whereas in the case of ME and all stages following ME data from other regions of Britain are available as well. The transition from OE to ME textual evidence is also not as neat as the historical linguist would wish, because there is a gap in transmission at the time of the Norman Conquest in 1066. The picture is further complicated by the fact that standardization has played a far more significant part in all periods following ME (cf. Nevalainen and van Ostade, 2006). As a consequence, one finds less variation across different texts from that period. As for dialectal variation, I have taken it to be justifiable to abstract away from it for the purposes of this chapter. The only extant study that systematically includes dialect variation, Sheen (1988), shows that there are no significant inter-dialectal differences with respect to the expression of reciprocity in ME, apart from minor variations within the set of available strategy subtypes. The same seems to hold for eModE and also PDE.

In general, the grammar of reciprocity develops in such a way that, on the one hand, the number of conventionally used strategies is reduced to a small number of constructions, and, on the other, the forms and functions of those strategies that are available in PDE have undergone some inconspicuous but crucial changes. Both types of change can be seen as a result of an ongoing integration of linguistic items into the grammatical system of English ('grammaticalization' in the widest sense). Roughly, the most important changes leading to the present system took place in a period covering late ME and eModE, where the two forms *each other* and *one another* were established as fixed argument expressions in reciprocal sentences and other competing forms such as *either other* disappeared. The option of spelling out reciprocal situations in the ways described in Chapter 3, section 3.3, has of course always remained available, but these strategies have become restricted functionally as a result of the expansion of more grammaticalized reciprocal strategies. In the following, I will go through the relevant changes that the attested reciprocal strategies have undergone. Since several of the strategies identified in König and Kokutani's (2006) typology of reciprocal constructions are also found in early English,[1] I will take these authors' typology as a guideline.

3.2 TYPES OF RECIPROCAL MARKING

König and Kokutani (2006) distinguish the following types of monoclausal reciprocal strategies:[2]

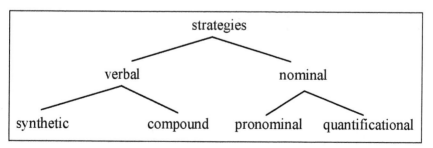

Figure 3.1 Types of reciprocal strategy; from König and Kokutani (2006).

The main distinction is between nominal and verbal strategies. Verbal strategies can be subdivided into synthetic and compound strategies. Nominal strategies, in turn, can be subdivided into pronominal and bipartite strategies. The latter distinction concerns the internal make-up of the nominal reciprocal marker. Bipartite markers[3] typically consist of a quantifier and the alterity word 'other', the two being fused to a single word to different degrees, depending on the language. (Bipartite markers that are composed of source expressions not observed in English, e.g. demonstratives, will not be explored here; for detailed discussion the reader is referred to Hanke [in prep.].) A paradigm example of this type is of course English *each other*. Pronominal reciprocal markers, by contrast, are 'free forms or clitics that are typically used also as reflexive markers' (König and Kokutani, 2006: 279).

Of the reciprocal strategies distinguished here, early English primarily makes use of the two types of nominal strategy: pronominal and bipartite. With respect to the two verbal strategies it cannot be claimed with certainty that early English possessed either of them. Whether one regards the intransitive use of a restricted number of verbs as an instance of the synthetic strategy depends on one's exact analysis of these verbs: are they the result of applying a reciprocal construction to transitive verbs? Are they distinct lexical entries, viz. intransitive verbs being simply used as such? Discussion of this issue is provided in Chapter 4. For the time being we may consider it a reciprocal strategy on a par with the other two.

It would probably stretch the extension of the verbal type too much, but if anything it would be this type which covers the reciprocal use of certain adverbials in early English. Note also that Evans (2008) adds an adverbial type ('modifier strategy') to his typology. As shown in the following, in contrast to PDE, employing certain collective or reciprocal adverbials was a frequent means of expressing reciprocity. Let us now look at the different early English strategies in more detail.

An important way of expressing reciprocity in OE was the employment of either simple object pronouns or reflexives (i.e. pronouns in combination with the intensifier *self*) filling the slot of the object argument. Mitchell (1985: 116–117) and Visser (1963: 439–440) list a number of OE examples of this type:

(1) gif hi   hi   gemetaþ
    if they them met
    'when they meet with each other.' [Boeth. (Sedgefield) 63, 10]

(2) þæt ða aglæcean   hy   eft   gemetton.
    that the adversaries them often met
    'It was not long until those foes met again.' [Beowulf, 2591]

(3) hu   hie hie selfe mid missellican gefeohtum fordydon.
    how they them self with many   battles   killed
    'how they killed one another in many battles.' [Orosius (Bateley) 77, 8]

(4) þe hie to gode hæfdon ge eac him selfum betweonum
    that they to God had   and also them selves   between
    ' . . . which they had to God, and also among themselves.' [Orosius
    (Bateley) 38, 25]

It is difficult to find 'pure' OE instances of reciprocal sentences with object pronouns in combination with *self*. Apart from (3), Mitchell (1985: 117), for instance, cites only sentences which—in addition to the complex reflexive— also display the preposition *betweonan/betwynan*. In (4), cited by Mitchell (1985: 117) as an example of a complex reflexive expressing reciprocity, the reflexive figures in a construction that denotes what Gast and Haas (2008) term 'collective reflexivity' (see Chapter 2). Note that it is not only the OE original, but also the PDE translation that allows the use of a reflexive in what seems to be a reciprocal context.

As argued with respect to modern European languages in Gast and Haas (2008), and described for PDE in Chapter 2, such uses of the reflexive in combination with prepositions like *between* and *among* should be ana- lyzed as having not a reciprocal but rather a reflexive meaning. The latter interacts with the meaning of the preposition in the following way: it refers to a situation in which the action denoted by the verb is in some way car- ried out among the members of the group denoted by the subject. It is not necessary, therefore, to regard the reflexive expression in this use as having both a reflexive and a reciprocal meaning. Also, in this way it is no longer surprising that in PDE as well as in a number of other European languages, reflexives can generally not be used for the expression of reciprocity, except in combination with one of the aforementioned prepositions.

OE examples like (4) appear to fall into the same category. In other words, they do not demonstrate that OE complex reflexives could have a reciprocal meaning, whereas (3) is a clear instance of this type. The fact that many of the commonly cited alleged instances of complex reflexives in OE expressing reciprocity are really examples of collective reflexivity and therefore not of reciprocity proper is in line with statements to the effect that the reciprocal use of *self*-forms in OE is rather rare and becomes more frequent only in ME (see, e.g. Faiß, 1989: 178). Collective reflexive struc- tures, by contrast, are argued to be the most frequent reciprocal strategy in OE by Einenkel (1916: 138).

In the examples that follow, the relevant prepositions are used with sim- ple object pronouns not marked for reflexivity:

(5) hwylce twa sint þonne wiðerweardran betwuh him
    which two are then more.contrary between them
    'Which two are then more contrary to each other . . . ' [King Alfred's
    Old English Version of Boethius, Ch. XVI, 16]

(6) sawul and lichama, þe nu on ðisum life him betweonan winnað.
    soul and body that now in this life them between strive

' . . . soul and body, which now in this life strive with each other.'
[Homilies of Ælfric I, 272]

(7) þæt þa   cynegas seht   naman him   betwynan
    that the kings   in.agreement take   them between
    'that the kings should make peace with each other . . . ' [Anglo-Saxon
    Chronicles, A.D 1016, MS C]

As noted by Visser (1963: 441), the fact that *betweonan* and its variants
followed the pronoun more often than preceding it should not automatically lead us to conclude that *betweonan* was interpreted as an adverbial
adjunct following the reciprocal object. To him, the more plausible analysis
is to view the pronoun as the complement of *betweonan*. In fact, the case
marking of third-person pronouns in this position seems to be governed
by the preposition (Visser, 1963: 441). Another question concerning the
syntax of these structures is the one of whether the prepositional phrase
headed by the preposition *betweonan* is itself an adjunct or whether it is
rather governed by the verb. The answer to this question hinges both on
one's interpretation of some more general syntactic changes in the history
of English and on one's theoretical perspective. As far as the former point
is concerned, it will be argued that in general earlier English argument,
realization is more liberal in the sense of allowing the non-expression of
arguments, specifically objects. As a consequence, it may be possible that
the phrases involving *between* in the earlier examples are not as strictly
required by the predicate as we would expect from a PDE perspective.

In order to answer this question, one's theoretical perspective is also relevant because there are different views on whether a clause is simply a spelling
out of the predicates and its arguments, or a more or less abstract structure
that is itself related to a certain meaning or function. If one takes the first
perspective, the string *between* + pronoun in sentences like (5)–(7) is either a
complement of the relevant verb or an adjunct, and this is exactly the decision
that is far from easy to make here. If one takes a constructionist perspective,
the two aforementioned options are not the only possible ones. I propose to
consider the option that the structure in (5)–(7) is part of a semi-schematic
reciprocal construction that consists of a verb which may be transitive (and
thus normally requiring an object) and a phrase that in turn consists of the
preposition *betweoh* and an objective pronoun, the latter two elements being
able to occur in either order. The construction as a whole has the function of
expressing reciprocal relations.[4] Crucially, what distinguishes this construction from an ordinary transitive clause is the fact that it sanctions the non-
expression of the predicate's direct object. In turn, the syntactic function of
the phrase containing *between* can only be determined with respect to the
construction as a whole. In other words, it is neither a complement of the
verb nor an adjunct to a complete verb phrase.

Does this now mean that reflexive forms could not really be used to
express reciprocity in OE? This is definitely not the case. Note that OE

did not have a separate class of reflexive pronouns (or 'anaphors') comparable to the PDE forms of the type x-*self*. With certain verbs, simple object pronouns of all persons could be used with a reflexive reading. In late OE at the latest, the 'emphatic' *self* could be added to the pronoun, but in contrast to later stages of English it was still morphosyntactically independent of it.[5] Pronominal expressions with a reflexive meaning were able to express reciprocity until relatively recently (eModE), irrespective of whether the relevant items were specialized reflexives or rather, if they were ordinary object pronouns that could be used reflexively. Considering the chronology of events, however, it is striking that the point at which complex reflexive forms became the standard variant (cf. Visser, 1963: §454ff.) seems to coincide with the period in which these expressions lost the potential to express reciprocity. Both changes are attributed to the time of Shakespeare. Is this a pure coincidence or do the two changes in some way correlate?

Plank (2008) suggests that there is such a correlation: 'Once firmly entrenched, new and purpose-built reflexives are perhaps inclined for a while to remain dedicated to just that single function' (348). I take this quote to mean that reflexives became unavailable for the expression of reciprocity because they became conventionalized in a form that was transparently specialized for the expression of reflexivity. I consider there to be a problem with Plank's account: if the option of expressing reciprocity had been lost for reflexives just because they had become specialized for reflexivity, this is either a circular statement (given that reflexivity and reciprocity had been the only meanings the relevant forms could express[6]), or it implies that it is the emphatically reflexive meaning of the *self* element in the newly formed anaphors which preempted the reciprocal reading. But then we would have expected the impossibility of a reciprocal meaning much earlier, namely, in all cases in which *self* was added to the object pronoun. If, as has been repeatedly suggested in the literature (see, for example, König and Siemund, 2000; Keenan 2002: 346–347; Lange 2007), the compound reflexive had gradually lost its emphatic nature—the *self* element having been an intensifier to start with—it would be particularly surprising if reciprocity was part of the form's meaning at the stage at which the emphatic meaning component of the reflexive was still present, whilst it was lost at that stage at which the emphatic component, in turn, was no longer present (or at least to a lesser degree). But this is apparently the development that we observe. An explanation for why PDE reflexives may not express reciprocity must therefore be somewhat different. I propose that for the reasons given, there is nothing inherent in English reflexives to prevent them from being markers of reciprocity in addition to reflexivity.[7] It seems more probable that the reason for the PDE state of affairs has to be sought in the grammaticalization of the specialized reciprocal forms *each other* and *one another* (Haas, 2007).

The later development of the two reciprocals is best characterized as grammaticalization, if the latter is taken to be context expansion, both in the sense of occurring in a wider range of semantic and syntactic contexts and in the sense of gaining ground with respect to alternative strategies of expressing the same meaning. Presumably, then, the loss of reciprocal readings in eModE *self*-forms is due to the expansion of specialized reciprocal expressions.

A class of related strategies involves adverbs with a collective meaning or ones designating role reversal (see also Plank, 2008). The former type includes adverbs like *together*, i.e. adverbs expressing that the action denoted by the verb is jointly carried out by the participants that the subject denotes. The latter type comprises those adverbs that have a more narrowly reciprocal meaning, i.e. they express that the event or situation denoted by the verb holds reciprocally (cf. PDE *mutually*). Late ME examples of the first type of adverb include the following from Malory's *Morte Darthure* (see also Spies, 1897: 184; Jespersen, 1927: 332):

(8) *And thenne they sware to gyders that none of hem shold neuer fyghte ageynst other* . . . [Book 8, ch. xlj]

(9) *and so hurtled to gyders lyke two rammes that eyther felle to the erthe So at the last they smote to gyders that both her swerdys met euen to gyders.* [Book 1, ch. xxiij]

(10) *and so they loued to gyder more hotter than they did to fore hand.* [Book 18, ch. i]

(11) *thenne they put up their suerdes and kyssed hertely to gyders* . . . [Book 8, ch. xl]

The strategy—or rather the class of strategies—that seems most pertinent when it comes to accounting for the development of the modern reciprocals *each other* and *one another* involves combinations of two expressions that can be described as quantificational in the widest sense. Since the development of these structures will be more thoroughly discussed later, I will only give an example at this point and refer to the reader to sections 3.3 and 3.4 (for an overview, see Kahlas-Tarkka, 2004):

(12) wæron ealle on þæt gebæd-hus   gegaderode mid
     were   all   in the house.of.prayer gathered   with
     gebigedum cneowum and eadmodum gebede heora
     bended   knees   and humble   prayer of.them
     ælc oþerne   grette
     each other.ACC greeted
     ' . . . they were all gathered in the house of prayer with bended knees and humble prayer, and greeted each other.' [Ælfric, Lives of Saints, 8, 114]

Let us conclude this general overview by reconsidering the ways in which the expression of reciprocity has changed from OE to PDE. We can observe a striking general tendency. Not only have some of the available strategies been ousted, but the remaining default strategy, viz. the reciprocal construction involving one of the two expressions *each other* and *one another*, has also become more grammaticalized in the sense of being an integral part of the grammatical system of the language. More specifically, the two expressions are now a sort of pronoun that stands in a paradigmatic relationship with reflexives and other objective pronouns. The latter is a property which makes the PDE reciprocals crucially different from several of the strategies that were available in earlier stages of English. In sentences with the reciprocal (*each other* or *one another*), the latter fills an argument position. In other words, the verb's argument structure is always preserved by the reciprocal (or, in terms of construction grammar: the participant roles of the verb and the argument roles of the construction do not conflict).

If we compare this state of affairs to the situation in OE, the difference turns out to be the following: OE had a number of reciprocal strategies in which the two (or more) participants were denoted by a single syntactic argument and the remaining argument position was left unfilled. This is, of course, not unfamiliar to students of PDE, since the latter allows a number of verbs to occur intransitively in reciprocal contexts. As will be argued in more detail later (section 3.6), however, I take these to be different types of alternations. Let us now take in more detail how the English reciprocals have developed.

3.3 DIACHRONY OF THE RECIPROCALS

The reciprocal expressions *each other* and *one another* as they are used today are the result of a series of morphosyntactic and semantic changes. As a first step in this development, OE expressed reciprocal relations by using structures resembling a PDE sentence of the type *Each man helped the others*. But their status in the system is different: whereas in today's English such structures are relatively rare compared to reciprocal sentences involving one of the two expressions *each other* and *one another* (see Chapter 5), OE did not have the latter strategy at its disposal, the former type being correspondingly more widespread. Sentences of this type displayed diversity in the sense of making use of different component expressions. Consider (13), where the quantifiers are *ægðer*, *æghwæþer*, *gehwilc* and *ælc*:

(13) a. &   gebidde   hira   ægðer   for   oðer
        and prayed   of.them   either   for   other
        'and either of them prayed for the other . . . ' [Gregory the Great, Pastoral Care]

b. æghwæþrum wæs bealohycgendra brogan fram oðrum
   either.DAT   was evil   terror   from other.DAT
   'In each of the foes there was terror of the other.' [Beowulf, 2562]

c. 7   æghwæþer oþerne oftrædlice ut   dræfde
   and either   other   frequently out   forced
   'and they displaced each other several times.' [Anglo-Saxon Chronicle, A.D. 887, MS A]

d. and   het   gehwilcne oðerne aðwean fram fulum synnum
   and bid   each.ACC other   wash from foul   sins
   'and commanded each to wash the other from foul sins . . . ' [Ælfric,
   Hom. II, 14]

e. %   tihte   ælc oðerne to gode mid god   gebisnunge
   and stimulated each other to good by good example
   'and let everyone stimulate another to good by good example.'
   [Ælfric, Hom. I, 10]

Discussing Germanic in general, Plank (2008) also lists 'mid-scale' quantifiers (*several*, *many* etc.) as constituting the first part of this construction.
He does not provide evidence for their occurrence in reciprocal constructions. As far as English is concerned, I have not come across reciprocal sentences involving mid-scale quantifiers, but of course I cannot exclude their
existence. It is interesting to note, however, that from a cross-linguistic
point of view mid-scale quantifiers do not ever seem to constitute the first
part of a bipartite reciprocal marker (Hanke, in prep.).

At any rate, the variety of quantifiers in OE was larger than today's variety
in the following way: whereas in PDE reciprocity may of course be expressed
by any semantically appropriate quantifier in a transparent structure like
Either of the two frowned upon the other, such sentences have a different status from the corresponding structures in earlier English. In earlier English all
reciprocal sentences employing quantifiers and the alterity word were transparent in the same way: the reciprocal meaning was derived directly from
the combination of the quantified subject, the verb meaning and the alterity
word. This has not become impossible, yet the conventional way of expressing reciprocity with ordinary transitive verbs (i.e. excluding symmetric and
prototypically reciprocal verbs) today is to fill an argument position with one
of the reciprocals: *each other* or *one another*. For these reciprocal expressions
there is no choice between different quantifiers, given that reciprocals like
any other, *every other* or *either other* are impossible.[8] As argued in detail
in Chapter 5, the two types of reciprocal sentences—the basic reciprocal construction and the split quantificational construction—are not totally synonymous in PDE, and there is thus a functional niche for the latter even today. In
OE (and later), by contrast, there was no such choice. This means that what
is now a transparent structure filling a functional niche in the grammar of
reciprocity was once one of the central ways of expressing reciprocity.

In OE the different combinations of quantifier and alterity word were not all equally common. Kahlas-Tarkka (2004: 128) extracted reciprocal sentences involving the aforementioned quantifiers from the Helsinki Corpus and the Toronto material for the Dictionary of Old English and provides the following frequencies: '75 instances of *ælc* [. . .], 10 of *æghwilc* and *gehwilc* each, three of *gehwa*, and none of the infrequent word *æghwa* "every"'. The rarity of *gehwa* and *aeghwa* in reciprocal constructions can easily be explained by their rarity in general, according to Kahlas-Tarkka (2004: 128). As far as the higher frequency of *ælc* as opposed to *æghwilc*, *gehwilc* and *gehwa* is concerned, it would be tempting to make reference to the difference in meaning between PDE *each* and *every*. *Each* is claimed to be more strongly distributive than *every*. Furthermore, *each* usually 'involves some pairing of two domains' (McCawley, 1977: 374). Consider the following sentences from McCawley (1977), where this principle explains the oddity of (14) c., as opposed to the corresponding sentences with other quantifiers.

(14) a. Take all of the apples.
    b. Take every one of the apples.
    c. ?Take each of the apples.
    d. Take each of the apples and weigh it.
    e. Take any one of the apples and weigh it.

The pairing function of *each* appears to be particularly suitable for reciprocal sentences of the bipartite type: single individuals are paired in such a way that one of the reciprocal situation types results. At least from a diachronic point of view this line of argumentation is not convincing, however. Kahlas-Tarkka (1987) shows that the subtle semantic aspects distinguishing PDE *each* from other universal quantifiers are a relatively late development. It would be inaccurate, therefore, to explain the frequency contrast cited earlier by making reference to the special semantic properties of PDE *each* as opposed to those of *every* and *all*.

Formal Changes

How have bipartite reciprocals evolved historically? In a nutshell, the development of quantifier and alterity word into an invariable expression—apart from changes in the position of the relevant items—comprises changes in the inflection on the verb and the two items themselves. As for verbal inflection, it is the change from singular to plural agreement that indicates that the quantifier is no longer analyzed as the subject of the clause. The subject slot is then filled by another noun, which has to be plural and denote all participants involved in the reciprocal relation. We can depict this change schematically as follows:

(15) a. Each knight fights the other.
b. The knights fight each other.

The situation in OE is almost invariably one in which the quantifier in reciprocal sentences occupies an argument slot distinct from the one occupied by the alterity word. The examples in (13) show that the quantifier does not have to be in the nominative. Sentence (13) b., for instance, has *æghwæþrum* in the dative[9] and in (13) d. *gehwilcne* has an accusative form, being part of an 'Exceptional Case Marking' (ECM) (or 'AcI') construction. In the majority of cases, however, the quantifier displays nominative case and the alterity word is marked for an objective or oblique case. Furthermore, it should be noted that the quantifier can either stand alone, as in (13) c., be the head of a possessive phrase (cf. [13] a.), or function as a determiner (or 'pre-nominal modifier') of a full noun or a post-verbal quantifier, as will be discussed in more detail later in relation to the emergence of reciprocal pronouns.

Let us briefly survey the morphological properties of the alterity word in OE, with some projection to later changes. The word *oðer*, which did not only mean 'other', but also functioned as the ordinal numeral 'second', is declined like an adjective. It is special in this regard in that it always follows the strong inflection. The fact is worth mentioning, among other things, because the dative forms are identical in the singular and the plural. As a consequence, it is often impossible to determine whether in an OE reciprocal sentence the alterity word is singular or plural, which makes it harder to examine the correlation between the number of participants and the number specification of the alterity word. To exemplify this point with a PDE example, in sentences involving a dative form of the alterity word a contrast such as the following would not be visible in OE:

(16) a. The two priests each gave a bible to the other.
b. The three priests each gave a bible to the others.

As discussed in relation to the lexicalization of the reciprocal in the following, the alterity word can show plural agreement in reciprocal sentences with more than two participants, if it is syntactically separate from the quantifier. Apart from this syncretism, however, OE shows more formal variability than the corresponding PDE forms. Specifically, there is inflection for case on the alterity word, i.e. it inflects for dative, accusative and genitive case.

As is commonly known, this situation changed in ME, which was a period characterized by the reduction of inflectional morphology. The alterity word *oðer* was no exception to this development, with a complication, however. It did not simply lose all inflectional marking, with number being regularly marked on *other* today (*other* [Sg.]–*others* [Pl.]). What did change was the morphological exponent of the plural. As pointed out by Einenkel (1903), the substitution of the plural suffix was not at all a sudden change:

> Die alte substantivische plural-form *opre* ist in ihren regelrechten laut-lichen verjüngungen *oth(e)re other* noch bis etwa zur mitte des 16. jah-rhunderts in reichlichem gebrauche. Von dieser zeit an wird der bereits gegen ende der me. Periode sporadisch auftauchende neue plural *others* häufiger. Doch ist [. . .] der alte plural nicht selten noch im 17. jahr-hundert zu beobachten. [The old substantival plural form *opre* is in the form of its regularly developed variant *oth(e)re other*, commonly used until the middle of the sixteenth century. From this time on the new plural form *others*, already occurring sporadically at the end of the ME period, becomes more frequent. Nevertheless, the old plural form can still be observed in the seventeenth century; my translation.] (521)

Case marking on *other* became obsolete in ME, thus making the emerging reciprocal expression more invariable formally.

With respect to bipartite reciprocal marking in general, the situation did not change considerably in ME. The data collected by Sheen (1988) show remarkable variation in the expressions making up the structure under dis-cussion. The number of sentences he compiled certainly does not allow us to draw any statistically significant conclusions as to the dominant status of one or another structure. What Sheen's (1988) examples do demonstrate, however, is that ME retains the aforementioned variability in the position of the quantifiers that will turn out to be an important prerequisite for the genesis of the later reciprocals of the type *each other*. To be sure, the same positional freedom already existed in OE. But apparently, it is only in ME that the univerbation of the two elements takes place. It is not unreasonable to assume that the increasing formal invariance of the two expressions con-stituting the reciprocal-to-be facilitated the reanalysis as a single expres-sion. Consider the following examples from Malory's *Morte Darthure*, where the two elements are adjacent and follow the verb, thus in a position that supposedly led to their reanalysis as a reciprocal expression:

(17) a. how they smote eche other. [25/22]
   b. I wil wil said Balan that we do and we wil helpe eche other . . . [83/17]
   c. and they brysed their helmes and their hauberks and wounded eyther other. [142/13]
   d. . . . they graunted eyther other to rest . . . [238/35]
   e. Soo they went vnto bataille ageyne and wounded euerych other dolefully. [18/97]

Similar examples can be found in many other ME texts. Example (18) gives two instances:

(18) a. Kindeli eche other clipt and kessed ful oft. [a1375, William of Pal-
erne, 1833]

  b. Men of the lond. .robbede eche oþer for socour of þe peril of honger
þat þey sigh hem schulde befalle. [a1387, John Trevisa, Higden's
Polychronicon, 5.229]

In eModE *each other* and *one another* established themselves as the main
strategy of expressing reciprocity with ordinary transitive verbs. Which
types of grammatical change were responsible for this development will be
discussed in the following section.

3.4 TYPES OF CHANGE IN THE DEVELOPMENT OF *EACH OTHER* AND *ONE ANOTHER*

Up to now I have remained rather neutral in regard to the issue of what
kind of grammatical change the formation of the two reciprocal expressions
each other and *one another* exemplify. Plank (2008: 362) calls it 'grammaticalization', without, however, discussing arguments for or against this
particular choice of terminology. The same holds for Raumolin-Brunberg
(1997) and Kahlas-Tarkka (2004).[10]

Apart from grammaticalization, lexicalization appears to be a serious
alternative. It is certainly not the only alternative, and we will see later that
especially for *one another* analogy and borrowing may also play a role.
Yet in this section I will focus on grammaticalization and lexicalization.
In order to apply this distinction to the formation and later development
of *each other* and *one another*, it has to be clear how to best draw the line
between the two phenomena in the first place. One should not start from
the assumption, of course, that both of the English reciprocals must have
developed in exactly the same way. Although not much is known about
the exact development of *one another*—Plank (2008), for example, tacitly
assumes that reciprocal expressions involving quantifiers other than *each*
have developed in the same way as those including *each*—it is not implausible to assume that this has not been the case, especially in the early stages
of their history. For this reason, I will first concentrate on the development
of *each other* (see also Haas, 2007) and discuss the special properties of
one another separately in section 3.5.

The search for the best way of distinguishing lexicalization and grammaticalization has become a major topic in the grammaticalization literature in recent years (Wischer, 2000; Brinton, 2002; Himmelmann, 2004;
Brinton and Traugott, 2005; Lindstroem, 2005; Fischer, 2007; Trousdale,
2008). Many problems are due to the fact that linguists do not always agree
on how to define the two processes. Clearly, if there were precise definitions
of both lexicalization and grammaticalization and if the description of the
formal and functional components of a given instance of language change

is adequate, one should be able to assign it to one of the two phenomena. As convincingly argued by Himmelmann (2004), an important step in this direction would be to discount the 'box metaphor' of grammaticalization. According to the box metaphor, grammaticalization is taken to be a shift of linguistic items from the lexicon to the grammar. This cannot account for some instances of change that are usually considered to be grammaticalization, among other things those which involve source expressions that are already grammatical.[11]

I will argue later that the genesis of the reciprocal *each other* is an example of this dilemma. Furthermore, for a number of items such as derivational affixes and function words, linguists do not agree on whether they are part of the lexicon or part of the grammar. By the same token, it is not obvious why the expression *each other* is 'more grammatical' than its source expressions *each* and *other*. From a more general and theoretical point of view, the strict partition of a given language into a lexicon on the one hand and a grammar on the other has also turned out to be problematical. All those theoretical frameworks, most prominently construction grammar, recognizing that patterns larger than words display semantically and syntactically idiosyncratic properties and have to be represented as independent items, concede that a strict division cannot be made between the lexicon as an open set of formally and semantically idiosyncratic words and the grammar as a finite set of totally regular rules building sentences in a syntactically and semantically transparent manner (see, among others, Fillmore et al., 1988; Culicover, 1999; Jackendoff, 2002; Michaelis, 2003; Culicover and Jackendoff, 2005; Goldberg, 2005).

Himmelmann (2004), whose position in this respect conforms to the one of Bybee (1988) and Bybee and Dahl (1989), opts for a 'process-based approach'. What this means is that grammaticalization and lexicalization are defined by making reference to the diachronic processes that linguistic items and constructions undergo. In accordance with what is normally attributed to the two phenomena anyway, Himmelmann then defines grammaticalization as semantic/pragmatic and syntactic context expansion[12] and lexicalization as the co-occurrence of univerbation and fossilization (for detailed discussion and exemplification, see Himmelmann, 2004). In the following, I argue that, along the lines of this approach, a satisfying answer to the question of whether the formation of *each other* is a case of grammaticalization or lexicalization can only be given by making reference to a process-based definition of the two phenomena (see also Haas, 2007).[13]

Lexicalization of the Reciprocal *Each Other*

The historical development of the reciprocal *each other* was surveyed earlier. Here I focus on those aspects of its formation that are pertinent to the issue of lexicalization. This includes the univerbation of the two elements making up the reciprocal, as well as possible symptoms of fossilization thereof, but also the fact that *each other* (and initially its 'pre-univerbated' variant) had competed with a number of similar strategies before replacing the latter and thus expanding the contexts in which it could occur.

As for the univerbation of *each* and *other*, an important step was the stage between ME and early eModE where the two items must have been reanalyzed as a unit, or—more specifically—as a nominal constituent being able to fill argument positions. Since no obvious signs of morphological or phonological fusion can be observed for this stage, the first clear sign of unit status are those reciprocal sentences in which *each* and *other* occur in positions where the grammar would not allow them to occur if they fulfilled independent functions in the sentence. Reciprocal sentences involving prepositional phrases are a case in point (see also Plank, 2008). In (19) the relevant change is illustrated by two examples providing the state of affairs preceding the reanalysis ([19] a.–b.) and one example providing the state of affairs following reanalysis ([19] c.).

(19) a. And there vppon they cast eche to other their gloves . . . [Helsinki Corpus, ME IV (1420–1500)]
b. They foynen ech at oother wonder longe. [Chaucer, Canterbury Tales, Knight's Tale, 1654]
c. I praie God send them comfort of eche other. [1546, John Johnson 481; cited in Raumolin Brunberg 1997]

Since English syntax did not allow quantifiers to float behind a preposition, sentences like (19) c. can only be accounted for if we assume that the string *each other* was treated as a single noun phrase. In order to qualify as lexicalization as defined in the preceding section, the formation of *each other* should also exhibit fossilization. Again, the process of fossilization is taken here to consist of the component elements of a complex expression shedding their independent meanings. This happens when speakers come to interpret a complex expression as a single whole. In other words, the complex expression loses its semantic transparency, and may change its meaning in such a way that the independent meanings of the hitherto component elements can no longer be taken to build up the meaning of the whole.

On the formal side, two types of change would indicate fossilization. First, the newly formed unit may preserve formal properties that the component expressions had exhibited at the point before they began to form a unit. Second, morphological material may be lost. This can also concern exponents of inflectional categories. The latter type of formal fossilization becomes particularly obvious if those items that make up the newly formed unit are still used independently of the fossilized expression. We will see that the element *other* has come to show inflectional behaviour that diverges from that of the independent use of the same form after it formed a unit with *each*.

Univerbation in the narrow sense of morphological fusion cannot be observed in the case of the reciprocal.[14] Instead we have to turn to the other properties mentioned earlier: morphological properties that are either productive elsewhere today and lost in the form at issue, or the conservation of otherwise obsolete morphology. From the point of view of PDE it seems that the former option applies to *each other*. Consider plural inflection on *other* when used independently, in contrast with being the second part of the reciprocal *each other*:

(20) a. John, Harry and George know each other.
  b. John and Harry know each other.
  c. John, Harry and George each know the others.
  d. John and Harry each know the other.

The PDE data in (20) demonstrate that with respect to plural marking, the element *other* as part of the reciprocal behaves differently from its counterpart outside the reciprocal (see also McCawley, 1988: 355). Sentences (20) a. and (20) b. make use of the reciprocal, while (20) c. and (20) d. spell out the reciprocal situation. In the present context it is crucial that the form of the alterity word can vary according to the number of participants in (20) c. and (20) d., while it is invariably singular in (20) a. and (20) b.

In what way does the form of other in (20) c. and (20) d. depend on the number of participants? The sentences in (20) all express strong reciprocity, i.e. every participant in the set denoted by the subject acts on every other participant in that set. For sentences like (20) c. and (20) d., in which the reciprocal relation between the participants listed by the subject noun phrase is spelled out by what we called the 'split quantificational strategy' in Chapter 2, the reciprocal meaning is arrived at in the following way: *each* in (20) c. and (20) d. quantifies over the sets {john,harry,george} and {john,harry} respectively. Each individual in the set is then put into a relation with the denotatum of the object, i.e. *the others* in the case of (20) c. and *the other* in the case of (20) d. Since reciprocal sentences involving stative verbs such as *know* and a relatively small number of participants always display strong reciprocity (see Chapter 2), the alterity word in the sentences at issue refers to two individuals in (20) c. and one individual in (20) d. This number is the total number of individuals in the subject set less the one individual picked out by *each* for any possible relation.[15] The same effect should be expected for the alterity word in (20) a. and (20) b. if it were an independent word contributing to the sentence meaning parallel to its counterparts in (20) c. and (20) d. Since this is not the case I take the invariability of *other* to be an indicator of fossilization.

From the diachronic point of view, the reasons for the alterity word as part of the reciprocal *each other* having a singular form as opposed to a plural form are not as easy to determine. When we consider the sentences in (20) and roughly identify (20) c. and (20) d. with the pattern that gave rise to the PDE reciprocal *each other*, different options come to mind. The singular form as employed in contexts with two participants might have been generalized to those contexts involving more than two participants. Another reason for the PDE state of affairs may be that the plural form of the alterity word was first frozen as part of the invariable reciprocal and later shed as a result of phonological erosion. It appears that neither of these two scenarios can tell the whole story. At the time when the univerbation of *each* and *other* must have taken place, namely late ME or an early stage of eModE, the word *other* was not obligatorily marked for number (see Einenkel, 1903: 521; Jespersen, 1914: 459–460; Curme, 1935: 174). It is therefore possible that the reciprocal generalized the option of leaving the plural uncoded. This scenario would differ from the first of the two possible developments mentioned earlier in that it was not the singular form that was generalized, but rather the invariable form that could be used in all cases at that time. Whatever the exact chronology, plural marking on the reciprocal did not in any way become obligatory for the reciprocal at the time when plural marking became obligatory for nouns in general, and thus also for the nominal use of *other* (*the other* versus *the others*).

The Fate of the Definite Article

Another feature that distinguishes (20) a. and (20) b. from (20) c. and (20) d. is the absence of the definite article preceding *other*. In PDE *other* in its nominal use must be preceded by a determiner. The only context where a determiner need not be added is the use of *other* as an indefinite plural (e.g. *Others would do a better job*). The absence of the definite article—or an indefinite article for that matter—is thus evidence of fossilization. Note that the significance of *other* lacking a determiner cannot be explained away by saying that it is a plural form. It was pointed out earlier that a compositional semantics of reciprocal sentences with two participants requires the alterity word to be singular.

Unfortunately, the historical side of this state of affairs is again more complex than the synchronically detectable symptoms of lexicalization. In other words, whereas there is no doubt that the lack of an article in the PDE reciprocal *each other* indicates lexicalization, it is less clear exactly which developments have led to this situation. As in the case of plural marking, there are two logically possible scenarios: either there was a determiner when the two elements were reanalyzed as a unit, or there was no determiner when univerbation happened. Now, at the time when *each* and *other* seem to have fused into one lexeme, the overt determination of nouns was not yet obligatory in all contexts. To be sure, the use of definite articles goes back as far as OE (Mitchell, 1985: 131–132). Yet the PDE situation in which the obligatory use of articles is systematically specified for any syntactic context had not been reached at the time when the univerbation of the reciprocal took place. An exploratory search in two eModE corpora (the eModE part of the Helsinki Corpus and Lampeter) has shown that *other* varies as to the presence or absence of the definite article, both in reciprocal and non-reciprocal contexts. One thus finds instances of definite *other* with and without an article, and there does not seem to be any difference in meaning between the variants. Curme (1935) supports this observation when he states: 'A peculiarity of this older usage was the absence of the definite article before *other* for definite reference' (159).

Stress Placement

Stress placement also provides support for a lexicalization analysis of *each other*. Compare the sentences in (21):

(21) a. Stephen, Jane and Sue hate each other.
　　 b. Stephen, Jane and Sue each hate the others.

The reciprocal *each other* in the basic reciprocal construction in (21) a. is invariably stressed on the second syllable. As a consequence, it is impossible to assign stress to one of the two elements in order to focus on a single semantic component of the reciprocal. This restriction does not hold for a sentence like (21) b., in which the two elements are evidently independent words. Let us now see in more detail what types of stress assignment are possible for the two sentences.

(22) a. Stephen, Jane and Sue HATE each other.
　　 b. Stephen, Jane and Sue hate each OTHER.
　　 c. *Stephen, Jane and Sue hate EACH other.
　　 d. Stephen, Jane and Sue each HATE the others.
　　 e. Stephen, Jane and Sue each hate the OTHERS.
　　 f. Stephen, Jane and Sue EACH hate the others.

In the most natural interpretation, (21) a. would carry its main stress on the verb (see [22] a.). Alternatively, *other* can receive stress. In this case, the reciprocal nature of the proposition is emphasized (see [22] b.) if contrasted to a reflexive relation, for instance. In the latter case we have to assume that the entire reciprocal is focused, *other* being the focus exponent. Stress on *each* is not possible, as shown in (22) c. Example (21) b. is different. Either the verb, the quantifier *each* or the alterity word may carry the main stress. In each case, the semantic effect is a different one. With stress on the verb, as in (22) d., the sentence has a predicate focus interpretation (Lambrecht, 1994: 226), i.e. it is asserted that the stressed predicate holds, as opposed to alternative predicates that would be compatible with the remainder of the proposition. With stress on the alterity word (see [22] e.), by contrast, the effect would be similar to the one that is achieved if (21) a. is stressed on the reciprocal. Therefore, a possible continuation of (22) e. could be: *Stephen, Jane and Sue each hate the OTHERS, not themselves.* In addition, there is the option of stressing the quantifier *each*. In (22) f. the maximal quantification over the set denoted by the subject is focused. In this case one may continue by saying: *Stephen, Jane and Sue EACH hate the others, not only Stephen and Jane.* To sum up, (21) b. allows more focusing options than (21) a., an observation that is fully compatible with the more general claim that the reciprocal *each other* is a lexicalized unit the two parts of which cannot be individually accessed for semantic interpretation (and stress).

Since lexicalization is a type of language change, putting forward the argument based on stress amounts to the claim that prior to the lexicalization of the reciprocal, stress assignment was in fact free to the extent that it is in the PDE spell-out variant in (21) b. Given our severely limited evidence of sentence stress in earlier stages of English, it is impossible to bring forward direct evidence here. As with other changes that the basic reciprocal strategy and its source structures have undergone, however, I am assuming that those syntactic structures that led to the lexicalization of the reciprocal in ME and eModE basically correspond to the spell-out strategy of PDE.

Why Are There No 'Reciprocal Verbs' in English?

The final question I would like to raise in this section concerns the locus of reciprocal marking. Recall that from a cross-linguistic point of view there are different options of where reciprocal marking is located in the clause (see König and Kokutani, 2006). The most basic distinction is the one between those reciprocal markers that function as morphologically independent argument expressions, on the one hand, and bound reciprocal morphemes affixed on verbs, on the other. Viewed from this perspective, the development of the English reciprocal clearly led to the former type. It is a nominal expression occupying argument slots in the clause. But would it not also have been possible for English to develop 'reciprocal verbs' by universe-verbating the relevant verbs with the alterity word in source constructions like *Stephen, Jane and Sue (each) hate others*? In other languages, among them Germanic languages such as Swedish and Danish and Romance languages like Spanish and Italian, verbs followed by a middle suffix in reciprocal contexts have been conventionalized as fixed units, and very often the respective verb stems no longer even occur without the suffix.

Why, then, has *each other* univerbated? Firstly, string frequency is likely to have been a contributing factor. Crucially, the string frequency of the string *each + other* is much higher than the string frequency of any verb followed by *each other* or *other*, for that matter. This discrepancy can easily be made clear by imagining a paradigm of different verbs, each of them combining with the reciprocal (Table 3.1).

It is obvious that going down the rows of Table 3.1, the collocation of *each* and *other* remains invariable while the verbs differ, rendering the string frequency of *each+other* a multiple of the string frequencies that the

Table 3.1 String Frequency of *Each Other*

Verb	Quantifier	Alterity Word
see	*each*	*other*
hear	*each*	*other*
tickle	*each*	*other*
admire	*each*	*other*
. . .	*each*	*other*

individual verbs followed by the reciprocal exhibit (on how frequency determines the formation on new structures, see, *inter alia*, Bybee and Hopper, 2000; Krug, 2003; Bybee, 2006; Gast, 2007: 42–45; Haspelmath, 2008a). Secondly, those verbs that are and have probably always been used most frequently in reciprocal contexts are syntactically intransitive (symmetric and prototypically reciprocal verbs) and thus do not require a noun phrase in object position. To give an example, in the novel *Small World* by David Lodge, thirty-two instances of the basic reciprocal construction face fifty-two examples of intransitive verbs used reciprocally—*meet* (n = 22) and *kiss* (n = 6) being the most frequent ones; note that non-intransitive uses of the relevant verbs were not included in this count. The other languages mentioned earlier are different in that these verbs also combine with the reflexive that is destined to become or already is a middle marker. In Italian, for example, the translations of intransitive *meet* and *kiss* are *incontrar-si* and *baciar-si*, respectively. The element *-si* is the reflexive and middle marking suffix that lacks a counterpart in English. Recall that the English reflexive x-*self* does not normally cover the middle uses under discussion (but see Chapter 5, section 5.3). In this way, whereas in those languages the verbs which are most frequent in reciprocal contexts could serve as the first component of the univerbation under discussion, they did not enter the picture in English in the first place.

Another factor that presumably made the historical scenario just sketched more unlikely is the fact that *each other* is more frequent as a prepositional complement than as a direct or indirect object. In *Small World*, the majority of the thirty-two instances of the basic reciprocal construction involve a preposition (twenty-one examples). To further underline this point, I examined the three PDE corpora FLOB, LOB and BROWN for the relative frequencies of the reciprocals *each other* and *one another* in different syntactic positions, assuming that the asymmetry at issue has probably not changed a lot throughout the more recent history of English.[16] Table 3.2 provides the results of this count.

As for the discrepancy between the frequency of the direct object and that of the prepositional complement, Table 3.2 shows that reciprocals in the position of prepositional complements are consistently more frequent

Table 3.2   Frequency of the Reciprocals *Each Other* and *One Another* in Different Syntactic Positions

	LOB	BROWN	FLOB
Direct Object	48	42	27
Indirect Object	1	2	1
Prep. Complement	68	76	65
Possessor	3	0	11
Other	1	2	0

than reciprocals in direct object position throughout the three corpora. The contrast as such is not statistically significant ($\chi^2 = 3.235$ (df = 2), p > 0.20), but at least the table shows that a large portion of reciprocal sentences, namely, those where prepositions precede the alterity word, cannot have served as a source structure for the univerbation of verb and reciprocal.

To sum up, the data show that a large portion of reciprocal sentences in English cannot have served as a source structure for the hypothetical development under discussion. Would it be more realistic for the quantifier to undergo univerbation with the verb? To be sure, at the point where quantifier and *other* were not yet univerbated the quantifier was able to follow the verb. I also mentioned that in reciprocal sentences involving prepositions, the alterity word follows the preposition at this stage. Notably, verb and quantifier are not separated by a preposition in the many sentences where the alterity is preceded by a preposition. Since the alterity word is crucial in conveying the reciprocal meaning of the relevant sentences, it would be strange for the verb to go together with the quantifier only, however. Whereas reciprocal sentences displaying the alterity word but not the quantifier word have always occurred (see Chapter 2, section 2.5), the reverse case—a reciprocal sentence involving the quantifier but no alterity word—is not documented and would in fact be unexpected, given that in this structure a valency position would be left unfilled. The latter, unexpected, scenario is illustrated in (23):

(23) a. Adam and Eve looked each at (the) other.
　　b. Adam and Eve looked-each at (the) other.
　　c. Adam and Eve looked-each at ((the) other).

Note that at the next step this scenario should lead to the omission of the alterity word, because reciprocity would now be marked on the verb. In this case, in turn, the preposition (*at* in [23]) would lose its complement, an improbable result. In sum, I think that one can safely conclude that such a development is unlikely and has in fact not occurred in the history of English.

Grammaticalization

As argued in Haas (2007: 43–47), the development of *each other* does not only qualify as lexicalization. At the same time, it exhibits those properties that should be understood as being criterial of grammaticalization: semantic/pragmatic and syntactic context expansion. One reason why, along the lines of Himmelmann (2004), I opted for these criteria has to do with the grammatical status of the source expressions *each* and *other*. Traditionally, grammaticalization is defined as the process whereby a lexical expression develops into a grammatical expression in a particular syntactic construction. To the extent that the categories 'lexical' and 'grammatical' can be distinguished, this definition works quite well for the majority of cases discussed in the literature. The development of the English reciprocal turns out to be a case where the definition is not easily applicable, however. Both source elements, *each* and *other* (we will consider *one another* later), would normally be categorized as grammatical expressions. The word *each* belongs to the closed class of quantifiers and it is not obvious that reciprocity is in any way 'more grammatical' than ordinary quantification. With *other* the situation is similar: in some grammars it is classified as an adjective, but then it behaves more like a determiner than an adjective syntactically. In any case its meaning is more abstract than that of prototypical adjectives denoting dimension, age, value or colour. And again, comparing the meaning of *other* to the concept of reciprocity, it would seem ad hoc to attribute a lesser degree of 'grammaticalness' to the former and a higher degree of 'grammaticalness' to the latter. However, the matter is even more complex. Strictly speaking, if one tries to compare the degrees to which a single item A and a compound [AB] are grammatical (as opposed to lexical), one does not compare one and the same form at different historical stages. The new form *each other* can only be traced back as far as it actually existed as a unit. Before that point in time there were only the simple words which were about to undergo univerbation. This restricts the search for changing degrees of 'grammaticalness' to the period after the univerbation, and thus the lexicalization, of *each* and *other*. What we *can* observe in this period is indeed syntactic context expansion.

Earlier, I mentioned the occurrence of the reciprocal in prepositional phrases. The crucial change became visible when *each other* could follow the preposition as a unit. Assuming that univerbation had to take place in direct object position in order for the reciprocal to be admissible in prepositional phrases, context expansion thus took place (DO > DO, PP). A further syntactic context in which the reciprocal became possible is the 'genitive construction' with *each other* as a pre-nominal possessor. The first examples of possessive reciprocals date from the late sixteenth century (cf. Visser, 1963: 446; Raumolin-Brunberg, 1997: 230):

(24) a. They strained one another's hand. [1590, from Visser, 1963: 446]

    b. for lakke of knowledge often of eche other's proceedings we may entre into a confusion of things . . . [1547, cited from Raumolin-Brunberg, 1997: 230]

More recently, reciprocals began to occur in the subject position of subordinate clauses (see also Chapter 2). Reciprocals in subject position have consistently been considered incorrect by prescriptive grammarians (see, for instance, Partridge, 1957: 101). Yet structures such as the ones illustrated in Chapter 2 are commonly used in PDE. The first instances of such structures are again hard to trace, given that reciprocal sentences are generally relatively rare. There is an isolated example from 1658:

(25) Be not angry my dear, if thou hast not a Smock to thy back I would have thee, but in knowing what each other hath, we shall know the better how to improve it, do thou the same by me, . . . [17]

In any event it seems safe to assume that reciprocals in subject position were not well established before the late nineteenth century. Bolinger (1990) regards them as 'a construction that has become commonplace in the past half-century' (267). The reciprocal may now also occur in the subject position of non-finite clauses:

(26) Children were playing and throwing a ball for each other to catch. [HTY 841]

Reciprocal sentences involving collective nouns in subject position (cf. the examples in [27]) could not be found in earlier stages of English either, which suggests a recent development.

(27) a. . . . it may mean that our group will support each other by saying nothing about each other's judgements, competencies or foibles. [AN5 519]
    b. I don't know how I'd cope as a solo artist because we're a real support group to each other. [CBC 10341]

Other likely instances of context expansion concern the appearance of *each other* in syntactic slots, such as the predicative noun phrase following a copular verb (cf. [28]), or the fronted noun phrase in a cleft construction (cf. [29]).

(28) a. Underlying time banks is a growing recognition, a consensus, that the greatest untapped resource we have is each other.[18]

(29) a. Each of the characters soon realise that they themselves are the instruments of hell, and it is each other who will force them to reveal their deepest and darkest secrets.[19]
    b. And, in the main, it is each other they prey upon and kill.[20]

Can the context expansion of the basic reciprocal construction also be linked to changes in frequency? It has already been mentioned that there was a development—roughly starting in late ME—such that spell-out structures of the split quantificational type (e.g. *Each* (N) V *the other(s)*), as well as the other types discussed earlier (above all the reciprocal use of reflexives, the strategies involving the preposition *between* and the one employing adverbs such as *together* in post-verbal position) lost ground, while the use of the basic reciprocal construction with the marker *each other* (for some time also involving *either other* and later *one another*) in turn gained ground. At the same time it was argued that the spell-out construction of the type *each . . . the other* has not and will probably never disappear completely, given that it is a transparent spelling out of reciprocal relations that conforms to the grammatical rules of PDE. Let me therefore point out how the statement according to which the lexicalized reciprocals have gained ground at the expense of the spell-out type can nevertheless be justified.

The proportion of spell-out constructions to reciprocal sentences as a whole seems to be much higher in earlier stages of English than in PDE. In other words, although the spell-out strategy has not completely disappeared in favour of *each other* and *one another*, the reciprocals have clearly gained ground on the spell-out strategy in terms of frequency. I compared the relative frequency of *each other* and the *each . . . the other* in the eModE (and early ModE) Lampeter Corpus, on the one hand, and the PDE corpus FLOB, on the other. If we compare Lampeter and FLOB, we get the following frequencies (see Table 3.3): 102 occurrences of *each other* versus three occurrences of *each . . . the other* in FLOB, as opposed to seventy occurrences of *each other* versus sixteen occurrences of *each . . . the other* in the Lampeter Corpus.

This distribution shows that the reciprocal is significantly more frequent in PDE than in eModE ($\chi^2 = 13.11$ (df = 1), p < 0.001). The contrast remains statistically significant if we add all instances of *one another* in the two corpora (seventy-one in Lampeter and thirty-three in FLOB) to the figures for *each other*. What these figures also show is that the reciprocal was already more frequent than the spell-out strategy at the time covered by the Lampeter Corpus (1640–1740). The expansion of *each other* at the expense of *each . . . the other* must therefore have started in the early phase of eModE at the latest, which accords with the evidence that at that time the lexicalized reciprocal came into being. It is interesting to note that the variety of

Table 3.3   The Relative Frequency of Basic and Split
               Quantificational Construction in eModE and PDE

	Lampeter	*FLOB*
each other	70	102
each . . . the other	21	3

forms has also been reduced in the case of the spell-out strategy. Poutsma (1926: 1070), for example, provides the following list of combinations from the eModE and ModE periods, 'all of them now obsolete or archaic in this function' (1926: 1070).

(30) a. *both . . . either*: They are both in either's power. [Shakespeare, Tempest, 1, 2, 449]

　　b. *each . . . each*: You two glare each at each like panthers now. [Browning, In a Balcony, 102]

　　c. *each . . . either*: For each had warded either in the fight. [Tennyson, Coming of Arthur, 130]

　　d. *either . . . either*: While he spoke | Closed his death-drowsing eyes, and slept the sleep | With Baltin, either locked in either's arms. [Tennyson, Balin and Balan, 605]

As will be discussed in more detail in Chapter 5, the spell-out strategy has come to occupy a functional niche as an alternative to the use of the lexicalized and grammaticalized reciprocals *each other* and *one another* in PDE. It should therefore not be too surprising that, due to the general tendency 'one form = one function', the variety of forms corresponding to this single function has also been reduced. In other words, although the spell-out strategy is assumed here to be a transparent spelling out of reciprocal situations, due to functional specialization to the expression of distinct-events reciprocal situations, conventionalization seems to have taken place, at least for the split quantificational subtype (to be distinguished from clause coordination and the other ways of spelling out reciprocity; see Chapter 2). Specifically, the alterity word has become fixed as a second part. This would explain why the structures in (30) have become obsolete; however, they are not excluded as categorically as reciprocals of the type *any other*, *every other* or *either other*. Clearly, the formation of the latter forms is categorically excluded because the two existing forms *each other* and *one another* are lexicalized expressions that are not regularly composed like an ordinary noun phrase. They are rather products of lexicalization and grammaticalization processes and thus complex syntactic entities only from a historical point of view. Consequently, they do not represent a productive pattern of noun phrase formation, which we would need in order to build up the reciprocals *any other*, *every other* or *either other*.

Let us sum up the discussion of how the reciprocal *each other* was formed and has developed, and specifically which processes of language change have been relevant for its development. It is obvious that the expression originates in structures that spell out a reciprocal relation by using the quantifier *each* and the alterity word *other*. Since it was possible for the two items to be adjacent in reciprocal sentences, both in sentences where the quantifier functioned as the subject of the clause and in those cases where it was added to an independent plural subject, the formation of the nominal reciprocal expression was made possible. In a period spanning from late ME to the early phase of eModE, the two items must have been reanalyzed as a single nominal expression being able to fill argument slots. This emergence of a new linguistic item qualifies as lexicalization, first because two independent words undergo univerbation and second because fossilization has been taking place. Further changes related to the newly formed reciprocal have been characterized as grammaticalization, the latter being defined as semantic/pragmatic and syntactic context expansion.

Having established that the development of *each other* is best characterized as the co-occurrence of lexicalization and grammaticalization, I addressed the question of why it is the quantifier *each* and the alterity word *other* that have undergone univerbation, as opposed to the option that the verb and any or both of these items coalesce. It was argued that the absence of such a hypothetical development is not surprising, given that the string frequency of *each+other* is much higher than the string frequency of any verb in combination with *(the) other*, on the one hand, and the univerbation of verb and quantifier, omitting the alterity word, is excluded for syntactic reasons, on the other.

3.5 *ONE ANOTHER* AND THE ISSUE OF FLOATING QUANTIFIERS

In the preceding sections the focus has been on the lexicalization of the reciprocal *each other*, which in turn made possible its grammaticalization (in the sense of context expansion). Let us now return to the issue of how the quantifier came to be adjacent to the alterity word in the first place, and to what extent the alleged history of *each other* carries over to the second reciprocal *one another*.

Plank (2008) provides the most explicit treatment of the formation of bipartite reciprocal expressions in Germanic to date. He exemplifies his scenario with English sentences in which the expressions *one*, *either* and *each* are listed as alternative choices in the relevant position (see Plank, 2008: 360). In this way the different items appear to behave identically. Yet, such a treatment of *one* really begs the question of whether these items have all come to be permitted in the position adjacent to the alterity word in the same way. In other words, it is not self-evident that the plausible scenario commonly assumed for *each over* carries over to *one another*.

Was *One* Able to 'Float'?

Recall that Plank (2008) assumes the variable position of the quantifier *each* in OE and ME to be a crucial prerequisite for the formation of the reciprocal. The following sequence of sentences from Plank (2008: 363) is meant to illustrate the steps in the development that he proposes:

(31) a. The (one) earl fought with the (other) earl, and the other/latter
        (earl) fought with the one/former (earl).
     b. Earl(s) fought with earl(s).
     c. Earl(s) fought with other(s).
     d. One/either/each . . . earl fought with (the/an) other.
     e. The earls fought one/either/each/ . . . with (the/an) other.
     f. The earls fought with one/either/each/ . . . (the/an) other.

What does this scenario, as assumed by Plank (2008), imply for the formation of *each other* and *one another*? With respect to possible differences
between the two reciprocals, (31) d.–e. are the relevant steps (the assumed
steps in [31] a.–c. will be discussed later). Consider the post-verbal position
of the quantifier in (31) e. We may call this phenomenon 'quantifier float', in
analogy to generative analyses of the corresponding phenomenon in PDE.[21]
Again, the crucial difference between PDE, on the one hand, and OE and
ME, on the other, is that the latter allowed *each* in the position following
the main verb, while the former is more restrictive and excludes this option.
If one takes *one another* to have been formed identically to *each other*, this
implies that *one* (or, more specifically, its ME source expression *an*) was
positionally flexible in the same way.

The literature on the counterparts of PDE *one* in earlier English (see Rissanen, 1967; Mitchell, 1985) do not explicitly mention the possibility of the
numeral occurring in a post-verbal position. Rissanen (1967) observes that
'the position of *one* within the phrase offers interesting alternatives. Most of
the syntactic types where the place of *one* is "exceptional" probably aim at
heightened emphasis' (312). According to Rissanen, putting emphasis on *one*
is tantamount to indicating exclusiveness, one of the functions of *one* that
he works out (for the corresponding structures in ME, see Mustanoja, 1960:
293). Considering the meaning of reciprocal sentences, it does not seem likely
that the reciprocal use of *one* and *another*, and thus their eventual univerbation, goes back to such an 'emphatic' use of *one*. In reciprocal sentences
exclusiveness is not normally emphasized. Note that in reciprocal situations,
not one exclusive individual but rather a set of at least two individuals are
involved. From this set the reciprocal use of *one* picks out either of the two
(or every individual in groups larger than two) and treats them all equally,
i.e. it does not assign an exclusive status to any of the individuals. Rissanen
(1967) describes this type as one in which 'one refers to either of two persons
or things, or to any person or thing among a group of many' and links it to
the formation of the reciprocal *one another* when he says that '[t]he modern
reciprocal use of *one another* seems to have developed mainly from this type'
(95). Now, if the emphatic use of *one* cannot be the source for the adjacency
of *one* and the alterity word, what are the alternatives?

Could *one* be a floating quantifier, just like *each*? From the point of view
of PDE it is not surprising that *one* does not behave like floating quantifiers. Those PDE quantifiers that occur in the relevant positions following

the auxiliary or preceding the main verb, viz. *all, each* and *both*, quantify over the complete set introduced by the subject.[22] If *one* were a floating quantifier, that is to say a quantifier that interacts with a set of individuals that is already introduced by the subject, it would restrict the predication to only one of those individuals. Yet in such a case the introduction of the remaining individuals by the subject would be redundant. In sum, from the point of view of PDE it is expected that also in earlier stages of English the expression *one* did not behave distributionally like the expressions that have been called 'floating quantifiers'.

Alternative Scenarios of the Genesis of *One Another*

Even though it seems to be excluded for *one* to have come to occupy the position adjacent to the alterity word via the 'quantifier float' process, as implicitly proposed by Plank (2008), there are other structures that may have been the basis for the univerbation of the reciprocal. Indeed, it was always possible for *one* to occur post-verbally, but only in interaction with the alterity word. Consider the following random example cited by Einenkel (1903: 524):

> (32) they toke leue one of other. [Caxton's Blanchardyn and Eglatine, ed. L. Kellner, London 1890, 94, 6]

Example (32) shows that at the stage where the univerbation of the PDE reciprocals is assumed to have taken place, it was indeed possible for the expression *one* to appear in a position separated from the subject. Importantly, however, this position was available for *one* only in those cases where it interacted with the alterity word. This restriction appears to be compatible with the semantic constraint discussed earlier, in that the entire set of individuals referred to by the subject is also covered by the post-verbal expressions taking up the reference of the subject, viz. *one* and *other*. Although the expression *one* in cases like (32) is syntactically distinct from floated quantifiers such as *each, both* and *all*, it may lead to the same result: in those cases in which the verb does not govern a prepositional complement but rather a direct object, quantifier and alterity word come to stand adjacent to each other and their reanalysis as a single reciprocal expression would become possible (see also Einenkel, 1903: 523).

What the historical data attesting these source structures cannot tell us is the syntactic status of what follows the verb in (32) and similar examples. One option would be to regard it as a reduced clause that functions as a type of afterthought. The relevant diachronic scenario could be sketched as follows:

(33) a. The knights hugged; one hugged another.
    b. The knights hugged$_i$; one e_i another.
    c. The knights hugged one another.

During the first stage, represented here by (33) a., there are two clauses: the first clause has a plural subject denoting all participants involved in the reciprocal situation. In the first clause, therefore, the reciprocal nature of the situation is only implied. It can then be spelt out by adding a second clause in which the verb is repeated, its subject and object being *one* and *(an)other* respectively. In the second stage the verb is left out. On the basis of the historical data, I assume that the option of leaving out the verb in the second clause had always been possible and that this was in fact the default option. The third stage represents the reanalysis of the complex *one + another* as the direct object of the (first) verb. This explanation of the formation of *one another* should also work for other languages that have reciprocal expressions of the same type.

It has to be kept in mind, however, that the alleged reduced clause is not always preceded by a complete clause. More specifically, whereas *hug* in (33) a. and b. can be analyzed as an intransitive (or intransitivized) verb, the reciprocal use of which is underlined by adding a reduced clause that spells out the reciprocal nature of the situation, the construction occurs also with transitive verbs (but see section 3.6 on the problem of classifying verbs as intransitive or transitive if used reciprocally in eModE). Consider the eModE example in (34):

(34) Withont anoying the one the other. [OED, s.v. *one* 11]

A scenario that would be better compatible with this fact is one in which the alterity word indeed functions as the complement of the transitive verb, while the status of *(the) one* was that of an adjunct. The fact that reciprocal sentences of the type illustrated by the ME example in (35) (see also Visser, 1963: 443–444) have always been an option in English seems to lend support to such an analysis:

(35) And how they sware that for wele nor woo they shold not leue other [Malory, Morte Dartur, 1, xij]

Here, the alterity word is not accompanied by a quantifier, neither one making part of the antecedent noun phrase nor one in an adverbial position. The possibility of leaving out the quantifier when spelling out a reciprocal situation is thus an option and can be taken to suggest that the quantifier is analyzed as an adjunct also in the structure exemplified in (32).

Revisiting *Each Other*

When one considers such scenarios for the development of *one another*, the question arises of whether the genesis of *each other* should not be accounted for in the same way. Visser (1963) already conceives of the reciprocal as originating in a reduced clause:

The type '*his suna* . . . ðenoden ælc oðrum', '*hie* beheoldon ælc oðerne' differs from all the types discussed above in that it consists of a subject in the form of a noun or a personal pronoun + verb + *each* (*either*) *other*. If *each* or *either* on this type still functions as a subject, it follows that we have to do with sentences with two subjects, a phenomenon of frequent occurrence in older English [. . .] and not unusual in modern English [. . .]. The original meaning of 'They kissed each other' may therefore have been 'They kissed; each . . . other'. (445)

Since the main focus of this chapter is on those stages of development that are responsible for shaping the PDE system of reciprocal marking, I cannot provide a conclusive answer to the issue of how the English reciprocals reached the state prior to their lexicalization. From a cross-linguistic point of view, the modified reduced-clause scenario sketched earlier appears to be the one that is compatible with data from more languages than the floating quantifier scenario. Even though bipartite reciprocal markers and their development have been neglected in most of the literature on reciprocity, the floating quantifier scenario as proposed by Plank (2008) seems inapplicable to a large number of reciprocal constructions across languages (see Hanke, in prep., for details).

The Earlier History of the Reciprocals

Having examined the possible ways in which *each other* and *one another* may have come to be reciprocal expressions in argument positions, let us now briefly consider those stages that, according to Plank, precede (31) d.–(31) e. The reality of Plank's first two steps is hard to ascertain or disprove. Plank himself does not provide evidence for the existence and relevance of such structures in the history of English reciprocals. Concerning the noun phrase repetition strategy as illustrated in (31) e., he states: 'In historical handbooks it goes often unnoticed, presumably because it is syntactically so inconspicuous. Proper documentation would be desirable, also for other parts of the diachronic story told here, but is beyond the modest scope of the present paper' (2008: 359). In my examination of OE texts I have not come across reciprocals of this type. Although their existence cannot be excluded, of course, I think one should at least be cautious and not simply assume them to be crucial steps towards the structures in (31) d.–(31) f. It is certainly not necessary that speakers start from a cumbersome clause repetition strategy as in (31) a. and/or the noun phrase repetition strategy in (31) b. in order to form sentences like (31) d., (31) e. or (31) f. Structures like the one in (31) c. are attested from OE on, as mentioned in the previous section, but I would not consider them to be a prerequisite for the formation of what Plank assumes to be later stages. It might be helpful to consider the PDE situation at this point. All kinds of spell-out strategies are available for the expression of reciprocal situations in PDE. In this way, the spell-out construction of the split quantificational types (*each . . . other/one . . . another*) are also and have always been transparent means of expressing reciprocity. Therefore, I see no reason for ordering them in a historical sequence to the effect that one was the prerequisite for the formation of the other.

3.6 INTRANSITIVE VERBS AND THE ISSUE OF SYMMETRY

We preliminarily defined symmetric predicates as lexical items the meaning of which involves a necessarily bidirectional relation. In this section, I will take the preliminary definition as a starting point and ask whether and how the behaviour of these predicates has changed throughout the history of English.

Historical Survey

In English, there has always been a class of verbs with inherently reciprocal meaning. If we take the standard example of a symmetric predicate *meet*, we observe that its OE predecessor *gemetan*, just like its PDE counterpart, was used both transitively and intransitively:

(36) Se   bið   gefeana fægrast þonne hy   æt frymðe   gemetað
     that shall.be joys.GEN fairest when they at beginning meet
     'That shall be the fairest of joys, when they at the beginning meet.'
     [GuthA 83,1]

(37) þa   metton hie   Leonantius
     then met   they Leonantius
     ' . . . they met Leonantius.' [Orosius (Bateley), Hist.,III.xi.78]

OE verbs other than *gemetan* are rarely mentioned in the literature. It is beyond doubt, however, that a number of symmetric and prototypically reciprocal verbs could be used in this way.

Middle and Early Modern English

In ME too, the relevant structure is well attested. The main difference between OE and ME seems to be that ME generally shows a more pronounced tendency to use allegedly transitive verbs intransitively. As pointed out by Mustanoja (1960), the change may be due to the increasing morphological simplification of the English verb in that period:

> Throughout its history, though particularly in the Modern English period, the English language has shown a remarkable tendency to develop intransitive functions for transitive verbs. The development has been

accelerated by the morphological simplification completed within the Middle English period, which, for example, led to the disappearance of the formal distinction between the transitive *ja*-class and the intransitive *o*-class of weak verbs—a distinction which even in OE is no longer strictly observed. (429)

Moving on to eModE, Shakespeare's plays offer several instances of intransitive verbs used in a reciprocal sense, including ones that do not allow the intransitive use in PDE. Schmidt (1875), Jespersen (1927: 332) and Franz (1939: 282) list the following examples:

(38) a. you and I have known [The Tragedy of Antony and Cleopatra, II, 6, 68]
  b. we have known together in Orleans [Cymbeline, I, 4, 36]
  c. upon the next occasion that we meet with visages displayed to talk and greet [Love Labour's Lost V, 2, 142–3]
  d. That sundered friends greet in the hour of death. [Henry VI A, IV, 3,42]
  e. never two ladies loved as they doe [As You Like It, I, 1, 117]
  f. One woe doth tread upon another's heele, so fast they follow. [Hamlet, IV, 7, 165]
  g. How haue ye done since we last saw in France? [The Famous History of the Life of King Henry VIII, I, 1, 2]

It is difficult to find such usages outside Shakespeare's work, and as far as the verbs *know, greet, love, follow, hate* and *see* are concerned, it is only in Shakespeare's plays where the intransitive uses are reported in the literature (see Visser, 1963: 145).[23] Note that in descriptions of reciprocity in PDE, it is often reported that the set of verbs that could be used intransitively in a reciprocal sense has undergone slight changes in the history of English (see, for instance, Kjellmer, 1982: 242). The data underlying such claims are typically the examples from Shakespeare, leading one to the conclusion that in eModE more verbs could be used intransitively than in PDE. It seems, however, that those verbs which exemplify the alleged fluidity are either restricted to a single author in their occurrence, or are obsolete in PDE, so that the flexibility of the verb set under discussion becomes less convincing.

Consider the verbs listed by Visser (1963: 144–145). The ones that are not possible in intransitive reciprocal use today are *halse, greet, know, love, see*. Of these, the only verbs that are not cited in Shakespeare's work are *halse* and *cut*. Of these two verbs, in turn, the former is obsolete both transitively and intransitively in PDE. It cannot, therefore, be stated that *halse* has lost the potential of being used intransitively, given that the verb has disappeared altogether. As for *cut*, the transitive use of the relevant sense has become restricted to the collocation *cut sb. dead*. Hence, it is again not the case that a prototypically reciprocal verb has lost the potential of being used intransitively, given that the contexts in which the sense occurs have become more restricted in general.

Poutsma (1926: 153–155) provides another list of Late ModE instances, including the verbs *salute, call, cross, kiss, fraternize, harmonize, join, separate* and *unite*. Again, among these verbs we cannot find one that is a clear instance of the change we are looking for, this time involving a contrast between Late ModE and PDE. The verb *call* is still in use in PDE, although not in the intransitive structure we are interested in. Poutsma's (1926: 153) example does not represent an unambiguously reciprocal use of intransitive call, however:

(39) Distant parties (sc. of penguins) salute in this way and continue calling till they get pretty close. [Shackleton, The Heart of the Antartic, App. I, 346]

The event of calling in (39) may be interpreted as an undirected action carried out by each of the two groups of penguins (or, more specifically, each of the individual penguins in the two groups). Crucially, it is not necessary to view the event as involving two groups of participants acting on each other. Still, the frequently cited examples from Shakespeare remain, and they need to be accounted for.

It has been noted that eModE in general, and Shakespeare in particular, was relatively liberal in using transitive verbs intransitively (Blake, 2002: 143). We may, therefore, entertain the hypothesis that what seems to us a diachronic change in the set of verbs being specified as intransitive is really a consequence of a more general change: eModE allowed more flexibility with respect to the argument structure constructions a given verb may be used in. (Note also that there does not seem to be a verb which occurs intransitively and transitively in PDE, but only transitively in eModE.) What is it that has changed then? If the change under discussion is a consequence of a more general change in argument realization options, we should not want to imply that the set of symmetric predicates as such has undergone a change. But this is what statements in the literature often suggest. Let us therefore ask what can actually change. It is commonly stated that symmetric verbs in English have the property of allowing an intransitive argument realization, the two or more participants of the event being jointly realized as the subject (cf. Chapter 4). Note, however, that the argument realization patterns that a given verb occurs in are logically independent of the verb's meaning. Consequently, it is theoretically possible that a certain verb allowed the intransitive argument realization at some point in the history of English but ceases to be used intransitively at a later stage, the meaning of the verb involving symmetry all along (cf. PDE *resemble* as an example of a semantically symmetric verb that does not allow the intransitive argument realization). I am abstracting away here from those meaning components that are presumably *effects of* the argument realization the relevant verbs occur in (see Chapter 4). The question we have to ask is therefore the following: has the verb meaning changed in such a way that the loss of the intransitive argument realization goes together with a loss of symmetric meaning, or has the meaning of the verb stayed the same, whereas the argument realization options of the language have changed independently of individual verb meanings?

As for the history of argument structure alternations in general, it is commonly assumed that they are a relatively recent development, at least partially due to loss of case marking and the allegedly concomitant loss of word order freedom since ME. Moreover, it appears that in earlier stages of English it was easier than in PDE to leave certain arguments (especially objects) unexpressed. Ohlander (1943) provides data suggesting that object omission in OE and ME was less restricted than in ModE (see also Visser, 1963: 144–145; van Gelderen, 2000: 147–149; Gast 2006: 214). It is therefore not implausible to assume that the higher propensity of 'object drop' in earlier English contributed to those instances of seemingly intransitive use of verbs in reciprocal sentences.

The Role of Auxiliaries

A test for the transitivity status of verbs in eModE—apart from their actual occurrence in the relevant argument structure frame—is their choice of auxiliaries. Intransitive verbs take *be* as their auxiliary (e.g. in compound tenses), whereas transitive verbs combine with *have*. Obviously, the latter has been generalized to all verbs in PDE, and even earlier *be* had been losing ground for some time (see Denison, 1993: 344–370). Apart from a number of idiosyncrasies, those intransitive verbs that denoted a change of state ('mutative verbs' in the historical literature) also came to be combined with *have* (cf. Jespersen, 1931: 29–46). Yet, it would be interesting to see how the verbs under discussion behave with respect to this parameter. In Shakespeare's work, *meet* almost exclusively combines with *be*. I checked all instances of the form *met* and found nineteen examples of the auxiliary *be* in the relevant contexts, as opposed to only two occurrences of auxiliary *have*. Here are some pertinent examples:

(40) a. Are we all met? [A Midsummer Night's Dream, 3, 1, 1]
   b. A crew of patches, rude mechanicals that work for bread upon Athenian stalls, were met together to rehearse a play. [A Midsummer Night's Dream, 3, 2, 9]
   c. Peace to this meeting, wherefor we are met. [Henry V, 5, 2, 1]

More generally, a number of studies, summarized in Rydén and Brorström (1987: 131), show that intransitive *meet* with auxiliary *be* was commonly used in ME and eModE. Concerning the few instances of auxiliary *have* with this verb, they bring forward the hypothesis that intransitive *meet* with auxiliary *have* goes back to influence from the transitive use of *meet*, which of course combined only with *have*.

By contrast, those verbs we are mainly interested in at this point, e.g. *greet* and *know*, do not occur in a context requiring an auxiliary in Shakespeare's work, except for the two examples (38) a. and b. involving *know* cited earlier. It is of course dangerous to draw any conclusions on the basis of two examples only; nevertheless, I take it to be noteworthy that the only two occurrences of *know* in the present perfect tense involving a plural subject take *have* as their auxiliary. The verb, *know* in the sense of 'get to know each other', relevant here is mutative in that there is a change from the state of not knowing each other to the state of knowing each other. The same holds for *meet*. In the relevant sense, it denotes a change from the state of not being together to the state of being together. Since *meet* takes *be* as its auxiliary, it would therefore not be totally unreasonable to entertain the hypothesis that the two verbs do not have the same status.

Keeping in mind that, on the basis of the sparse data I looked at, any conclusion is highly speculative, the facts concerning auxiliary choice support the assumption of two classes of verbs. On the one hand, there are those verbs which are not only able to occur without an object, but which are also treated as properly intransitive verbs by the grammar of eModE, as shown by their co-occurrence with the auxiliary *be*. The verb *meet* is probably the clearest example of this group. On the other hand, we find verbs that may occur without an object, but which do not exhibit typical intransitive behaviour in terms of auxiliary choice. Here, *know* would be an example. Coming back to the issue of whether earlier stages of English had more verbs of the PDE type *They met/kissed/embraced*, it seems that those verbs that are candidates for constituting this larger group in fact have a different status. The statement according to which English has seen considerable fluctuation in the set of intransitive prototypically reciprocal verbs should therefore be taken with a pinch of salt. One has to take into account more general syntactic changes as well as changes in the meaning and use of individual verbs.

This concludes our survey of historical changes in reciprocal constructions. We observed a general development that fits very well with what the situation in PDE looks like. Chapter 5 will bring together the diachronic picture, on the one hand, and the competition between the reciprocal constructions of PDE, on the other. But before this, a class of constructions that so far has been discussed only in passing will be investigated in some detail: the different realizations of symmetric and prototypically reciprocal verbs.

4 Intransitive Verbs Expressing Reciprocity

4.1 INTRODUCTION

In this chapter, I will have a closer look at those reciprocal sentences that contain symmetric or prototypically reciprocal verbs. In Chapter 1, I subscribed to the view that functional contrasts between constructions—the term 'functional' here encompassing what is traditionally divided into 'semantic' and 'pragmatic' aspects—are pertinent to the analysis of grammatical structures. With regard to the realm of reciprocity, this view implies that in order to provide a comprehensive analysis of this domain in English we also have to consider symmetric and prototypically reciprocal verbs from this perspective and describe the factors that are responsible for speakers' choices between the variable syntactic realizations of these predicates. It should also be kept in mind that, as outlined in Chapter 3, the system of reciprocal constructions in English has undergone changes to the effect that variation of expressive means has been reduced and the surviving constructions have formed a well-organized system of constructions on which meanings, i.e. different construals of reciprocal situations, are mapped. In this way, the present chapter investigates alternations within the domain of reciprocal constructions that are available to symmetric and prototypically reciprocal verbs. Under the reasonable assumption that sentences involving these verbs are not synonymous across different argument realization patterns, we will consider which factors determine the choice between the intransitive and the transitive realization of symmetric and prototypically reciprocal verbs. A more general, but related, issue that we will come across is the notion of symmetry as a property of predicates. We will now begin by looking at the way in which symmetry is usually defined in studies on the subject.

Traditionally, the defining property of 'symmetric predicates' is taken to be a bidirectional relationship of the type 'if (aRb) then (bRa)' (cf. Partee et al., 1993: 40–41). For example, the predicate 'be similar' is symmetric, since for all possible pairs of arguments the relation of being similar is bidirectional. Thus, if Bill is similar to Harry, Harry is by definition similar to Bill as well. A verbal predicate that is commonly used to illustrate the notion of symmetry is *meet*. Consider the following statement from Dimitriadis (2008b: 377):

> (1) By definition, a two-place predicate is symmetric if exchanging its two arguments always preserves truth values; so X *met* Y is symmetric, but X *saw* Y is not (since X might see Y without Y seeing X).

Effectively, (1) claims that the sentences X *met* Y and Y *met* X are synonymous, since in any situation with a given truth value the arguments can be exchanged and thus the two sentences are always assumed to be true in the same situations. As soon as we take a more comprehensive view of meaning, however, it becomes obvious that the arguments of symmetric verbs are often not exchanged freely and in unprincipled ways (see also Baldi, 1975; Dimitriadis, 2008a: 346–348; 2008b: 398–402). A number of factors can be identified which determine the choice between the variant realization options.

4.2 ARE 'SYMMETRY ALTERNATIONS' MEANING-PRESERVING?

Consider the examples in (2) (Dong, 1970: 13):

> (2) a. The truck collided with the lamppost.
> b. *The truck and the lamppost collided.
> c. *The lamppost collided with the truck.

Apparently, the arguments of the verb *collide* cannot be freely exchanged without making the resulting sentence ungrammatical. The clearest argument against the assumption of synonymy is thus the ungrammaticality or at least unacceptability of one of the alternation variants. This is what several studies show in relation to different verbs. I will now review these studies, considering *meet* in more detail later.

In this way, we will also come across various attempts at determining the factors responsible for the choice between the different variants. As will become clear from the survey following, linguists first tried to ascribe the argument realization of the relevant verbs to a single factor. It has since become clearer that a single factor is unlikely to account for all cases.

Agentivity and Proto-Roles

Not flinching from a tabooed group of expressions, Dong (1970) carefully analyzes the syntactic behaviour of *fuck* and semantically similar verbs. He starts from Lakoff and Peters' (1969) analysis according to which the different argument realization variants of symmetric predicates are related to each other via meaning-preserving transformations and shows that there are clear counterexamples.

On the one hand, one finds examples of seemingly symmetric events which can be expressed by the transitive variant, but do not allow the intransitive variant (cf. Dong, 1970: 12–15). On the other hand, Dong's examples make it clear that with the transitive variant the distribution of arguments in the subject and object positions is not arbitrary, but crucially depends on subtle properties of the participants and the event expressed (for details, see Dong, 1970: 12–15). This implies, of course, that the transitive realization of a symmetric predicate need not always express exactly the same state of affairs as the corresponding intransitive variant.

Dong's (1970) explanation for the observed difference between intransitive and non-intransitive argument realization makes reference to the thematic role of Agent. An event with two participants may have either one or two Agents. In the intransitive variant, where both participants are encoded as a joint subject, both are Agents. Syntactically, agency is implemented by introducing the covert verb DO as the main verb taking the agentive noun phrase as its subject. Dowty (1979) adopts Dong's analysis and describes the meaning difference it is meant to capture as follows: 'The difference in meaning between such pairs of sentences is just whether one or both individuals are asserted to be voluntary participants in the act' (16).

Later, Dowty (1991: 586) concedes that the relevant contrast is not sufficiently characterized in terms of 'voluntary participation' and makes reference to his notion of 'proto-role entailments'. Such entailments are semantic properties that a given verb assigns to its participants. They are divided into two sets, one containing typical properties of Agents and the other typical properties of Patients. A participant exhibiting the full list of Agent properties is called 'proto-agent', whilst a participant with the complete set of Patient properties is called 'proto-patient'. These properties, or 'entailments', are assumed to determine argument realization in that the participant combining the highest number of proto-agent entailments is realized as syntactic subject, whereas the participant with the highest number of proto-patient entailments is realized as syntactic object. What makes Dowty's (1991) theory more attractive than other theories of argument realization is the fact that no fixed set of properties is required for a participant to be realized as either subject or object. Instead, the relative closeness to a role prototype is responsible for the assignment of syntactic functions, a view that seems to account well for the PDE situation in which the syntactic functions of subject and direct object may host a highly divergent set of semantic roles.

The crucial examples that Dowty brings forward against the DO analysis sketched earlier describe events involving inanimate or non-human animate participants for which agency or volition are not at issue.

(3) a. The ship passed the lighthouse in the night.
   b. The snake separated from its skin.
   c. The ivy gradually intertwined with the trellis.

(4) a. (#) The ship and the lighthouse passed in the night.
   b. (#) The snake and its skin separated.
   c. (#) The ivy and the trellis gradually intertwined

The acceptability contrast between (3) and (4) seems to go back to the fact that one of the participants is in motion whereas the other is not. The two arguments are therefore excluded from the joint subject realization of the intransitive variant. Only the transitive variant, with the moving participant as subject and the stationary participant as object or oblique, may render the asymmetry. Apart from volition and motion, Dowty does not discuss cases of other proto-role entailments determining the subject choice with the predicates at issue, but he appears to suggest that theoretically any entailment from his list may be relevant. 'Voluntary participation' or 'initiative' is also relevant in the following examples from Allan (1987: 64):

(5) a. I gave the four of them a lift back from the party. Mary fought with Paul all the way home in the back of the car; it was awful.
   b. I gave the four of them a lift back from the party. Paul fought with Mary all the way home in the back of the car; it was awful.

As Allan (1987: 64) notes, (5) a. suggests that Mary, i.e. the subject participant, 'started the fight or was at least the principal contender'. Conversely, in (5) b. Paul is taken to be the one to start the fight.

Adverbial Modification

The meaning contribution of adverbs modifying symmetric verbs also sheds light on the issue we are interested in. Fillmore (1972: 11–12) compares the following pair of sentences:

(6) a. John and Fred willingly agree.
   b. John willingly agrees with Fred.

Since (6) b. is not a paraphrase of (6) a., it is tempting to conclude that in general the intransitive and the non-intransitive variants of symmetric verbs differ in meaning. Fillmore does not go that far, but notes that in a non-intransitive argument realization of *agree* the two participants are encoded by separate noun phrases, and this makes it possible for them to be separately accessed by modifying expressions. This phenomenon is also relevant for embedded clauses:

It may be the case that in the symmetric predicate itself, there is no necessarily semantic difference that accompanies one subject choice over another. Once a choice has been made, however, the sentence is limited as to the embedding context which will welcome it. (Fillmore, 1972: 12)

Consider (7):

(7) John enjoyed meeting Mary.

Here, according to Fillmore, the choice of *John* as subject of the matrix clause forces the speaker to choose *John* as the (covert) subject of the embedded clause also and thus to opt for the transitive variant of *meet*. The event denoted by the verb *meet* itself, however, is taken to be constantly symmetric (see McCawley, 1970 on comparable asymmetries in the use of the adjective *similar*).

Empathy

Kuno and Kaburaki (1977) approach the acceptability of transitive symmetric verbs from the perspective of 'empathy', which they define as 'the speaker's identification, with varying degrees, with a person who participates in the event that he describes in a sentence' (628). Using the following examples, they examine transitive uses of *marry* and *meet* and conclude that the speaker's empathy must always be placed on the subject of the clause.

(8) a. John married Jane.
   b. Jane married John.
   c. John married his present wife in 1960.
   d. ?John's present wife married him in 1960.
   e. ?A 17-year-old girl married John.
   f. ??A 17-year-old girl married me.

(9) a. John met Mary on the street.
   b. Mary met John on the street.
   c. John met his wife on the street.
   d. John's wife met him on the street.
   e. *An eight-foot tall girl met John on the street.
   f. *John met me on the street.

The oddness of (8) d.–f., as well as the ungrammaticality of (9) e.–f. (Kuno and Kaburaki's judgments), is thus explained by saying that the speaker's empathy in these sentences could exclusively be directed at the object referents, given that any combination of personal pronouns, bare proper names and indefinite noun phrases is only compatible with the following (simplified) empathy hierarchy:

(10) personal pronouns > proper names > full noun phrases

According to (10), a sentence like (9) e. is not possible because the subject (a full noun phrase) is lower on the empathy hierarchy than the object (a proper name). Similarly, the subject in (9) f. is lower on the hierarchy than the object (a personal pronoun), which is incompatible with the default distribution of subject and object in sentences involving symmetric predicates.

Figure-Ground

Talmy (1978, 2000) demonstrates that the opposition between 'Figure' and 'Ground', a well-established notion in cognitive psychology, is crucial for various syntactic phenomena. He defines the Figure as 'a moving or conceptually movable entity whose path, site, or orientation is conceived of as a variable, the particular value of which is the relevant issue' (2000: 312). The Ground, on the other hand, is 'a reference entity, one that has a stationary setting relative to a reference frame, with respect to which the Figure's path, site, or orientation is characterized' (2000: 312). Talmy also applies the Figure–Ground contrast to situations in which the contrast in terms of motion defined earlier can only be understood in a more abstract sense. In this context, he discusses the varying acceptability of symmetric predicates in their non-intransitive use (cf. also Gleitman et al., 1996). In (11), the a-variant is better than the b-variant because the object is construed as Ground and the subject as Figure. Thus, in (11) a. Madonna is correctly construed as a reference point, whereas the speaker's sister is construed as having the 'variability whose particular value is at issue' (Talmy, 2000: 312). The opposite distribution, as shown in (11) b., would only be acceptable in the less likely situation of the speaker's sister providing a better reference point than Madonna.

(11) a. My sister resembles Madonna.
　　b. ?Madonna resembles my sister.

In this way, Talmy concludes that the Figure–Ground opposition plays a role in the realization of symmetric predicates. Unfortunately, he does not elaborate on how this dichotomy interacts with other possible factors.

Gradedness and the Role of Clause Structure

Gleitman et al. (1996), the only large-scale experimental study of the meaning and syntactic behaviour of symmetric predicates, tackles several issues addressed in this chapter. Two of their main insights can be summarized as follows: firstly, speakers can be shown to perceive the 'symmetry' of predicates to be graded. There is a consistent cline from more to less 'symmetric', suggesting that there is no clear-cut boundary between ordinary transitive predicates and what we called 'prototypically reciprocal predicates', and none between the latter and 'symmetric predicates' either. Secondly, if predicates occur in non-intransitive syntactic structures the situation expressed is perceived to be asymmetric. As for argument realization, the authors reject the assumption of a distinct verbal entry for every realization frame of alternating predicates; rather, they attribute the meaning differences between the variants to the interaction of a single lexeme with the meaning contribution of the respective syntactic structures in which the predicates occur.[1] Like Talmy (2000), Gleitman et al. (1996) attribute the choice between variants to the Figure–Ground asymmetry. Their experiments confirm that it is often not inherent properties of the relevant referents which determine argument realization. Rather, the assignment of Figure and Ground to arguments is conversely a result of their argument realization. In other words, a hearer construes the subject as Figure and the object as Ground (see also Langacker, 1991: 308). Problems arise if inherent properties of the referents contradict the respective assignment, as shown by the oddity of Talmy's example (11) b. (see also Polinsky, 1996). Given the fact that very often the syntactic position of the relevant noun phrases triggers the choice between the interpretation as Figure or Ground, I find it difficult to analyze the Figure–Ground contrast as a factor *determining* the choice between the transitive and the intransitive variant. If a transitive clause always triggers a Figure–Ground dichotomy such that the subject is interpreted as Figure and the object as Ground, it would be circular—at least to a certain extent, i.e. excluding cases in which inherent properties of the noun phrase referents exclude one of these options—to argue for a given instance that the speaker opts for the transitive variant with a particular distribution of noun phrases *because* the subject participant is Figure and the object participant is Ground. To put it differently, the Figure–Ground contrast may often be an epiphenomenon, whereas the speaker opts for the respective realization for other reasons. Apart from this issue, Gleitman et al. (1996), like the other authors discussed earlier, restrict their attention to one determining factor of the alternation, viz. the Figure–Ground contrast, arguably implying that other factors are not relevant.

Transitivity and Subjective Construal

Langacker (1987; 1991: 311–316) briefly discusses symmetric predicates in the context of transitivity and grammatical relations. Like the authors discussed earlier, he also observes that symmetry alternations are not meaning-preserving once one no longer restricts one's attention to truth-conditional aspects of meaning. Langacker approaches symmetric predicates as a potential problem for his account of the transitive clause construction.

After having proposed 'asymmetric interaction' as the minimal semantic feature of transitive clauses, he considers the symmetric verbs *intersect* and *resemble* and notes that the objective state of affairs expressed by transitive clauses involving these verbs does not show any asymmetry. This means that one has to go for a more abstract definition, including reference to the subjective construal of a given state of affairs by the speaker. Note that the verbs treated by Langacker—*intersect* and *resemble*—appear to leave less room for 'objective' asymmetries than *meet*.

To conclude the section on previous research, several linguists have been concerned with the argument realization of symmetric predicates from different theoretical perspectives. It seems, however, that none of them gives a comprehensive account of all the factors involved. Either a single factor is explicitly proposed as the only relevant one, or a single factor has been investigated and the issue of how pertinent other factors are has not been broached. An exception is Dowty (1991), who implies that potentially all of his proto-role entailments could determine the choice between the variants. Yet he considers only one factor (motion). As mentioned earlier, another problem with his account is the exclusion of topicality, a move that seems to be due to theory-internal considerations (cf. Dowty, 1991: 563–564) and the minor role that this factor plays in the large majority of verb alternations—it is not normally necessary as a factor when it comes to accounting for subject and object choice with transitive verbs. The 'entailments' that he holds responsible for argument selection are taken to be entailments of the respective verb meanings and the thematic roles with which these are associated (see also Carlson, 1998: 38–39), something that topicality is definitely not. Yet, this move does not do justice to the alternation at issue, because topicality does play a role.

Having concluded that alternations involving symmetric predicates do not alter the truth-conditions of the sentence, Dowty leaves open how to deal with them in his theory. Since information structure asymmetries are often responsible for choosing between one variant and the other—as will be shown later—it seems that Dowty (1991) misses a generalization here. An appropriate modification would be to give up the restriction saying that all meaning components which determine the argument realization of a given verb have to be inherent in the lexical meaning. However, there do not appear to be any convincing arguments for setting up a categorical boundary between 'non-lexical' and 'lexical' determinants of argument realization, apart from the fact that, at least for *meet*, the 'lexical' factors usually outrank the 'non-lexical' ones. Incidentally, it has been shown for object alternations such as the dative alternation that the choice between variants can be due to information structure only (cf. Arnold et al., 2000; Levin and Rappaport Hovav, 2005: 216–219). Not including them in a theory of alternations cannot, therefore, be a conclusive step.

As for the concept of empathy, it does not seem to explain the distribution of noun phrases in all transitive uses of symmetric predicates, either.

There are contexts, for example, where a sentence like (9) f. is possible (cf. example [23] following). Another drawback is the fact that what Kuno and Kaburaki (1977) call 'empathy' is really a bundle of factors, including, among other things, information structure and the animacy status of participants. These factors are closely related, but my data will show that in the context of symmetric predicates it is better to keep them apart.[2] Information structure and those factors often subsumed in the 'Extended Animacy Hierarchy' should be especially held distinct.

More generally, it is problematic that Kuno and Kaburaki's (1977) and also Talmy's (2000) contributions to the analysis of symmetric verbs and argument structure restrict their attention to only one factor, empathy in the former, and the Figure–Ground opposition in the latter. The possibility that empathy, on the one hand, and Figure–Ground, on the other, may be crucially related or even reducible to other factors should be considered more seriously. Allan (1987: 54, n.5) makes a similar point regarding the alleged centrality of the Figure–Ground opposition when he says: 'Most of the examples given in Talmy (1978) seem to me to be governed by the topic < comment and/or given < new hierarchies and not, or not only, by figure < ground'. I also suspect that the notion of empathy—Zubin (1979: 473) shows that it is not easy to operationalize in the first place—may coincide with or be reducible to topicality in most of the cases.

4.3 THE CASE OF *MEET*

In what follows I will consider the verb *meet* and its syntactic behaviour in more detail, thus illustrating the role of different syntactic, semantic and pragmatic factors as determinants of argument realization. As well as showing that argument structure alternations in the area of symmetric predicates are associated with a set of factors that cannot be sensibly reduced to one overarching determinant, this section will be a further step towards a comprehensive description of reciprocity in English. Recall that the usage-based constructional view of grammar adopted here takes grammatical constructions to be symbolic, i.e. they have both a form and a meaning side. In consequence, knowing meaning differences between alternating constructions is vital to their grammatical analysis.

The reasons for choosing *meet* as the object of study are threefold. First, *meet* is often described (at least implicitly) as the prototypical symmetric predicate, and in fact the meaning of the word appears to leave little room for potentially non-symmetric meaning components (henceforth 'asymmetries'). The second reason for choosing *meet* is that the verb is relatively frequent in the BNC (31,535 occurrences). This allows us to make fine-grained observations as to its distribution in different syntactic configurations and semantic as well as pragmatic contexts. The third argument in favour of the verb *meet* is historical. Within the class of symmetric predicates this verb seems to be the only one with a native Germanic root. In contrast to other members of the class, which have mostly been borrowed from French or Latin, it is thus possible to trace back the history of *meet* to the oldest stages of written English. (The history of *meet* and similar verbs was discussed in Chapter 3.)

Note that the discussion in this chapter is not based on a quantitative study. My aim here is not to determine the frequency of the verb in different syntactic, semantic and pragmatic contexts, but rather, firstly, to pin down those factors that determine the choice between argument realizations and their interactions with each other and, secondly, to approach the more general question of what this implies for the linguistic (as opposed to the logical) notion of symmetry in general.

Let us repeat what is at issue. The verb *meet* may be realized in three different argument structure configurations, as illustrated in the following examples:

(12) a. Trevor and Willie met.
     b. Trevor met Willie.
     c. Trevor met with Willie.

Two major syntactic types can then be distinguished, represented by (12) a. on the one hand, and (12) b. as well as (12) c. on the other. The first type involves a single noun phrase functioning as subject. The single noun phrase in (12) a. refers to all the participants that take part in the event denoted by the verb, in this case Trevor and Willie. The second type, represented by (12) b.–c., differs crucially from the first one in that the two participants are now distributed over distinct syntactic positions, namely, either subject and object (cf. [12] b.) or subject and prepositional complement (cf. [12] c.). As far as (12) c. is concerned, it seems that this construction is very similar to structures in other languages that have been termed 'discontinuous reciprocals' (cf. Dimitriadis, 2008a: 335–340; see Plank, 2006 for a detailed treatment of this construction type in German). The only major difference, it seems, is that the formal structure of the construction in (12) c. is not restricted to reciprocal sentences (it can also describe a purely collective situation, as in *Trevor watched TV with Willie*), whereas in the case of the discontinuous reciprocal in other languages like Greek and Bosnian-Croatian-Serbian the structure is unambiguously reciprocal, given the presence of a reflexive expression that is incompatible with a purely collective situation.

Whether we should think of this as one verb that is compatible with different argument realization types or rather with distinct verbs, each licensing one single argument structure will be discussed in more detail later. For now the working hypothesis is the one outlined by Fillmore (1972):

It must be agreed that no theory of grammar should be constrained in such a way that it has to recognize two different verbs *meet*, two different verbs *agree*, etc. in order to distinguish the intransitive from the non-intransitive of use these forms. (11)

Surprisingly, the frequency distribution of the two types under discussion is highly skewed in my sample taken from the BNC: type (12) a. is rather infrequent. Out of a total of 1,440 sentences with *meet* there are only 284 examples of the intransitive realization (excluding passives).

Types of Factors Determining Argument Realization

The factors responsible for the choice between the different variants in (12) can be divided into two major types. One type comprises factors that affect the meaning of the sentence such that the relevant event is interpreted as being asymmetric in some way. Let us illustrate this with the prototypically reciprocal verb *embrace*. Whereas the sentence *Willie and Kate embraced* designates a symmetric situation, meaning that the subevents carried out by the two participants are identical, the situation described by the sentence *Willie embraced Kate* is asymmetric in the sense that it requires Willie to put his arms around Kate, but not vice versa. As I mentioned earlier, such asymmetries are less clearly detectable with properly symmetric predicates like *meet*. Nevertheless, they are comparable to the case of *embrace* mentioned above.

The other type of factor that should be isolated does not involve asymmetries of this type. With respect to *meet*, this means that there are cases of the verb being used transitively that do not involve any clear asymmetry with respect to the meeting event. Such factors concern, for example, information structure or what I will describe as 'separate reference'.

Separate Reference

What happens in the case of 'separate reference' is that for reasons independent of how symmetric or asymmetric the speaker might want to present the meeting event, the different participants of the event have to be expressed by distinct noun phrases. Consider first the case of relative clauses. Sometimes, the verb appears inside a relative clause modifying only one of the two (or more) participants. In such a case, the coding of the two participants as a single noun phrase would be syntactically impossible. In other words, the second participant cannot be introduced as part of the relativizer:

(13) a. . . . said David Missen, the lover of sex therapist Sara Dale, alias Miss Whiplash, who met Courtney when the pair became involved in the Life Shield Association. [CBF 360]

    b. The mega-rich sheik, who met the queen at Claridges in July 1989, has spared no expense on the island, 11 miles long and five miles wide. [CH7 8729]

   c. For an example of innovative action in relation to norms we can return to the couple we met earlier. [EDH 409]

   d. Being a mother has a certain status after all. It makes you a grown-up person, something you can't feel, if, like a girl I met in Barnsley, [. . .]. [EG0 1176]

What all the examples in (13) thus have in common is that the transitive construction involving *meet* cannot be transformed into an intransitive construction. Attempts at expressing the relationship intransitively result in ungrammaticality, or at least a serious distortion of the proposition to be expressed, as shown in (14):[3]

(14) a. * . . . the lover of sex therapist Sara Dale, alias Miss Whiplash, who and Courtney/Courtney and who met when the pair became involved in the Life Shield Association.

   b. *The mega-rich sheikh, the queen and who met at Claridges in July 1989, has spared no expense on the island, 11 miles long and five miles wide.

   c. *For an example of innovative action in relation to norms we can return to the couple we and it/they met earlier.

   d. *Being a mother has a certain status after all, it makes you a grown-up person, something you can't feel, if, like a girl I and her met in Barnsley . . .

A similar case is provided by the information question in (15) a. and the impossible alternation in (15) b.:

(15) a. Who met them on the beaches? [CBF 3448]
   b. *Who and they met on the beaches?

Again, a transitive clause structure is the only possible way of encoding the proposition at issue, given that the grammar of English does not allow the coordination of a nominal and a question word, except for echo-questions, which would require a special intonation contour. It is important to note that irrespective of whether the transitive realization eventually induces an asymmetric construal on the situation, this need not be the motivation for employing the transitive variant in the first place. For the purpose of questioning one of the two participants that are involved in the meeting situation in (15), the only available realization of the verb is the transitive one in (15) a.

   Imperative sentences likewise require separate reference. Imperative sentences involving the verb *meet* typically have only one of the participants as their understood subject. Consider (16):

(16) Merril, meet Bob, my half-brother. [HA7 1667]

The speaker of (16) requests only Merril, not Rob, to engage in a meeting event. This is independent of the symmetric nature of the meeting event itself, however. In other words, Rob's participation in the event is necessary for the event to take place, but it is not profiled (16). In this way the speaker makes reference to a distinct subevent of Merril taking part in a meeting event with Rob. As in the other cases of separate reference, this does not imply any kind of asymmetry in the nature of the event itself. It is the syntactic nature of imperative clauses which makes it impossible to address only one of the participants but at the same time encode both of them as the single argument of the intransitive construction (compare the ungrammaticality of *ø and Bob meet!*). Here are some further examples:

(17) a. It read 'Meet us at 8 o'clock on Boxing Night' and specified a place. [CCC 436]
   b. Come along on Tuesday 11 September, 6 to 8 pm, meet the Pallants and join us for champagne and informal modelling. [ED9 121]
   c. Come and have a glass of wine and meet David Wallington. [FSC 549]
   d. Come along between March 21–24 and meet all your favourite television cooks, chefs and food and wine authors. [G2E 159]

Is what I have called 'separate reference' really an independent factor when it comes to the choice between intransitive and transitive realization of symmetric verbs? As mentioned earlier, separate reference as required by the syntactic construction in which the symmetric verb appears does not exclude an asymmetric interpretation of the event. In addition, the asymmetrical coding of participants—they are realized in syntactically distinct slots—may correlate with an information structural asymmetry. Thus the participant to whom the relative pronoun in (13) b. refers, for example, is more topical inside the relative clause than the queen. Note, however, that the reason for using *meet* transitively in such a case is not just to render an asymmetry in topicality, but rather to modify a single participant by means of a relative clause. Hence, I think that separate reference as a determinant of argument realization cannot simply be reduced to one of the other factors, e.g. topicality, to which we now turn.

Information Structure

The next factor that turns out to be relevant for the choice between different syntactic realizations of *meet* and its arguments is information structure, and in particular topicality. The notion of 'topic' plays a role in many different research traditions and has therefore been defined in several similar, but non-identical, ways. A fundamental distinction that one can make is the one between discourse topic and sentence topic. The latter concerns the topic as (the referent of) that noun phrase in a sentence about which something is said (or 'predicated'). The former notion takes topic to be the mentally most accessible element at a particular point in discourse. Roughly, the first type of definition is tied to the sentence level, whereas the second only makes sense if the discourse/text preceding the sentence at issue is taken into account (for discussions of definitions of topic, see Lambrecht, 1994; Jacobs, 2001; Krifka, 2007). In most cases, the two coincide, viz. the most accessible element at a given point in discourse is highly likely to also be the one about which something is predicated. This is also the case with *meet* in its transitive realization. Yet, I will take the notion of discourse topic to be the primary one here. In this way, I will regard a noun phrase A as 'more topical' than a noun phrase B if, at the point in discourse under consideration, the referent of A is more accessible than the referent of B.

In contrast to the preceding section, I am thus interested in cases in which one of two participants is chosen as subject in a situation where both would be grammatically possible subjects and where the reciprocal event is again not necessarily interpreted as being asymmetric. Indeed, the data demonstrate that in many cases the topicality status of the different participants seems to explain the choice both between a transitive and an intransitive use as well as the possible distributions of participants in a transitive clause. If we assume a scale of topicality or accessibility (cf. Givón, 1983; Ariel, 1990), we can predict that the more topical participant is realized as the subject of a transitive clause and the less topical participant as the object. The following examples represent instances of the transitive realization that do not suggest anything other than information–structural asymmetries between the two participants:

(18) a. She underwent a lumpectomy and then a course of radiotherapy, and was due to start drug treatment when she met another cancer patient. [A1X 104]
   b. She met Andy while working on a production of Carmen at Sky Television, and at their wedding, her two outfits stole the show. [A7P 937]
   c. 'Was there anyone else who was important to her–I mean before she met Mr Hawick, of course?' he asked vaguely. [AB9 1379]
   d. She recalls that she met her ex-husband, cameraman Danny Mindel, on a place going to the Seychelles and, after chatting for ages, asked if she could kiss him. [K3P 72]
   e. It was at the Camp that Alison met husband Jeff–who actually lived a few miles away back home! [HP6 301]

It is crucial here that although the two participants are different with respect to their information–structural status, the meeting event as such may be interpreted as being perfectly symmetric. Example (18) a., for instance, does not require the subject referent (*she*) to take the initiative while the object referent (*another cancer patient*) remains passive, a type of event structural asymmetry often associated with the transitive realization of *meet*. Moreover, in contrast to the examples in the preceding section, it is syntactically and semantically possible to realize the participants in (18) as the joint subject of an intransitive clause. Yet, such a transformation would change the information structure. Consider again example (18) c. The subject referent (*she*) of the clause involving *meet* is more topical than the object referent (*Mr. Hawick*). An intransitive realization of the type *I mean before she and Mr. Hawick met, of course?* is possible, but dispreferred because two participants of divergent topicality would be encoded by a joint noun phrase. The fact that the alternative variant is in principle available in such cases shows, however, that the realization has a different status than the one involving separate reference.

One might object that it is not really topicality, but empathy (or 'perspective') which determines the choice of the subject in the preceding examples.[4] As I argued more generally in my overview of previous research, I doubt that one can show empathy to be totally independent of topicality. With respect to the examples in (18), this view seems to be supported. For each of the sentences in (18) it can be argued that the speaker identifies him- or herself with the person expressed as subject. But how would the subject choice in these cases be justified if the speaker did not identify with any of the participants more than with the other, except for the fact that he or she is talking about the subject participant at that moment? If we call this 'empathy', it boils down to equating empathy and topicality. I propose therefore to speak of empathy only in those cases in which it can be clearly shown that identification with a participant goes beyond higher activation in discourse, viz. topicality—see Kuno and Kaburaki (1977) as well as Kuno (1987) for a number of other syntactic phenomena argued to be triggered by empathy distinctions.

Event Structure

Let us now consider corpus examples in which the transitive construction seems to correlate with an asymmetrical interpretation of the meeting situation. We are thus going beyond asymmetries in information structure, on the one hand, and separate reference, on the other. Such asymmetries include restrictions on inherent properties of the participants, as well as the ways in which the subevents are carried out by the respective participants. The two types of asymmetry often correlate. For example, an inanimate participant never has control of the action it carries out. Note that for the moment I will take a rather unrestricted approach to the data and assume that the different senses of *meet* that are commonly distinguished in dictionaries are facets of a single sense, with different interpretations arising from contextual information and the meaning contribution of the relevant syntactic construction. This simplified view will be modified later.

A contrast in animacy between the two participants leads to the following regularity:

(19) a. A pair of participants, such that one is animate and the other inanimate, are not jointly coded as the subject of the intransitive variant.

b. A pair of participants, such that one is animate and the other inanimate, are realized as the subject and the object of the transitive variant respectively.

This generalization follows from the well-established animacy hierarchy (Croft, 2003: 128–132) and is taken to include cases where one participant is human and the other non-human animate. The latter would then behave like an inanimate object. Furthermore, it has to be kept in mind that the generalization does not exclude instances of the intransitive type and the transitive type in which none of the participants are animate. The following examples illustrate the generalization in (19) b.:

(20) a. I should like to begin by making hasty sketches of the many things I meet. [CBN 12]

b. Did you know that 63 percent of all smart-ass know-alls meet a violent and hideous end? [A27 317]

c. It can probably best be described as the way you are feeling and thinking when you meet any situation. [CDK 2391]

d. Here you meet the Garbourn Road, a rough trackway which crosses over the pass. [CMD 440]

e. . . . the excitement that children show when they meet books, . . . [FSW 723]

f. . . . and to train staff in the best ways of dealing with violence if they meet it. [GXJ 3535]

g. He met his sentence smiling and waving to his friends. [ANK 1253]

h. We met the equivalent of this knife-edge, you will remember, in the story of the Grudgers and Cheats in Chapter 10. [ARR 623]

i. He met a particularly unpleasant death. [G15 2778]

Rare examples of the opposite type, i.e. inanimate subjects and animate objects, can be easily accounted for, since in these cases the inanimate subject is construed as the more agent-like entity. Incidentally, such cases show that the animacy restriction is merely a result of the event structure asymmetry and its prototypical participant distribution. To put it differently, in a transitive clause construction, the more agent-like participant will typically be realized as subject, while the less agent-like participant will typically be realized as object. Although in situations where animates interact with inanimates the former are usually more agent-like than the latter, the reverse mapping can occur and result in the inanimate participant being realized as subject.

Note, however, that topicality in the sense introduced earlier does not override an asymmetry on the level of the event. In this way it is not possible to exchange the arguments of a transitive clause involving *meet* by merely making the original object more topic-worthy:

(21) a. ?As for Garbourn Road, a rough trackway which crosses over the pass, it meets you here.
    b. ?As for Garbourn Road, a rough trackway which crosses over the pass, you and that road meet there.

(22) a. ?There had been speculation on the sentence for weeks. When it finally met the defendant, he smiled and waved to his friends.
    b. ?Harry had longed for the decision for weeks. When the sentence and he finally met, the defendant smiled and waved to his friends.

Let us be more specific in relation to those meaning components that make an event less symmetric. *Meet* is sensitive to motion as a semantic factor restricting possible argument realizations. Recall Dowty's (1991: 586) examples (3)–(4) earlier, where the factor of motion was shown to be relevant for other verbs. Sentence (23) illustrates how the transitive use of *meet* licenses an asymmetry in terms of motion:

(23) My father met me in the kitchen. [HWC 28]

Example (23) describes a situation in which the speaker hides from his father in the kitchen, where his father finally finds him. Note that the same situation is only inappropriately expressed by the intransitive variant or the transitive variant with the non-moving participant in subject position:

(24) a. #Me and my father met in the kitchen.
    b. #I met my father in the kitchen.

If we take the person hierarchy 1/2 < 3 to determine the inherent topicality of referents, (23) violates the aforementioned preference for topical arguments to be realized as subjects of the transitive variant. The first person pronoun *me* refers to a more topical participant than the full noun phrase *my father*. If information structure were the only factor determining the argument realization of symmetric predicates, (24) b. would be the expected variant. Apparently, however, the motion asymmetry is able to override information structure here. More generally, it seems that—in terms of argument realization—an asymmetry that concerns the structure of the event overrides asymmetries in information structure.

How Many Factors?

The preceding discussion implies that there is not just a single factor determining the argument realizations of *meet*, and supposedly of other symmetric verbs, but rather the interaction of several factors. The question arises of whether this is exceptional from the point of argument structure alternations in general. Linguists do not agree on this point, and the role of information structure especially has been controversially discussed. On the one hand, it is well known that information structure plays a role in word order variation in general, and in argument structure alternations in particular (cf. Levin and Rappaport Hovav, 2005: 217–219). What role information structure exactly plays and how it interacts with other factors is still a matter of dispute, on the other hand. Hawkins (1994, 2004), for example, claims that heaviness of constituents and processing considerations explain word order variation and that information structure as a determining factor can be neglected (cf. Hawkins, 2004: 122–123). Birner and Ward (1998) hold that only information structure correctly predicts word order alternations. Construction grammarians such as Goldberg (1995) in turn stress slight semantic differences between alternate constructions.[5] Few studies have really examined the interplay of different factors (Arnold et al., 2000: 34). As Arnold, Wasow and colleagues show for some English alternations, however, at least two factors, information structure and heaviness of constituents, are relevant and one cannot be reduced to the other (Arnold et al., 2000; Wasow, 2002).

Returning to our case study of symmetric verbs, it also seems to be the case here that their variable syntactic realizations cannot be reduced to a single determining factor. This concerns both the choice between intransitive and non-intransitive realization, on the one hand, and the order of arguments in the transitive variant, on the other. The data show that at least information structure, event semantics and the necessity of separate reference are determining factors. Heaviness of constituents is likely to come into play, as well, but will be neglected here. What makes the analysis of the data particularly difficult is that very often several factors apply to a sentence simultaneously.[6] As far as I can see, the case for information structure asymmetries being able to trigger transitivity alternations has not yet been made.

In any case it is important to stress that it cannot automatically be assumed that all of the factors that might be relevant in a given instance do actually determine the argument realization. This is illustrated in (25).

(25) . . . he took his diagonal path through the weeds every day to meet Buddy Rourke, . . . , so they could walk to school together, . . . [Updike, Villages, 12]

In the event described by (25) there could be a motion asymmetry such that the participant denoted by the pronoun *he* moves throughout the weeds in order to arrive at the location of Buddy Rourke. In fact, it is not clear from the context whether Buddy Rourke should be analyzed as a stationary participant or not. From what we saw in examples like (23), we know that such an asymmetry can determine the distribution of subject and object in a transitive clause. Now, in (25) there is also an asymmetry concerning the relative topicality of the two participants. The participant realized as the subject is clearly more topical than the one referred to by the object. He is the last participant mentioned in previous discourse and encoded as a pronoun in the clause at issue. The second participant, by contrast, is not activated to the same degree and correspondingly receives coding through a full noun phrase. In my view, one cannot tell for sure whether the argument realization as we observe it in (25) is a result of either the motion asymmetry, or the topicality asymmetry or both. In general, however, the interaction of several factors determining the choice between different syntactic constructions is a common phenomenon and there is no reason to assume the alternation under discussion is an exception. I would like to stress, however, that such cases do not contradict the view that the different factors are in principle independent of each other. Being independent of each other does not entail that the factors may not co-occur in usage.

4.4 HOW MANY MEANINGS?

So far I have described the argument realization of the verb *meet* under the working assumption that it has a single meaning which interacts with the semantics of the construction it occurs in (see also the earlier quote from Fillmore). This is an oversimplification, however. The uses of *meet* are varied and the question arises of whether they are stored as independent lexical entries, although in accordance with the usage-based model it will be assumed that the distinction between monosemy and polysemy is graded, related meanings being represented in a network the nodes of which are entrenched to different degrees, depending also on the frequency of the respective uses (see for instance Diessel, 2004: 13–40).

The relevant uses of *meet* are illustrated in the following examples (see also Haas, 2008: 256–257):

(26) a. I've only met her once.
   b. Not even in Paradise Street had Rose met that phenomenon. [B2M 304]
   c. However, in order to avoid unnecessary delays in meeting the expectations of the staff, [. . .] [B2M 304]
   d. Resistance was met by beatings, fines or imprisonment. [HH3 12618]
   e. She and her husband were met at the station by a small open carriage which took them to the palace. [ANR 650]

The use in (26) a. is the one that most linguists have in mind when they present *meet* as an example of a symmetric predicate. It may be called COME TOGETHER. In this use the two (or more) participants act in identical ways, which would conform to what we would want symmetric predicates to be like: the subevents are mirror images of each other. The event described in (26) b. is slightly different. There is a clear asymmetry in participation; the subject participant is moving and consciously attends to the entity denoted by the object, but the reverse does not hold. In sentences of this type, the object can refer not only to inanimate entities, but also to animates (including humans) that remain passive in a similar way. I will call this the COME ACROSS use of *meet*. Those uses of *meet* that I described in terms of event structure asymmetries earlier basically falls into this class. The use types illustrated in (26) c.–e. share with the latter type the non-identical participation that the two participants exhibit, and historically they seem to be extensions of the 'come across' use (Haas, 2007: 35). The use in (26) c. will be called STANDARD, because the referent of the active subject fulfil (or attempts to fulfil) a standard, requirement or need, as specified by the object. Example (26) d. shows a use of *meet* that is similar to the 'standard' use in that the active object (or passive subject in the actual example) also acts as a reference point or stimulus. It is nevertheless semantically distinct, since the event here is not predetermined by the reference point. There is an event which functions as a reaction to the stimulus denoted by the passive subject (hence REACTION). The reading in (26) e., finally, exemplifies what could be called the ARRIVAL use of *meet*: the active object or passive subject refers to a person, a group of persons or a means of transport conducted by the latter, waiting for and then receiving the other participant, typically at an airport, a station or any other place that is construed as an arrival point of that kind. Recall that all the examples discussed in the context of information structure, separate reference or event structure asymmetries in the earlier section fall in the class of either 'come together' or 'come across'. Strictly speaking, as soon as there is an event structure asymmetry, the definition of a symmetric predicate and thus the 'come together' sense would not be fulfilled. Example (23), for instance, thus belongs in the class 'come across'.

We will not be concerned here with the question of whether all of the uses of *meet* illustrated earlier constitute distinct senses (see Haas, 2007, for some discussion). What I would like to stress, however, is that the syntax of these different uses of the verb generally follows well-known principles of argument realization. Note, for instance, that in the case of the 'arrival' use of *meet* it is always the more active participant that is coded as either the subject of the active variant or as the adjunct agent-phrase of the passive variant (the latter option is illustrated by [26] e.). The 'standard' and 'reaction' uses behave similarly. 'Come across', which is arguably much less distinct semantically from 'come together' than the remaining three types, likewise exhibits a semantically motivated pattern of argument realization.

Asymmetries with respect to the animacy status of the participants or the parameter of movement (moving versus stationary participants) inhibit an intransitive realization (**Not even in Paradise Street had Rose and that phenomenon met*), on the one hand, and restrict the mapping of participants over argument positions in the case of the transitive variant (*#Not even in Paradise street had that phenomenon met Rose*[7]), on the other.

What does this imply for the question of whether *meet* is a 'symmetric predicate'? Firstly, the use types 'standard', 'reaction' and 'arrival', although certainly semantically related to 'come across' and 'come together', are not symmetric in the sense intended in the literature. The same holds for 'come across', if we take it to be an autonomous sense, i.e. independent of 'come together' in the mind of the speaker (see Croft and Cruse, 2004: 109–140 on the distinctness of polysemous senses). Secondly, it was pointed out that it is often difficult to tell for sure whether a given non-intransitive realization of *meet* (including the transitive variant and the variant involving the preposition *with*) is merely due to information structure or the need to refer to the two participants separately (see the earlier discussion of 'separate reference'), or whether either of these two factors interacts with an event structure asymmetry. Recall that in examples like (25), the situation as described in the sentence, as well as the context, is compatible with either of these types of analysis. One can therefore expect that the instances of *meet* that are properly 'symmetric' are even fewer (cf. also Carlson, 1998: 37–38 on symmetric predicates in general).

Even though the preceding discussion thus shows that statements of the type 'The verb *meet* is a symmetric predicate' should be qualified, it does not make the assumption of a class of 'symmetric predicates' invalid. As long as there are those uses in which symmetry definitely holds—intransitively realized *meet* and those non-intransitive uses that are due to separate reference and information structure asymmetries—it appears that we can safely consider a subset of the uses of *meet* symmetric. At the same time there is reason to believe—for the aforementioned reasons—that sentences expressing strictly symmetric situations are more marginal than often seems to be assumed in studies that take truth-conditional identity between pairs of sentences of the type in (27) to be a sufficient condition for classifying V as 'symmetric':

(27) a. A V$_{\text{SYMM}}$ B
  b. B V$_{\text{SYMM}}$ A

The Status of Symmetric Verbs Used Intransitively

There is another complication that we have to take into account when asking to what degree allegedly symmetric predicates are really symmetric, and this concerns the intransitive variant. In Chapter 5 it will be shown in which way the intransitive realization of symmetric and prototypically reciprocal verbs competes with the basic reciprocal construction. I will argue that with respect to the parameter single event/collective versus distinct events/distributive the intransitive realization tends to express a single event in which the two (or more) participants take part in the relevant event as a collective entity, at least to a higher degree than in the case of the basic reciprocal construction. What does this have to do with the issue of symmetry? The two issues are related in that the logical definition of symmetry normally assumed in discussion of verbs like *meet* suggests that the participants taking part in the event act on each other in a bidirectional manner, i.e. participant A acts on participant B in some way, and the very same event is mirrored in the opposite direction, B acting on A. When it now comes to the question of what 'symmetry' actually means in intransitive sentences involving allegedly symmetric verbs, we have to keep in mind the following: if the discussion in Chapter 5 is on the right track, this type of sentence is the type of reciprocal one most clearly associates with a single-event construal. Here we have to ask in which way such sentences are related to the well-known type of sentence involving 'collective predicates'. Are they perhaps examples of collective predications, after all, having less to do with the bidirectional type of event characteristic of reciprocity than one would expect?

Brisson (2003) defines a collective predicate as 'one that requires a plural argument; or a predicate that with a plural argument has an interpretation that is different from the interpretation that comes from universally quantifying over the parts of the plural argument' (144). Common examples of collective predicates are *gather, be a big group* and *be a happy couple* (Lasersohn, 1990; Dowty, 1987). It seems that collective predicates share at least one important property with verbs like *meet*: there is identical participation by all participants (cf. Dowty, 1987 for detailed discussion of what this means in the case of collective predicates). What is it that distinguishes them from symmetric verbs then? In chapter 2, section 2.7, I discussed Kemmer's (1997) observation that a prototypical reciprocal situation is related to a prototypical collective situation through an intermediate 'indirect bilateral' type. Let us briefly look at her quote again:

> In the ['indirect bilateral'] type, on the other hand, the affectedness is indirect rather than direct. [. . .] The focus of such constructions is not on affectedness of the participants by the verbal action, but on mutual interaction. [. . .] each participant must adjust his/her actions to a considerable extent to those of the partner, or the mutual activity designated cannot be said to take place. The sense of accompaniment in carrying out some overarching event is therefore considerably strengthened compared to the reciprocal. (237)

As mentioned in Chapter 2, Kemmer does not specifically discuss symmetric and prototypically reciprocal verbs, instead taking as a starting point what she calls the 'prototypical reciprocal situation' type expressed by the basic reciprocal construction. We will see in the next chapter that the contrast between the intransitive use of symmetric and prototypically reciprocal verbs, on the one hand, and the use of these verbs in the basic reciprocal construction (the verb in combination with *each other/one another*), on the other, is indeed associated with the semantic contrast described earlier. Again, what does this imply for the characterization of symmetric verbs? When realized intransitively, these verbs do require the participants jointly denoted by the subject to exhibit identical participation, yet by virtue of being expressed as a single subject of an intransitive construction, the situation tends to be construed as a single event collectively carried out or undergone by the participants. In this way, the 'symmetric' situations are strictly speaking symmetric only in the sense of there being identical participation by two or more individuals, not in the sense of there being two more clearly distinguishable subevents that are mirror images of each other.

Since there are differences between verbs with respect to the contrast in construal under discussion—verbs describing dynamic events like *meet* leave more room for differing interpretations than stative verbs, especially those designating purely geometrical configurations such as *intersect*—it is certainly not true that all allegedly 'symmetric' verbs are generally construed as expressing a collective situation. Eventually, the degree to which a given verb can be interpreted as expressing a collective event, as opposed to a set of two or more distinct bidirectional events, depends on the lexical meaning of the verb. A detailed comparison of all verbs commonly categorized as 'symmetric' (let alone non-verbal symmetric predicates) is beyond the scope of this study. What should have become clear, however, is firstly that the interpretation of reciprocal sentences in general and of intransitive reciprocal sentences in particular involves at least two dimensions: the degree to which subevents are construed as being distinct from each other and the degree to which the two or more participants participate identically in the larger event. Secondly, and this is an aspect that a logical definition of symmetry does not capture, the intransitive realization of verbs like *meet* differs from the transitive realization not only in that identical participation is required, but also in that an interpretation of two identical subevents being mirror images of each other gives way to the interpretation of a single collective event. Thus, coming back to the question of the status of symmetric verbs in English, it seems that they are ambivalent in a way: when used transitively, strictly identical participation is rarely upheld (cf. the discussion of *meet* in the preceding section), and when used intransitively, the idea that they are used to describe two or more distinguishable events that stand in a relation of symmetry cannot be upheld. The upshot of this, in my view, is that while it is certainly sensible to identify a class of verbs that appear to carry reciprocity in their lexical meaning, one should be careful not to simply attribute the strict logical notion of symmetry to natural language verbs. Instead, I propose to view symmetry as a two-dimensional property whose value in a given reciprocal sentence depends both on the kind of situation the verb refers to and on the kind of construction the verb occurs in.

In the following chapter, we will come across data that substantiate the claim that I took for granted in the preceding discussion. The intransitive clause construction and the basic reciprocal construction impose different construals on the events denoted by symmetric and prototypically reciprocal verbs. In addition, it will be argued that for those verbs that do not allow an intransitive realization, the same kind of contrast in event construal (single event versus distinct events) can nevertheless be linguistically expressed, taking into account conditions on using reciprocal constructions of the spell-out type.

5 Reciprocity in English
A Comprehensive Perspective

In this chapter the focus will be on the competition between the reciprocal strategies of PDE. To this end, I will build on the observations made in the preceding chapters and add further data supporting my claims on the functional differentiation between the intransitive variant described in the preceding chapter, the basic reciprocal construction and what I termed spell-out constructions. The structure of the chapter is as follows. First I will discuss cross-linguistic data concerning functional splits between variable reciprocal constructions that have long been known and ask to what extent these generalizations can be carried over to the situation in PDE. I will then survey previous research on functional splits in English and present quantitative data that support claims on these splits. Furthermore, I will attempt to describe the complete picture, i.e. the interaction between all three of the aforementioned constructions.

5.1 FUNCTIONAL SPLITS IN RECIPROCAL CONSTRUCTIONS

Kissing (Each Other) in English and Other Languages

It has long been known that the two sentences in (1) are not completely synonymous.[1]

(1) a. Kate and Willie kissed.
    b. Kate and Willie kissed each other.

Whereas (1) a. describes a unitary kissing event, (1) b. can be used to describe two or more possibly successive one-way kissing events. Such a contrast is detectable for many predicates in English and other languages. Generally, if there is a choice between formally different reciprocal constructions (typically for a limited class of naturally reciprocal predicates), the more parsimoniously coded reciprocal constructions have a one-event interpretation, while the less parsimoniously coded reciprocal constructions have a distinct-events interpretation (Dong, 1970: 11–14; Dowty, 1991: 583–584; Kemmer, 1993b; Carlson, 1998: 42; Wierzbicka, 2009). Detailed discussion of German data can be found in Wandruzska (1973) and Plank (2006); on other languages see Nedjalkov (2007b: 318–319), volumes 2 and 3 of Nedjalkov (2007c) and Maslova (2008: 244–245).

The distinction exemplified in (1) in turn correlates with particular classes of verbs such that in the relevant languages symmetric and prototypically reciprocal verbs tend to combine with the light marker, while all other verbs combine with the heavy marker. What Kemmer (1993b: 111) also notes is that what is a contrast between heavy and light forms in one language may turn up as a contrast between overt marking and intransitive use of the relevant verbs in another language. A language of the latter type is English, as illustrated in (1) b., and the most widely cited example of the single-event versus distinct-event effect is the variable use of the verb *kiss* (Kemmer, 1993b: 111).

If languages have two reciprocal markers at their disposal, one of them is often a reduced reflexive pronoun that has come to express a variety of 'middle' functions, and reciprocity is one of these middle functions. It may also be a verbal affix of reflexive or other origin. The second item is usually a specialized reciprocal expression similar to the English expressions *each other* and *one another* in terms of its internal make-up. That a reduced reflexive pronoun often expresses middle meanings is motivated by the special status of reflexive clauses in terms of argument structure. Following Hopper and Thompson (1980), transitivity is a multidimensional property of clauses that goes beyond the mere presence or absence of a second argument. From this point of view, the values in reflexive clauses for some of the dimensions listed by Hopper and Thompson (1980) diverge from those that are present in prototypical transitive clauses. Most obviously, as opposed to prototypical transitive clauses the referent of the subject and the referent of the object are not distinct. As shown, for example, by Gaby (2001: 19–23) for Australian languages, this semantic property of reflexive predications is often reflected in formal properties of the relevant clauses. This may concern case marking, cross-referencing and of course the overt presence of arguments. Now, the special transitivity status of reflexive clauses makes them amenable to developing further in the direction of reduced transitivity, something which motivates the reduction of reflexive pronouns to middle markers (see also Gast and Haas, 2008).

Concerning the interaction of markers with verb classes, note that the heavy marker naturally combines with those verbs that do not allow the light marker. The number of verbs repelled from the light marker, among other things, depends on the productivity of the marker. In Swedish, for instance, the light form has been reduced to a verbal suffix, which is still moderately productive but not able to attach to every transitive verb (see Nedjalkov, 2007a: 194–195, for further examples).[2]

Let us now consider a couple of languages that illustrate the formal and functional contrast under discussion. Whereas for pairs like (1) a.–b. from

English, it need not be necessary to think of two different word meanings—the event structure contrast being able to account for the meaning difference alone—the situation is different for other predicates. Pairs of this type abound in languages where reciprocity is marked by a reduced reflexive anaphor, i.e. a middle marker. Consider the examples from German in (2) and Swedish in (3):

(2) a. Gestern   hat   Katharina   Willie   gesehen.
      yesterday has   Kate   Willie   seen
      'Yesterday Kate saw Willie.'
   b. Gestern   haben   Katharina und   Willie   einander   gesehen
      yesterday have   Kate   and   Willie   one.another seen
      'Yesterday Kate and Willie saw each other.'
   c. Gestern   haben   Katharina und   Willie sich   gesehen.
      yesterday have   Kate   and   Willie REFL   seen
      'Yesterday Kate and Willie met.'

(3) a. Göran   ska   se   Pernilla.
      Göran   will   see   Pernilla
      'Göran will see Pernilla.'
   b. Göran   och   Pernilla   ska   se   varandra.
      Göran   and   Pernilla   will   see   each.other
      'Göran and Pernilla will see each other.'
   c. Göran   och   Pernilla   ska   ses.
      Göran   and   Pernilla   will   see-MM
      'Göran and Pernilla will meet.'

In the a-sentences the predicate 'see' is used in a syntactically unambiguously transitive sentence. If we compare the verb meaning in (2) a. and (3) a. to the meaning of the derived reciprocal verbs in the c-sentences we can observe that the meaning of *sich sehen* and *ses* in German and Swedish respectively cannot be compositionally derived from the basic meaning 'see' as it occurs in the a-sentences plus the meaning of the reciprocal marker. Thus the meaning 'meet' is not tantamount to 'see each other', but involves additional meaning components concerning social interaction and mutual awareness. Such combinations of verb and reciprocal marker have been lexicalized in the sense that a new intransitive lexeme is created. The lexicalizations exemplified in (2) c. and (3) c. are absent in the b-sentences, where the relevant verbs combine with the specialized reciprocal expressions *einander* in German and *varandra* in Swedish.

If there is a choice between two forms, the specialized reciprocal one need not be a free morpheme as opposed to an affix. The following examples from Gaby (2008: 284) show that the meaning contrast associated with the choice between a middle marker and a specialized reciprocal marker may be restricted to the level of morphology. The example in (4) is from Kuuk Thaayorre, a Paman language spoken on the west coast of Cape York Peninsula (Australia):[3]

(4) a. pul   nhaanhath-e-ø
     3DU.NOM   look.RDP-MM-NPST
     'They are looking into each other's eyes.'
   b. pul   meer-e   nhaat-rr-r
     3DU.NOM/ERG eye-ERG look-RECP-PST.PFV
     'They looked at *each other* (one after the other).'

The meaning difference between (4) a. and b. is again the one we are interested in. If the verb *nhaat* 'look' is combined with the middle suffix *-e*, the reciprocal situation is construed as a unitary event. In this particular case, this basically means that the two subevents take place simultaneously and that there is mutual cooperation of participants (Gaby, 2008: 284). The specialized reciprocal suffix *-rr*, by contrast, triggers a distinct-events reading: the two subevents take place one after the other and mutual cooperation is not essential.

We would expect the same pattern to hold in English, hence lexicalized intransitive reciprocal verbs contrasting with the basic reciprocal construction. Remember that the general pattern is the following: the light form is associated with single-event readings whereas the heavy form is associated with distinct-event readings. Either the light form obligatorily occurs with verbs that denote events construed as being unitary because they are symmetric or prototypically reciprocal in the first place, or they indicate a single-event construal of a reciprocal relation based on an ordinary transitive verb (see Kemmer, 1993b: 110–121, for ample illustration). Kemmer (1993b) shows that the idea of a two-form system applies to English as well. Those verbs which always take the light form in two-form languages roughly correspond to the intransitive verbs denoting reciprocal events in English. In this way, the intransitive argument realization in English corresponds to the light reciprocal forms in other languages. The expression *each other* can then be analyzed as a heavy form.

Subset Ambiguities

There is a context in which the addition of the overt reciprocal to a symmetric or prototypically reciprocal verb seems to be associated with the expression in truth-conditionally distinct situations. The attested example in (5) exhibits what I will call 'subset ambiguities':

(5) Through the country's long years of repression, artists, intellectuals and students met each other in the cafes, to swap ideas and information and to give each other solidarity. [AAX 121]

The possible readings of such a sentence are discussed at length in the formal semantic literature (cf. Scha and Stallard, 1988; Landman, 1989: 579;

Lasersohn, 1995; Schwarzschild, 1996). The readings that interest us here are the following:

(i) All artists, intellectuals and students are forming one undifferentiated set and all the members of this large set enter into a meeting relation (UNION reading).

(ii) Artists, intellectuals and students are separate groups and a meeting relation holds *between* the groups (INTER-GROUP reading).

(iii) Artists, intellectuals and students are separate groups and a meeting relation holds *within* the groups (INTRA-GROUP reading).

The intended reading of the corpus example is the one in (ii), which is highlighted by the sentence preceding (5) in the original text: *These imposing buildings from another era were the meeting point for elements that the establishment wanted to keep apart.* It is unlikely that the *establishment* just wanted to keep students apart from other students, intellectuals from other intellectuals and artists from other artists (the intra-group reading), rather than keep the different groups apart from each other. The union reading would not be incompatible with the intentions of the establishment in this example (note that truth-conditionally the two readings are compatible with each other), yet it seems safe to assume that the inter-group reading matches best what the *establishment* in (5) focused on most.

In this way, adding *each other* to a verb that does not normally need to combine with it appears to have the function of selecting reading (ii), or to put it differently: it has the function of triggering a distinct-events construal, which in this case selects for the inter-group reading. Why should this be the case, i.e. why should the distinct-events construal go together with the inter-group reading, as opposed to the union reading? This question brings us back to what was already mentioned earlier. Interpreting a situation as a unitary event, at least for situations involving human participants, would prototypically involve some action that is collectively carried out by the set of participants (see e.g. Lasersohn, 1990; Kemmer, 1993b: 123–124; Carlson, 1998: 41–42). This, in turn, has repercussions on how the participants themselves are construed; not merely as a set of individuals but as a single entity that is more than the sum of its parts (cf. Landman, 2000: 156). This contrast, usually termed 'collective' versus 'distributive' has for the most part been discussed in relation to noun phrase coordination and the issue of whether the latter can plausibly be derived from sentential coordination. Dik (1968), Wierzbicka (1980), Lakoff and Peters (1969) and Payne (1985: 17–23) discuss strategies of marking the referents of noun phrase conjuncts as 'separate'; Schwarzschild (1996: 103–104), Brisson (1998: 92–93) and Givón (2001: 15–24) consider more generally how the form of the subject noun phrase contributes to the assignment of collective versus distributive meaning. In the present context I take the collective construal of participants to be a concomitant of viewing the event in which the latter are involved as a single event.

For the subset ambiguities under discussion, I think it is reasonable to assume that the inter-group reading requires a distributive construal of the most salient subsets, which in this case are not the atomic individuals (each and every student, artist and intellectual) but the three groups: students, artists and intellectuals. A union reading, by contrast, views all individuals as an undifferentiated whole; the most salient subsets are not considered separately. It should be noted that the spell-out construction would not be a competitor in (5) (. . . *artists, intellectuals and students each met the other in the cafes, to swap ideas and information and to give each other solidarity*), because the quantifier *each* by necessity distributes down to the level of atomic individuals. In (5) these would be the individual students, artists and intellectuals. Exceptions are sentences where the quantifier determines a noun like *group* that refers directly to a subgroup:

(6) Brownies and Guides get together and each group entertains the others as part of the Programme. [G22 369]

Literature as early as Fiengo and Lasnik (1973: 448–450) noted that *each other* allows any salient subsets within the set of participants to be construed as reciprocal participants, whereas *each . . . the other* distributes more strictly.

In order to test whether the effect observed in (5) holds more generally I searched for instances of the lexeme MEET in combination with the reciprocal *each other* in the COCA. This query resulted in 217 instances in total, among which there are thirteen tokens displaying a (logically possible) subset ambiguity of the type in (5). All thirteen examples have the inter-group reading. Here are some of them:

(7) a. There are so many ways for different kinds of people to meet each other. That has never changed.
b. Iraqis and Americans need to learn more about each other, he says, and to meet each other.
c. We make it easier for buyers and sellers to meet each other.
d. When I reached the end of the line, where a park ranger kept visitors from going further, I joined the oohing and aahing at the spectacle of lava and waves surging up to meet each other like clashing superpowers.
e. Men and women are still meeting each other and vowing to spend their lives together.

This phenomenon of the reciprocal selecting for a reading in which the most salient subsets are singled out, as opposed to an interpretation in which all participants form an undifferentiated whole, is not restricted to the verb *meet*. This effect also seems to arise with *marry*, another symmetric verb that can be realized intransitively. Consider two examples from academic texts:

(8) a. . . . and Bakermans-Kranenburg's (in press) study showing that secure men and women (assessed via the AAI) marry each other more often than expected by chance.[4]

b. Any tendency for individuals from similar social backgrounds to marry each other will also lead to a positive marital correlation.[5]

Note that in (8) a. and b. it is not relations between two groups as such that are at issue, but rather relations between individual members of the two groups. Crucially, however, the sentences do not assert relations between any random pair of individuals. The only possible relations are between individuals from different groups. In general, one should not assume that the use of the reciprocal in these cases always has a disambiguating function. Especially the inter-group readings of the examples in (8) should be derivable from the context. It appears that the addition of the reciprocal is required anyway, due to the special type of distribution over salient subsets that is needed for the inter-group reading, and which is sanctioned by the basic reciprocal construction, not by the intransitive construction.

Let us now turn to the competition between basic and spell-out constructions, hence the alternation that—independently of the preceding data—has been argued to be associated with the single-event–distinct-events contrast as well.

Competition Between Basic and Spell-Out Construction

The distinction described in the previous section concerns grammaticalized means of reciprocal marking. In other words, both options represent constructions or markers that are firmly integrated into the grammatical system of the language, albeit not always specialized for the expression of reciprocity. In Kuuk Thaayorre, for instance, we are dealing with the choice between two suffixes, one of which is specialized for the expression of reciprocity and the other for the expression of middle functions, a single-event construal of reciprocal situations being one of them. The same holds for English, where the contrast is between the intransitive clause construction and the specialized reciprocal *each other/one another*. The former is again less specialized than the latter: depending on the type of verb, intransitive clauses can express a wide range of situation types and reciprocity is only one of them.

This is not where the range of reciprocal strategies ends, however. English, and presumably every other language, is able to spell out reciprocal situations by making use of non-specialized means, such as clause coordination or the *each . . . the other* type of construction (see Chapter 2 for a detailed description). Even though these reciprocal strategies are thus different from the ones discussed in the previous section, we also have to consider spell-out variants in order to understand the workings of the entire system. They are not part of the grammatical system in the strict sense, yet they seem to fulfil functions that their grammaticalized counterparts are not able to fulfil and in this way the two types compete with each other. In the following, the motivations for using the English spell-out constructions, with the main focus on the 'split quantificational' type *each . . . the other* will be described. In particular, I will give an account of the competition between this type of spell-out construction and the basic reciprocal construction. Frequency data from PDE corpora will complement both proposals made in the literature and non-quantitative observations made by the author.

It has repeatedly been observed in the literature that the basic reciprocal construction and the spell-out construction differ in that the former tends to be interpreted as expressing a single event, while the latter expresses distinct events making up the reciprocal situation; see, for example, Williams (1991), who uses this observation as an argument against Heim et al.'s (1991) derivational account of reciprocal sentences. Authors differ in whether they describe the contrast in terms of a contrast between a single-event interpretation and a distinct-events interpretation or a contrast in the way the participants are interpreted—collectively or distributively (cf. Fiengo and Lasnik, 1973: 454; Brisson, 1998: 39). As mentioned earlier, a single-event interpretation and a collective interpretation of the participants involved are actually tightly related to one another, and the same holds for the relation between a distinct-events interpretation and the distributive construal of participants.[6]

Fiengo and Lasnik (1973) observe that the basic reciprocal strategy 'characterizes the entire set' (454) and thus allows a vagueness that the spell-out strategy does not allow. According to Fiengo and Lasnik, what they call '*each-the-other* sentences . . . characterize each member of the set' (1973: 454). Furthermore, the authors observe the contrast between a one-event reading and a distinct-events reading (450–451), illustrated by (9)–(10):

(9) a. Each of the cars bumped into the other; the Pontiac bumped into the Plymouth on Monday, and the Plymouth bumped into the Pontiac on Tuesday.

   b. The cars bumped into each other; *the Pontiac bumped into the Plymouth on Monday, and the Plymouth bumped into the Pontiac on Tuesday.

(10) a. Each of the men stared at the other; John stared at Bill for three hours and then Bill stared at John for three hours.

   b. The men stared at each other; *John stared at Bill for three hours and then Bill stared at John for three hours.

The unacceptability of the continuations given in (9) b. and (10) b. is assumed to follow from the fact that in these examples one event at one time is referred to, whereas in (9) a. and (10) a., making use of the spell-out strategy, distinct events at different times are referred to. Unfortunately, in natural data the contrast at issue is not always as straightforward as in Fiengo and Lasnik's (1973) constructed examples. The relation between temporal simultaneity and a single-event interpretation, on the one hand, and non-simultaneity and a distinct-events interpretation, on the other, is evident. In many examples taken from corpus data the motivation for using the analytic reciprocal strategy does seem to be a construal of the reciprocal situation as two or more distinct events, but at the same time it is not always reducible to the contrast simultaneous versus non-simultaneous.

Bolinger (1987, 1990) also detects a systematic semantic contrast between the basic and the spell-out strategy. Viewing the issue from a diachronic point of view, he states the following:

> The present situation is that the older *each . . . the other* and *one . . . another* and the newer compounds *each other* and *one another* are competing on unequal terms. The newer form has shed its markedness, and the older one is reserved more or less for cases where the speaker needs to be extra precise, to avoid the 'blur' that the fusion of *each* and *other* into a single pronoun has created. What started out as a way of marking the construction as reciprocal has ended up once more—by way of fusion—close to the camp of the reflexive. (1990: 268)

Bolinger (1987, 1990) pins down the relevant contrast by using the terms 'mutuality' and 'commutation' (see Chapter 2 and the discussion of possible contrasts between *each other* and *one another*). I contend that his dichotomy easily translates into our opposition between single- and distinct-event readings, given that a focus on the bidirectionality (or 'commutation') of reciprocal situations indeed profiles the distinct events (or eventualities) making up the bidirectional relation. Conversely, a collective interpretation of the reciprocal participants and the related single-event interpretation of the reciprocal situation correspond to Bolinger's 'blur' and 'lack of precision', since distinct subevents are not distinguished. Bolinger (1987, 1990) argues that with two-participant sentences the two constructions differ semantically, too. He illustrates this with the following pair of examples ([11] b. is how the German title of an etching by Paul Klee, *Zwei Männer, einander in höherer Stellung vermutend, begegnen sich*, is translated into English):

(11) a. ?Two persons believing each other to be in a higher position.
   b. Two persons each believing the other to be in a higher position.

For (11), a single-event interpretation requires that the two participants believe the proposition p ('the other is in a higher position') jointly (viz.

collectively), but it is exactly this interpretation that is not easily compatible with the situation at issue, hence the oddness of (11) a. The expected interpretation—each participant believing p without being aware of their co-participant believing p as well—can be adequately expressed only by using the spell-out strategy in (11) b.

Interestingly, Bolinger claims that the meaning of the basic reciprocal construction is closer 'to the camp of the reflexive' (1990: 268) than the spell-out construction. Recall that in many languages single-event interpretations of reciprocal situations are expressed by grammatical markers which also express reflexivity, or at least historically derive from a reflexive marker. Now, if Bolinger is correct in relating the meaning of the basic reciprocal construction to reflexivity, this implies that not only the contrast between the English intransitive and the basic reciprocal construction corresponds to the one illustrated by the preceding Swedish and Kuuk Thaayorre examples, but also the one between the basic and the spell-out construction. This parallelism and its implications for a more comprehensive analysis of reciprocity in English will be the topic of section 5.2. But first, let us consider data that support the assumption under which there is a functional difference between basic and spell-out construction in English.

Qualitative and Quantitative Data

In what follows I will firstly provide some examples which illustrate how the use of the spell-out construction is associated with a distinct-events interpretation of reciprocal situations. Later, I will present quantitative data showing that those verbs whose meaning is more compatible with a distinct-events interpretation than other verbs are indeed significantly more frequent in that construction than verbs that are semantically neutral in this respect. Let us first consider two random examples illustrating the association between the distinct-events interpretation and the spell-out construction.

(12)   In the early Middle Ages, no real effort was made to go beyond the stereotypes entertained by Christians and Muslims alike. Each saw the other's religion as a menace; and their mutual polemics were really a part of theology.[7]

(13)   My own impression is that in both India and China there is a growing recognition, not only of the potential role of their countries, but also one of the other. They each see the other as already being a major player and one which is likely to become even more so in the future. They each recognize the importance of a better relationship between them.[8]

In order to clearly show how the two constructions are each associated with a different way of construing a reciprocal situation, we should go beyond anecdotal evidence and look for quantitative data that support the generalization. Indeed, there are problems with examples like the ones in (12) and (13). Firstly, by searching for sentences instantiating the spell-out construction one will not come across any counterevidence, for example, contexts that require a distinct-events interpretation but nevertheless show the basic reciprocal construction. Secondly, apart from some cases cited again and again in the literature (cars colliding with each other or men staring at each other), the semantic contrast under consideration here cannot easily be reduced to obvious differences such as the presence or absence of temporal simultaneity. In most cases the semantic effects are more subtle and concern factors like knowledge and intentions shared by the respective participants, something which cannot always be safely determined for corpus data.

I propose, therefore, to compare the relative frequencies of the two constructions, spell-out construction and basic reciprocal construction, across different verbs. The verbs are chosen according to their inherent propensity towards a distinct-events interpretation. To this end, I set up a list of verbs that fulfil at least one of the following properties, or more precisely: verbs which describe events for which at least one of the following properties would hold in a reciprocal context.

(14) a. The two (or more) subevents are not mutually agreed upon by the participants.
   b. The two (or more) participants do not appreciate the other's carrying out the same action as themselves.
   c. The two (or more) participants are not aware of the other participant(s) carrying out the same action as themselves.

In addition to fulfilling one of these conditions it will be necessary for the verb to be reasonably frequent in the corpus examined. On the basis of these considerations, I chose the following verbs:[9]

(15)   assume so. to X, suspect so. of X, accuse so. (of X), blame so. (for X), and regard so. as X.

As for the conditions in (14), *assume so. to X*, in the use that is relevant here, implicates that the participants are not aware of the other carrying out the same action as themselves (condition [14] c.). In fact, this is the crucial property of the situation described in Bolinger's example (11) involving the verb *believe so. to X*. The same holds for *suspect*, where we can add conditions (14) a. and b.: if person A suspects person B of property X and B likewise suspects A of X, there is unlikely to be mutual agreement and/

or appreciation of what the other is thinking. With *accuse* the situation is slightly different; given that accusation is public, the participants may well be aware of what the other is doing. Sentences (14) a. and b., however, are usually fulfilled. Mutual agreement and/or appreciation are absent for the action of accusing someone. The same holds for the verb *blame*, which differs slightly in meaning from *accuse*, yet in ways that are not relevant to the semantic components under discussion (whereas *blame* triggers the presupposition that the referent denoted by the object of the verb carried out the action they are blamed for, *accuse* does not trigger this presupposition; see Saeed, 2003: 107). The last verb on the list, *regard*, does not strictly require any of the conditions in (14), but I would claim that these components of a distinct-event interpretation are more likely with *regard* than with what I will call 'neutral' verbs. Interestingly, this hybrid status of *regard* is reflected in the relative frequency of the two relevant constructions, as will be discussed later. As neutral verbs, i.e. transitive verbs that do not have any inherent propensity to a distinct-events reading, I chose *understand*, *help*, *love* and *trust*. Using these verbs reciprocally would not normally make the hearer assume any of the states of affairs in (14). If two persons understand each other, the question of disagreeing upon their mutual understanding does not usually arise. Similarly, there is nothing in the lexical meaning of *understand* that would lead to the participants not appreciating the other's understanding. The restriction concerning mutual awareness is not relevant to *understand* either. If two persons understand each other, they may be both aware and unaware of the other's understanding, yet in contrast to the verbs in (15) the meaning of the verb is not associated with one of these options to a higher degree than with the other. I will assume that what I said about *understand* holds for *help*, *love* and *trust* just as well.

An exploratory investigation on the 100-million-word BNC did not yield a sufficient number of examples. Given the general rarity of reciprocal sentences, on the one hand, and the marginality of the spell-out construction, on the other, this is not surprising. My search of the COCA, which contains over 385 million words, turned out to be more fruitful. The search procedure I used was rather simple. First of all, in the case of the spell-out construction I restricted my attention to the *each . . . the other* type for practical reasons; since the reciprocal spell-out construction does not generally have a fixed form or any reliably recurring formal elements (consider, for example, clause coordination and its subtypes), it is not possible to automatically retrieve all instances of this construction from a corpus (in fact, the examples of spell-out constructions cited in Chapter 2 were encountered by scanning through entire texts manually). The subtype involving a quantifier and the string *the other*, by contrast, can be retrieved quite easily by searching for 'the other', preceded by any word form of the relevant verbal lexeme and then manually extracting all reciprocal sentences. Instances of the basic reciprocal strategy were retrieved by searching for all instances of *each other* and *one another*, again preceded by any word form of the relevant verbal lexeme. Note that in this corpus investigation I restricted my attention to verbs that do not select for a prepositional complement, assuming that the generalizations will carry over to sentences involving prepositional complements and also reciprocal constructions as part of adjuncts, for that matter.

Now, in order to set the resulting figures in the right context, we need to briefly digress to some more general considerations. It has been argued in the literature that reciprocal sentences are prototypically associated with a single-event construal, given that normally two or more human participants (collectively) carry out the same action, occupy the same roles and are aware of the other doing the same thing (see also Chapter 2, section 2.7). Evidence for this assumption is not difficult to come by. From a cross-linguistic point of view, it is above all the polysemy patterns of reciprocal markers that support such a conclusion. Very often, and especially in languages that morphologically mark reciprocity on the verb, the same marker is also employed for categories such as 'sociative' and 'collective' (see e.g. Lichtenberk, 2000; Nedjalkov, 2007b). On the basis of this kind of morphosyntactic evidence and more general considerations, Evans (forthcoming) proposes that in the analysis of reciprocal sentences involving human participants, a component of 'mutual intent to cooperate and/or reciprocate' should be assumed in addition to the component of a bidirectional relation. Traditionally, it is only the latter that is taken to define reciprocal situations and their expressions. As mentioned earlier, I propose not to define reciprocal constructions categorically as including a meaning component of mutual cooperation, but rather to regard the degree to which a given situation is construed as a single event as an independent parameter. At the same time, it has to be acknowledged that reciprocal situations prototypically involve a certain degree of single-event construal. Reciprocal sentences presenting a reciprocal situation as distinct events are thus marked in the sense of representing an unusual combination of properties and therefore being less frequent (see also Maslova, 2008: 246), and this is what we should take into account when considering the data from PDE. Specifically, this means that we should expect the basic construction to be more frequent than the spell-out construction overall, not only because it is the grammaticalized and therefore the default reciprocal construction, but also (and this is related to the latter point) because its association with single-event interpretations makes it suitable for the large majority of reciprocal situations.

The investigation yielded the following results (see Table 5.1). The verb *assume* is only rarely used in reciprocal contexts: ten instances in total. It is revealing, however, that all ten examples display the spell-out construction. We come across a similar situation with *suspect*, which, of the verbs under consideration, is the least frequent one in reciprocal contexts. Of the five occurrences in total, four are examples of the spell-out construction. All the other verbs are more frequently used in reciprocal contexts, yet there is a significant effect (see the following) such that the spell-out construction is more frequent than with verbs that are not in this group (see the following). The frequencies are given in Table 5.1 and Figure 5.1.

In order to show that the relative frequency of the spell-out construction with the relevant verbs is statistically significant I made use of the 'distinctive-collexeme analysis' as proposed by Gries and Stefanowitsch (2004). The idea behind this procedure is to determine the association strength between a lexeme, a verb for instance, and different constructions in which the lexeme occurs. For the purpose of calculating the extent to which the actual frequency of verb and construction deviates from what would be expected were there no association effect one also has to take into account the total frequency of the construction under consideration (cf. Gries and Stefanowitsch, 2004: 100–103, for the statistical background). This is crucial here, given that overall the basic reciprocal construction is much more frequent than the variant of the spell-out construction we are focusing on here (*each . . . the other*). Roughly speaking, it is not only a result where the spell-out construction is more frequent than the basic construction that would be significantly different from the usual situation. It would be similarly remarkable to come across cases where the spell-out construction is less frequent than the basic construction, but significantly more frequent than normally. Whether the latter is indeed the case from the statistical point of view can be demonstrated by applying distinctive-collexeme analysis.

The results in Table 5.1 show that the distribution of reciprocal constructions in interaction with the verbs *understand, help, love* and *trust* corresponds to what we would expect on the basis of what I just said about the markedness of distinct-events interpretations and thus the low frequency of the spell-out type of construction; if speakers use these verbs reciprocally, they employ the basic reciprocal construction in the vast majority of

Table 5.1 Frequency of Reciprocal Constructions with Different Verbs

	Basic reciprocal construction	Split quantificational spell-out construction	Proportion of split quantificational spell-out construction
assume so. to do sth.	0	10	100%
suspect so. of sth.	1	4	80%
accuse so. (of sth.)	64	55	46.2%
blame so. (for sth.)	86	49	36.3%
regard so. as X	15	4	21.05%
trust	225	8	3.4%
understand	475	13	2.7%
help	818	16	1.9%
love	1,007	4	0.5%

cases. The ratio of the spell-out construction ranges from 0.4 per cent for *love* to 3.4 per cent for *trust*. The verbs *help* and *understand* are situated in between, displaying a ratio of 1.9 per cent and 2.7 per cent, respectively. Those verbs, however, whose meaning makes one expect a higher proportion of instances involving the spell-out construction, can indeed be shown to be significantly more frequent in the spell-out construction. The tables that include the frequencies of the relevant verbs in the two constructions, and also the frequency of all other verbs combining with these constructions in the corpus, now allow us to calculate the expected frequencies and the level of significance to which the actual frequencies deviate from the expected frequencies. We need the former in order to see in which direction a potentially significant deviation goes: is the spell-out construction or the basic reciprocal construction more frequent than expected?

The logic of distinctive-collexeme analysis predicts that if the p value calculated from the aforementioned figures turns out to have a value taken to be significant in the statistical sense and a given construction has a higher (as opposed to lower) frequency than the expected frequency for a certain verb, then the preference of that verb for the construction at issue cannot be due to chance and needs to be explained. Indeed, the results of the count seem to confirm the hypothesis outlined here: although in terms of frequency the spell-out construction is rather marginal generally, it is significantly more frequent with those verbs whose meaning fits better the semantics of the construction ($\chi^2 = 1472.80$, $p < 0.001$ for *accuse*; $\chi^2 = 1009.16$, $p < 0.001$ for *blame*).

Given the general rarity of reciprocal sentences containing the verbs *assume* and *suspect* in the corpus, conclusions on the relative frequency of basic and spell-out construction for these verbs should only be made very cautiously. If we can conclude something from the fact that, in the set of verbs I looked at, these two are the only ones that are more frequently used in the spell-out construction than in the basic reciprocal construction it is the following: of the factors meant to make more explicit the contrast between single-event and distinct-events interpretation of reciprocal situations in (14) it is (14) c. that is most important. Both *assume* and *suspect* have a lexical meaning that—if the verbs are used in a reciprocal context—suggests mutual unawareness. The verbs *accuse* and *blame* are situated in between those verbs that prefer the spell-out construction (*assume* and *suspect*), on the one hand, and *regard*, on the other. The reason may well be that these two verbs conform to two of the relevant factors ([14] a. and [14] b.), while *regard* conforms to (14) a., but remains neutral to (14) b. and (14) c. The remaining verbs (*trust, understand, help* and *love*) represent the normal situation, i.e. the spell-out construction is a tiny minority. As already mentioned earlier, the meanings of these verbs are either neutral to the three factors at issue (*understand*), or even involve values opposite to those of the other verbs. Thus, a certain amount of mutual agreement, appreciation and awareness of the other's trusting, helping and loving seems to be the normal case with these verbs.

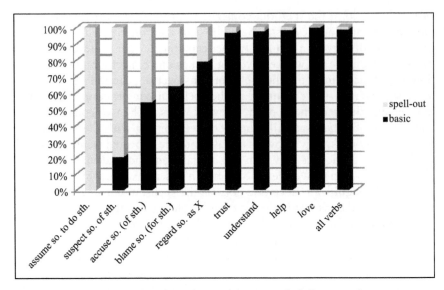

Figure 5.1   Frequency of reciprocal constructions with different verbs.

The data therefore show that verbs whose meaning is compatible with the distinct-events interpretation of reciprocal situations to a higher degree than other verbs also occur more frequently in the relevant construction. More generally, this substantiates the claim that there is a functional difference between the basic and the spell-out construction. Note, however, that we do not find a categorical association between a given verb and one of two logically possible reciprocal constructions. Whether a speaker uses either the basic or the spell-out reciprocal construction in combination does not only depend on the meaning of the verb alone, but also on the context, the way the relevant situation is conceptualized by the speaker and a number of other factors. To determine exactly how these factors interact in the choice between the two types of reciprocal construction is beyond the scope of this study. Yet, let me mention one factor that I would expect also to play a role. As a result of prescriptive pressure many speakers will tend to avoid the use of the reciprocals *each other* and *one another* in subject position, instead employing the split quantificational construction. Thus a sentence like (16) a. may be avoided by using the variant in (16) b.:

(16) a. We all read what each other had written anyway. [EE5 1248]
     b. We each read what the other had written anyway.

Without looking into the matter in more detail it is certainly premature to speculate on this, but note that choosing (16) b. in favour of (16) a. for the aforementioned reason does not invalidate the assumption that (16) a. is associated with a single-event interpretation to a higher degree than (16)

b. Note that normally the two variants of reciprocal sentences are truth-conditionally equivalent and uttering (16) b. instead of (16) a., for example, would not lead to a serious distortion of the message to be communicated. Using optimality theoretic terminology, whether a given speaker opts for (16) a. or (16) b. thus depends on which of the following two constraints is ranked higher: (i) avoid reciprocals in subject position; (ii) avoid spell-out constructions for the expression of reciprocal situations that are best construed as a single event. I leave this question to further research.

For the moment the crucial observation is that the meaning of verbs can influence the choice between two reciprocal constructions, proving incidentally that one would miss important generalizations if one considered the spell-out construction of the type *each . . . the other* to represent the underlying structure (or meaning) of the reciprocal *each other* (see also Chapter 2).

5.2 COMPETITION BETWEEN CONSTRUCTIONS: A MORE COMPREHENSIVE VIEW

One step in the direction of accounting for the competition between all three types of reciprocal construction in English can be found in Safir (2004). Like Kemmer (1993b), Safir examines the complementarity between 'light' and 'heavy' reciprocal marking, but more explicitly models it as a competition between different options, where the availability of a certain meaning for one marker depends on the availability of the other marker for a given verb. His main idea is that:

> if we take heavy markers of reciprocity to be the more relationally specific ones, then these markers will have the narrowest range of interpretation when they are in competition with semantically underspecified light markers but the widest range of interpretation when they are not by functional extension [. . .] where there is no competing form licensed, that is, when in English a predicate does not license the null reciprocal [the intransitive variant], then the overt one [*each other*] functionally extends to cover interpretations that it would not support when faced with a competitor. (2004: 225)

This insight provides us with an answer to the question of whether *each other*, the English 'heavy' reciprocal, always triggers a distinct-events interpretation. If competition is taken into account, the question must be answered in the negative; only when it competes with the light form, i.e. the intransitive variant in English, does the heavy form license a distinct-event interpretation. In this way, the necessity of a distinct-events reading depends on the availability of the light form with the same verb. Consider (17) and (18):

(17) a. Jim and Sue are kissing each other.
     b. Jim and Sue are kissing.

(18) a. Jim and Sue are observing each other.
     b. *Jim and Sue are observing.

The basic reciprocal construction involving *each other* in (17) a. competes with the lighter variant in (17) b. There is no competition in (18), by contrast; the predicate *observe* is not compatible with the intransitive construction and therefore the basic reciprocal construction in (18) a. is assumed to cover the single-event interpretation that is restricted to the intransitive variant with verbs such as *kiss*.

As discussed at length earlier, a similar type of competition can be observed for verbs of the *observe* type, verbs that are not compatible with an intransitive realization in reciprocal contexts. With the latter verbs the basic reciprocal construction is of course competing with the spell-out construction. Since the functional dimension which determines the competition—single-event versus distinct-events interpretation—is the same in the two cases, we arrive at the following picture. There is one functional parameter, and the two values of the parameter correspond to two ways of formally expressing the reciprocal situation at issue. Which of the forms corresponds to which value, in turn, depends on the availability of competing forms. The basic idea is illustrated by Table 5.2.

As can be seen in Table 5.2, there is either a choice between the intransitive construction and the basic reciprocal strategy, or between the basic and the spell-out construction. What does this imply for a characterization of what the reciprocals *each other* and *one another* mean? Clearly, they are specialized markers of reciprocity in PDE. Taking a more refined view of 'reciprocity', including the parameter of single-event versus distinct-events construal, however, we can now state that the value that the reciprocal assumes for this parameter depends on the availability of alternative reciprocal constructions for a given verb and thus eventually on the class of the verb.

This assumption is not only supported by the PDE data reviewed earlier, it is also compatible with the diachronic picture. The development of the reciprocal(s) is one of lexicalization and grammaticalization (see Chapter

Table 5.2 Competition Between Three Reciprocal Constructions

	intransitive construction	*basic reciprocal construction*	*spell-out reciprocal construction*
symmetric/prototypically reciprocal verbs	✓	✓	—
ordinary transitive verbs	—	✓	✓

3); it is above all the role of the universal distributive quantifier *each* that illustrates what has been happening here. The function of this expression in the PDE spell-out construction, and presumably also in the structures that gave rise to the development of the lexicalized reciprocal, is to indicate that the relevant event is carried out by each of the participants under consideration individually, and not by the set of individuals as a whole. Once lexicalization started to affect the syntactic status of the string *each other* and in this way also the meaning contribution of the quantifier, this universal and distributive component of meaning got lost and the semantic contribution of the new reciprocal changed. The range of situations with which it is compatible has become larger. This does not only concern the weaker types of reciprocity discussed in Chapter 2, section 2.8, but also those where not all participants denoted by the antecedent take part in the reciprocal situation (cf. the discussion of non-maximality in the context of Heim et al.'s [1991] account and its problems, Chapter 2, section 2.6).

On the other hand, the basic reciprocal construction, by virtue of being an explicit marker of reciprocity, is able to trigger a distinct-event construal with those verbs that without this expression occur in a construction that is not a reciprocal construction in the narrow sense, but a more general middle construction that assumes its reciprocal function from the relevant predicates. In other words, similar to Swedish, Kuuk Thaayorre (see [3] and [4] respectively) and many other languages, there is a detransitivizing construction which construes the two reciprocal subevents as a unitary one.[10] By adding one of the reciprocals *each other* and *one another* the clause is again made transitive, and this is iconically associated with what Kemmer calls a 'higher elaboration of events' and what I have called a distinct-events interpretation. The fact that the lexicalized reciprocal *each other/one another* is used in situations construed as single events with one group of verbs and in situations construed as distinct events with another group of verbs is not contradictory, in my view. The distinct-events effect seems to hold in exactly those cases where the use of an overt reciprocal marker is syntactically optional and can thus be exploited for a special effect.

5.3 INDEPENDENT EVIDENCE: ARIEL'S (2006) ANALYSIS OF REFLEXIVE PRONOUNS

Just like the reciprocals *each other* and *one another*, the English reflexives of the x-*self* series (*myself, yourself, himself, herself, ourselves, yourselves, themselves*) are normally taken to be well-behaved syntactic arguments, clearly differing from those reflexive expressions in other languages that have acquired (detransitivizing) middle functions. Yet, as Ariel (2006) can show, the picture is more complex (see also Ariel, 2008: 212–256) and, in my view, these findings from the domain of reflexivity lend further support to the competition view of PDE reciprocal constructions. There are uses of the English reflexive that may be analyzed as detransitivizing (e.g. *I cut myself shaving*), and this does not only concern its meaning contribution, but also its syntactic behaviour (see also Siemund, forthcoming). Specifically, with certain predicates the reflexive does not easily pass standard tests of argumenthood (e.g. coordination with other noun phrases). Concerning the motivation for this phenomenon, Ariel follows earlier proposals in the literature:

> As has been argued in the literature (Hopper and Thompson 1980, and Kemmer 1993 following them), reflexive clauses constitute an intermediate degree of transitivity. A reflexive construction may then be selected for this intermediate transitivity characteristic, rather than for the purely referential properties of the reflexive pronoun itself. In fact, we will also see how English reflexive markers may further shift their function to that of intransitive marking, which is what happened to the French *se*. (2006: 34)

The development under discussion is not as obvious as it is in languages where the relevant markers have also been formally reduced, but Ariel's (2006) and Siemund's (forthcoming) data clearly show that the relevant change has been underway. Given the observations presented in this chapter, the parallel to reciprocals is not far-fetched. Thus it seems that the effect of the reciprocal triggering a single-event reading, when used in competition with the analytic strategy, is comparable to the development described for the reflexive by Ariel. Interestingly, if the use of the reflexive is in competition with a syntactically intransitive realization of a given verb, an effect can be observed that seems to be analogous to the one described for the reciprocal earlier. Ariel (2006: 44) states 'that since reflexive clauses are intermediate in transitivity, they are at the same time higher in transitivity than intransitive clauses'. In this way, 'English reflexives are now used creatively, to either encode a lower transitivity than a transitive clause would have encoded, or a higher transitivity than that of an intransitive clause' (2006: 37). This is exactly the type of competition that was described for the reciprocal earlier. Semantically, similarities between reflexives and reciprocals are obvious: first and foremost, all participants are encoded jointly in both arguments, there being a special sort of co-reference between the subject and object participants. This gives both reflexive and reciprocal sentences an intermediate degree of transitivity. In Kemmer's (1993b) terminology, there is a low degree of participant distinguishability.

That there is still an important semantic difference between reflexive and reciprocal sentences can of course not be denied. Bhat (1981; 2004: 85–87) correctly notes the more complex type of co-reference in reciprocal as opposed to reflexive clauses, without, however, acknowledging how the inherent affinity between reflexives and a reduced degree of transitivity (*pace* Hopper and Thompson, 1980; Kemmer, 1993b; Ariel, 2006) corresponds to the tendency of reciprocal clauses towards shedding the distinctness of the reciprocal subevents:

> Notice that the reciprocal meaning does not refer to any particular individual (x or y) acting upon itself; that is, it does not refer to an individual being the Patient of an event of which it is also the Agent. The coreferentiality is only cumulative: if one splits the event denoted by it into two or more subevents, basing the split upon the action of individual Agents, there would no more be any coreferentiality occurring between the arguments. (Bhat, 1981: 41)

The analysis proposed by Moltmann (1992) comes closer to capturing the hybrid status of clauses of the basic reciprocal type. She assumes that the reciprocal meaning component, her 'reciprocity effect', is added to a reflexive interpretation of the relevant sentence:

> The semantic interpretation of a sentence such as [*The students work with each other*] has two parts. One is essentially the usual interpretation that [this sentence] would have if *each other* were disregarded as a reciprocal and instead interpreted as a simple plural anaphor coreferential with the students. [. . .] The second part consists in the specific reciprocity effect of *each other* as an association of parts of the three arguments that are involved in the first part of the interpretation. (413)

The 'three arguments' that Moltmann (1992) refers to are: the antecedent (*the students*), the reciprocal (*each other*) and a Davidsonian 'event argument' *e*, which need not concern us here. Roughly speaking, the meaning of the reciprocal is thus taken to be the meaning of a reflexive to which the 'reciprocity effect' is added. Note that this conception of reciprocity is not incompatible with the perspective taken in this book, at least as far as the following is concerned: the basic reciprocal construction in English, similarly to many other grammaticalized reciprocal constructions in other languages, resembles reflexive pronouns in developing collective (or sociative) meaning components. What I have tried to argue in this chapter was, among other things, that this property of reciprocals—totally obvious in languages whose reciprocal markers are also used as pure collective markers—can also be shown to be present in English, although it is less clearly notable.

To sum up this section, there is a revealing parallelism between the hybrid status of the basic reciprocal construction and certain aspects of the behaviour of reflexives, something which could easily be overlooked if one were not prepared to identify detransitivizing effects in reflexive and reciprocal sentences on the basis of what is happening in other languages.

5.4 MOTIVATING THE DISTRIBUTION OF RECIPROCAL CONSTRUCTIONS

The preceding sections have shown that a description of what the reciprocals *each other* and *one another* contribute to the meaning of a sentence has to go beyond a logical explication of reciprocal relations, independently of whether they are formalized in the system of predicate logic or not. We saw that it is necessary to take into account the manner in which speakers and hearers interpret the complex configuration of events that is characteristic of reciprocal situations: it may be understood as a set of two independent events that are mirror images of each other, yet it may also be construed to be a unitary event whose subevents are not as strongly profiled as the whole that they make up. I hope to have demonstrated that this functional parameter interacts in interesting ways with the syntactic constructions that English has available for the expression of reciprocity. Whereas the intransitive use of symmetric and prototypically reciprocal predicates is consistently associated with a single-event interpretation and the spell-out construction is consistently associated with a distinct-events interpretation, reciprocal sentences containing the reciprocal *each other* or *one another* (the 'basic reciprocal construction') can, in principle, be understood in both ways. This fact can easily be overlooked if the spell-out construction, and especially the *each . . . the other* subtype (termed 'split quantificational' earlier), is not taken into account as a serious competitor of the basic reciprocal construction.

The Spell-Out Constructions

From the point of view of the constructions involved, it is not surprising that the transitive clause construction, from which the basic reciprocal construction inherits part of its structure and meaning, covers a wider range of interpretations than the intransitive variant and the different types of spell-out construction. Let us first compare the basic reciprocal construction and the spell-out constructions. That the spell-out constructions—i.e. the split quantificational type, coordinated clauses each expressing one subevent of a reciprocal situation and other strategies of making reciprocal subevents explicit—are restricted to a distinct-events construal of reciprocal situations is motivated by their morphosyntactic make-up. In the case of coordinated clauses (e.g. *Our managers sued us, and we sued them*) we do not even have to assume any construction that has a reciprocal relation as part of its meaning. The reciprocal nature of the situation is compositionally derived from the coordination of (clauses denoting) two independent events that are mirror images of each other. Now, since it is implausible to assume a specialized reciprocal construction in this case, there cannot be a 'collectivizing' meaning component, i.e. a meaning component that caters for a single-event construal or a certain degree thereof. To be sure, coordination is a syntactic construction, also from the point of view of construction grammar. At the same time it is not a 'reciprocal construction' in the sense of reciprocity being part of the construction's meaning side.[11]

Other types of spell-out construction display more morphosyntactic integration of the reciprocal subevents, as discussed in Chapter 2. In the case of the split quantificational construction, for example, the participants are introduced by a single noun phrase, whereas in the case of clause coordination and the type involving the expression *vice versa* (see Chapter 2 for details) the two participants (or groups of participants) are each introduced by an independent noun phrase. The split quantificational construction (at least the most common subtype involving *each*) still expresses the distinctness of events transparently, simply by distributing over the relevant participants with the quantifier *each*. What all types of spell-out construction have in common, therefore, is a transparent expression of there being two or more events which together make up a reciprocal situation. This is, of course, fully compatible with the observations made in this chapter: spell-out constructions indeed compete with the basic reciprocal construction with respect to this functional parameter.

The Basic Reciprocal and the Intransitive Construction

The basic reciprocal construction has been characterized as a kind of hybrid entity. Depending on what it competes with, it can either reduce or increase the degree to which a reciprocal situation—which logically speaking is made up of two or more subevents—is viewed as a unitary event. Again, the functional character of the construction can be motivated by its morphosyntactic character, which is, in a way, in between the intransitive type and the spell-out constructions when it comes to the expression of the distinctness of events making up the reciprocal situation. Note the following contrast to the spell-out constructions: the participants in the basic reciprocal construction are neither introduced by distinct noun phrases nor is their distinctness marked by a distributive quantifier such as *each*. This also holds for the intransitive variant, so where is the difference? Recall that in a complex situation type like reciprocity a construal of distinct events naturally goes together with a construal of distinct participants, whereas a construal of a single event naturally goes together with what I called a 'collective' construal of the participants involved. It is first and foremost the way in which the participants are conceptualized which can be motivated by the morphosyntax of the intransitive variant, on the one hand, and the basic reciprocal construction, on the other. As discussed at length in Kemmer (1993b), detransitivization on the morphosyntactic side corresponds to the development of meanings commonly summarized as the 'middle voice'. What holds together these different 'middle' meanings, according to Kemmer, is a 'low distinguishability of participants', which she relates to a 'low elaboration of events' in her discussion of reciprocals. From this point of

view it is only natural that what looks like an impeccable transitive construction in English—the basic reciprocal construction—assumes middle
functions, namely, the single-event interpretation as a part of the reciprocal
meaning. To be sure, the English reciprocals *each other/one another* behave
like fully fledged argument expressions syntactically and, in this, contrast
with the intransitive variant. Yet, when it does not compete with the latter, as argued at length earlier, the basic reciprocal construction in part
extends to the middle area functionally. Otherwise, we could not explain
the semantic effects described for the contrast between basic and spell-
out construction. In sum, although the basic reciprocal construction has
not developed into an intransitive (or 'detransitivized') construction like
corresponding erstwhile transitive structures in other languages as far as
its syntax is concerned, it has assumed a hybrid position between proper
middle constructions, on the one hand, and prototypical transitive constructions with two clearly distinct arguments (Næss, 2007), on the other.
Note again that, just like reflexive clauses, reciprocal clauses of the basic
reciprocal type in English feature a reduced degree of transitivity only for
the fact that their two arguments do not refer to two distinct referents. The
non-distinctness of referents is even more pronounced in reciprocal clauses
than in reflexive clauses since the reciprocal expression cannot simply be
analyzed as being an anaphor that has the same referent as its antecedent—
see the earlier quote from Bhat (1981) and also Kemmer (1993b) and Gast
and Haas (2008) on why reciprocity is eventually a subtype of the middle
voice. All in all, it is reasonable to assume that the English basic reciprocal construction is situated in between the transitive clause construction
[NP1 V NP2] and the intransitive clause construction [NP1 V] functionally, although formally it looks and behaves very much like the former.
In Chapter 3, section 3.4, it was argued that for a number of reasons the
basic reciprocal construction in English has not developed into a properly
intransitive clause construction. One of them was indeed the fact that this
construction has a strong competitor: the intransitive clause construction,
which is the default option for those verbs that are most frequent in reciprocal contexts.

Summary and Conclusion

Let us sum up the preceding discussion. It should become obvious that the
mapping of functions (or meanings) onto the different types of reciprocal
constructions that PDE has available is not arbitrary, but rather motivated
by the inherent properties of these constructions. Thus, the spell-out constructions expressing reciprocal situations lend themselves to a distinct-
events construal because they transparently encode two or more distinct
events that together form a reciprocal situation. Similarly, the intransitive
clause construction lends itself to a single-event construal, given that such
a construal of reciprocal situations is ultimately a 'middle' situation type

which, across languages, is associated with reduced transitivity on the syntactic level. Last but not least, the basic reciprocal construction remains as the one that has to be able to cover both types of construal (single event and distinct events), depending on the type of reciprocal construction it competes with. Here we saw that a construction which has the syntactic structure of a well-behaved transitive construction,[12] but at the same time displays properties that deviate from the transitive prototype (first and foremost the non-distinctness of those referents that are indicated by the two syntactically distinct arguments), lends itself to fulfilling the hybrid character that the basic reciprocal construction seems to have acquired.

Notes

NOTES TO CHAPTER 1

1. A number of papers are concerned with more specialized issues in the realm of reciprocity from a cross-linguistic or typological point of view. Apart from those published in Frajzyngier and Curl (2000), Nedjalkov (2007c) and König and Gast (2008b), studies such as Latham (1844), Kaneko (1972), Baldi (1975), Bhat (1981: 40–51), Bosque (1985), Dench (1987), Knjazev (1998), van der Kerke (1998), Mohanan and Mohanan (1998), Davies (2000), Filip and Carlson (2001), MacKay and Trechsel (2003), Seidl and Dimitriadis (2003), Keenan and Razafimamonjy (2004), Maslova and Nedjalkov (2005), Bril (2005), Hüning (2006) and Behrens (2007) are typological investigations or studies on reciprocity in languages other than English.
2. See Croft (2004): 'A formalization is a means of representing theoretical hypotheses and their logical consequences; it is a tool, not an end in itself. A formalization is only as good as the hypotheses it represents in its axioms. If the hypotheses are wrong, then the formalism is useless' (642).
3. I follow Culicover and Jackendoff (2005: 3) in using the term 'mainstream generative grammar' (henceforth MGG) for a number of different theories that adhere to the basic principles advocated at some point by Noam Chomsky.
4. Recent attempts by Chomsky and colleagues at radically reducing the complexity of allegedly innate linguistic structures may be seen as partly being a reaction to such findings.
5. To accept this insight presupposes accepting that there is non-compositionality in grammar. Cf. Itkonen (2005):

   The true extent of non-compositionality has been discovered so recently that the majority of linguists, not to speak of philosophers, may not have fully digested it yet. The mainstream of philosophy of language as well as the philosophy of cognitive science take compositionality for granted. [. . .] [T]he entire edifice that philosophers and logicians have been constructing ever since Frege threatens to collapse if compositionality is abandoned. [. . .] They admit that 'idioms and other 'holophrastic constructions' are all exceptions, but—they assume—these are exceptions that prove the rule. However, this position, or a black-and-white distinction between 'holophrastic' and other constructions, can no longer be maintained. (100)

NOTES TO CHAPTER 2

1. The British National Corpus, version 2 (BNC World), 2001. Distributed by Oxford University Computing Services on behalf of the BNC Consortium.

URL: http://www.natcorp.ox.ac.uk/. Examples of usage taken from the BNC were obtained under the terms of the BNC End User Licence. Copyright in the individual texts cited resides with the original IPR holders.

2. It is well known that language data obtained via commercial Internet search engines is not necessarily reliable (cf. Lüdeling et al., 2007). For this reason, I only included examples from U.K. or U.S. websites, obtained via the Web-Corp interface (http://www.webcorp.org.uk/) and checked each example's validity. Furthermore, I excluded those structures from consideration which are extremely rare even on the Internet and might indeed involve errors.

3. See http://www.americancorpus.org.

4. Kemmer (1993b: 102) mentions the difference between the two verb classes and the situations they denote, but then collapses them under the term 'naturally reciprocal events'.

5. Considering the following PDE example, the reciprocal use of *themselves* does not appear to be categorically excluded in other contexts either:

> Elsewhere, while reduced vowels still mark distinctions, they tend to do so only as opposed to full vowels rather than opposed to themselves and the reduced vowel that is mostly involved is shwa [. . .] (Bolinger, 1986: 8).

The acceptability of the reciprocal reading in such examples varies between speakers. Furthermore, it should be noted that in the relevant sentences the *self*-form occurs in a contrastive context. The referent of *themselves*, that is, is being focused and contrasted to a set of alternatives. We may ask what is this particular context that favours the option of interpreting *themselves* reciprocally. Assuming that the meaning contribution of nominal reciprocals like *each other* can roughly be divided into an anaphoric component and one contributing the relational component of reciprocity, a division that is discussed in Bhat (1981: 41) and Moltmann (1992: 414), it seems that the contrastive use of *themselves* in Bolinger's examples stresses the anaphoric component to such an extent that the relational component can be left unexpressed and recovered from the context. But apparently, such a use of the reflexive that is not blocked by the lack of the relational component necessary for the reciprocal reading of the sentence is only marginally possible in PDE.

6. Source: http://pubpages.unh.edu/lch/Greenland_Arctic.pdf (accessed 15 June 2007).

7. The form *each the other* can in fact be found, but only in old translations of older texts or juridical texts that are also rather old. For this reason I do not consider them a productive reciprocal in PDE.

8. The scope relations of quantifier and negator differ between the respective variants. The argument to be made here does not hinge on this meaning difference, however.

9. It is interesting to note in this context that while modern reference grammars like Quirk et al. (1985) do not even mention reciprocal subjects (Huddleston and Pullum [2002: 1503] mention *each other* as the subject of a non-finite verbal complement, e.g. *They arranged for each other to be nominated by one of the directors*, but do not consider subjects of finite complement clauses), Jespersen (1924: 224) even provides an example from written English: *Miss C. and I are going to find out what each other are like*.

10. I disregard those structures that should not be expected to host a reciprocal in the relevant position, e.g. because the filler of the respective slot is fixed (e.g. to *it* in the case of extraposition) or otherwise irrelevant for a reciprocal (e.g. postposing, where the postposed noun phrase is heavy, viz. typically longer than a reciprocal).

11. Source: http://community.nytimes.com/rate-review/movies.nytimes.com/movie/443554/Bride-Wars/overview (accessed 5 July 2009).
12. Source: http://www.bbc.co.uk/radio4/history/inourtime/inourtime_comments_speed_light.shtml (accessed 15 June 2007).
13. Source: http://www.homebase-hols.com/exchangeagreement.shtml (accessed 22 June 2007).
14. Source: *Time Magazine*, 20 February 1931 (http://corpus.byu.edu/time/).
15. Source: http://www.sharrowpartnership.org.uk/whatsnew.html (accessed 29 January 2009).
16. This generalization is not contradicted by the cases discussed in Behrens (2007). She looks at a special type of reciprocal sentence in Greek, Hungarian, Bosnian-Croatian-Serbian and German, where a participant may be backgrounded and left unexpressed. Importantly, this is not the same as predicating a reciprocal relation of a single individual.
17. Source: http://www.bsu.edu/classes/carr/FCSHS482/chap10.html (accessed 7 May 2007).
18. Source: http://www.gro.gov.uk/Images/01chapters1–11_tcm693577.pdf (accessed 9 May 2007).
19. It has to be noted that Ngiyambaa, the language cited by Maslova and Nedjalkov as not allowing coordinated reciprocal antecedents, may indeed allow such subjects in reciprocal sentences. The grammar cited by the authors (Donaldson, 1980) is not clear about this. I am grateful to Thomas Hanke for pointing this out to me.
20. C-command is a structural relation in syntactic tree structures of generative grammar, defined as follows: 'Node A c-commands node B if and only if (i) A does not dominate B and B does not dominate A; and (ii) the first branching node dominating A also dominates B' (Haegeman, 1994: 134).
21. Source: http://query.nytimes.com/gst/fullpage.html?res=9E0CE7DA1431F9 3AA2575AC0A964958260 (accessed 3 July 2009).
22. Source: http://www.anorak.co.uk/strange-but-true/193076.html (accessed 2 February 2009).
23. Source: http://www.writersdelight.co.uk/blog/2009/01/noir-ats.html (accessed 2 February 2009).
24. Source: http://www.telegraph.co.uk/news/yourview/1555234/Which-best-represents-modern-Britain-Ascot-or-Glastonbury.html (accessed 2 February 2009).
25. As Bolinger (1987: 14) points out, the register differences—*each other* being more frequent in informal and *one another* in formal registers—may well be a result of the expressions' different shades of meaning.
26. The term 'mutuality' as referring to the collective component of reciprocal relations is actually not a good terminological choice. The word *mutual* can both mean 'reciprocally' and 'together'. Since these two meanings correspond exactly to the contrast at issue, I suggest using the unambiguous term 'collective' (and correspondingly 'collectivity') instead. Anyway, the fact that the terms 'mutual' and 'mutuality' exhibit this ambiguity is of course revealing in itself. It lends support to the assumption that the two components 'commutation', or 'bidirectionality' (see the following), and collectivity are highly intertwined in situations that we call 'reciprocal'. If Bolinger's observations are viewed from a more theoretical perspective, one wonders whether his connecting the 'precision' of *each other* to the word meaning of *each* amounts to Heim et al.'s (1991) hypothesis (reviewed in section 2.6) that the meaning of the former is directly derived from the interaction of the latter with the remainder of the sentence. This has to be answered in the negative, given that Bolinger (1987) views the meaning effect as a historical relic of

the lexical sources that once served to build up the reciprocal, viz. as 'persistence' (Hopper, 1991) in terms of grammaticalization (see also Chapter 3). That Bolinger is not proposing to directly derive the meaning of *each other* and *one another* from the meanings of its parts is also underlined by the fact that he demonstrates at length how reciprocal sentences of the basic reciprocal type differ in meaning from sentences of the spell-out type.

27. For the sake of completeness I should mention Stuurman (1987, 1989) as two further articles concerned with the contrast between *each other* and *one another*. They do not make a substantial contribution to the discussion, however. Stuurman advocates the somewhat bizarre position that the difference between the two reciprocals should follow from principles of (generative) grammar, even if there does not prove to be any difference: '[Y]es, the specific difference is of secondary importance, as long as we start from the assumption that there will be some difference' (Stuurman, 1989: 356).

28. Source: Interview with singer Bruce Dickinson on *Bruce Dickinson: Anthology*. DVD. Sanctuary Music. The example is revealing because there is a relatively long intonation break between the two clauses, which suggests that the two events making up the reciprocal situation were indeed processed independently, that is, one after the other, by the speaker.

29. It would of course be possible not to speak of reciprocal situations here. Given that there are different degrees to which logically distinct events are construed as a single event, however, it would be arbitrary to exclude the cases in (40) from the discussion. Syntactically, the cases in (40) are distinct from the cases focused on in this study in that the reciprocal situation is distributed over two clauses; see Evans (forthcoming) on the different degrees of grammaticalization in the expression of reciprocal subevents from a typological point of view.

30. The example is from Roberts (1991: 217), who attributes it to Mats Rooth (see also Heim et al., 1991: 69).

31. Among the eighty-four concordances that WebCorp returned for the search "each other's thoughts" I could not find a distinct events context such as the one in (50) b.

32. Heim et al.'s (1991) analysis is reminiscent of Dougherty's (1970) proposal according to which the sentence *The men are hitting each other* is transformationally derived from *Each of the men is hitting the others*. The most obvious difference between the two accounts is the direction of derivation, given that Heim et al. (1991) apply a movement operation to a sentence involving the basic reciprocal strategy, resulting in a 'logical form' roughly comparable to the analytic counterpart of this sentence. Since the problems that such a derivational account faces have been articulated mainly in reference to Heim et al. (1991), I will restrict the following discussion to the latter. Interestingly, Heim et al. (1991) do not mention Dougherty (1970) or the follow-up studies (Dougherty, 1971, 1974).

33. There is a third reading, paraphrasable as 'John thinks that he likes Mary and Mary thinks that she likes John', but it seems that this reading is even less salient than the contrast between the other two readings.

34. Sauerland (1994), who intends to maintain the general approach to the meaning of the reciprocal as advocated in Heim et al. (1991), addresses the issue brought up by Dalrymple et al. (1994). Concerning the representation of *each other* in which the two elements contribute to the meanings derivation independently he states: 'For now I will just assume that it is a grammatical necessity for an item that has the complex referential properties of a reciprocal to have a correspondingly complex structure' (Sauerland, 1994: 276). In a footnote he adds: 'Under this assumption it is not surprising that

a reciprocal-anaphor with a radically different realization like Chicheŵa *an* shows exactly the same behaviour as English *each other* (Dalrymple et al. 1994)' (1994: 276). I think that such a move is problematic for the following reasons. Firstly, it is strange to call Chicheŵa *an* an 'anaphor' (albeit with a 'radically different surface realization'), given that Dalrymple and colleagues have been at pains to argue that *an* should not be analyzed as an argument, but rather as a detransitivizing derivational affix. Secondly, the problem that reciprocal sentences often simply do not mean what the semantic contributions of *each* and *other* should trigger is still unaccounted for.

35. Of course, this negative conclusion should not generally rule out the possibility that in a given language reciprocity is compositionally derived from independent morphemes. Faller (2007), for example, argues that reciprocity in Cuzco Quechua is marked by two verbal suffixes, a marker of reflexivity and a marker of pluractionality.

36. For Fiengo and Lasnik (1973: 448–449) the 'weaker' meaning of (53) a. as opposed to (53) b. arises from partitioning the antecedent set into non-overlapping subgroups. According to their analysis, the strong relation present in (53) b. holds within each subgroup. This way of accounting for the meaning difference under discussion is problematic, since there may be weak reciprocity without there being strong reciprocity in non-overlapping subgroups. Imagine the following situation: A hits B, B hits A and C, D hits E and E hits D. For the sentence *They are hitting each other* there is no subgroup that contains C and displays strong reciprocity. Yet, the sentence could be felicitously uttered as referring to this situation.

37. *Hit*, included in the class under discussion by Jackendoff (1990: 116) and Huddleston and Pullum (2002: 302), is only used intransitively in the sense 'agree together', and this use is obsolete (cf. OED, s.v. hit).

38. The letters *j* and *m* here stand for *John* and *Mary* respectively, the two participants in the example referred to by Evans. Bill Croft (personal communication, 15 April 2004) also proposes that in a definition of reciprocity of the type (Rxy entails Ryx) one would have to specify (x+y) in addition to R.

39. There are exceptions to the claim that for two-participant situations strong reciprocity generally holds: (i) Kanskí's (1987) *There were two beds on top of each other* or (ii) Evans's (2008: 40) *They were chasing each other down the street*, the latter of which is accepted by some speakers with a reading involving two participants that have identical roles throughout the chase. The following is an authentic example which might have this reading: *The television showed two children chasing each other round a car, shrieking* [A0R 1942]. I will not discuss these cases—termed 'hyporeciprocal' by Langendoen and Magloire (2003: 258–259)—in the present chapter, apart from noting that their marginal status, both in English and cross-linguistically, seems to indicate the borderline case of what speakers construe as a reciprocal situation. Note that in both cases the speaker would utter the sentence if the assignment of roles to the respective participants is not crucial. In other words, (i) is not meant to make clear which of the two beds is on top and which is on the bottom. By the same token, it is not taken to be relevant in (ii) to identify the chasing participant on the one hand and the participant who is being chased on the other. It appears that abstracting away from the exact roles of the two participants in this way makes it easier to conceive of the situation as a reciprocal one. For an often-cited discussion of a similar phenomenon concerning the reciprocal-collective prefix *vei-* of Boumaa Fijian, see Dixon (1988: 177–179). In the example mentioned by Dixon, world knowledge selects for a specific assignment of the two participants to their respective roles in the interaction (e.g. a baby and its grandmother in a nursing situation).

40. Dalrymple et al. (1998: 168) provide a different sentence as an example of strong reciprocity. However, since their original example has been shown not to exhibit the strong reciprocity reading on closer inspection (see Bruening, 2004: 28), I chose the sentence given here.

41. Brisson (1998) shows how exceptions may be formalized by making reference to 'ill-fitting covers' (see also Schwarzschild, 1996). Malamud (2006) approaches maximality from the point of view of Decision Theory.

42. In addition, B, C, D and E all stare at the same pirate (A), which may also contribute to the incompatibility of the situation in Figure 2.2 and sentence (77). This additional property of the situation under discussion is independent of both the distinction between OWR and TWR and the issue of exceptions, however. I leave it open whether some sort of 'even distribution' of the reciprocal relation over the participant set is a further factor that can play a role. For now, the important point to note is that OWR as defined by Dalrymple et al. (1998) overgenerates, while TWR in combination with non-maximality seems to account for the acceptability judgments reported in Beck (2000a) and Bruening (2004).

43. I cannot do justice here to the extremely rich literature on reciprocal situation types. The interested reader is referred to studies such as Thielmann (1892: 343–344), Langendoen (1978, 1992), Higginbotham (1980, 1985), Moltmann (1992), Sauerland (1994, 1998), Sternefeld (1998), Beck (2000b, 2001), Schein (2003) and Mari (2006).

NOTES TO CHAPTER 3

1. I use the term 'early English' if there is no need to distinguish between Old and Middle English.

2. Evans (2008) offers a typology with a larger number of strategy types. The larger number of types is among other things due to the fact that Evans (2008) includes non-monoclausal strategies, i.e. mainly biclausal strategies, but also types that seem to fall in between the monoclausal versus biclausal distinction ('sesquiclausal constructions'). Importantly, non-monoclausal reciprocal strategies as described by Evans (2008: 79–88) cannot be found as grammaticalized construction in OE. Therefore, the exclusion of these types from König and Kokutani's typology is not a problem. See also König and Gast (2008a: 10–19), where different typologies of reciprocal constructions are compared.

3. König and Kokutani (2006: 276) call such markers 'quantificational', but since the complex expression may also consist of elements other than quantifiers, the term 'bipartite', being neutral as to the category of the source expressions, will be used here.

4. To be more precise, the function of the construction is the expression of reciprocal and/or collective relations between participants. (The relationship between collectivity and reciprocity in sentences that are commonly called 'reciprocal' was discussed in Chapter 2.) For simplicity's sake, I will only speak of 'reciprocal sentences' here.

5. See Visser (1963: 432–438), van Gelderen (2000: 28–32), König and Siemund (2000), Keenan (2002) and Gast (2006: 211–215) on the chronology.

6. I disregard the use as intensifier (or 'emphatic reflexive'), which is distributionally different.

7. Gast and Haas (2008) argue with reference to European languages other than English that reciprocal readings of reflexive pronouns typically arise via 'middle meanings' of the latter. Still, languages such as Polish provide

evidence of the fact that not only middle markers but also phonologically heavy reflexive anaphors may in certain circumstances acquire the potential of expressing reciprocity. It is thus not excluded for a non-middle reflexive such as English x-*self* to acquire or exhibit the reciprocal meaning potential.

8. It does not even make sense to say that speakers have a choice between *each* and *one* in the frame [_ *other*], since the alterity word does not remain constant. *Each* goes with the bare form *other*, *one* goes with the indefinite form *another*.

9. Since it does not play a role in the present discussion, I leave open whether such dative experiencers should be called 'subjects'. On the history of these constructions and possible syntactic analyses see Allen (1995) on English and Barðdal and Eithórsson (2005) on Germanic in general.

10. Raumolin-Brunberg (1997) states: 'On the whole the issue is about grammaticalization, if we interpret it here as a process in which grammatical items become more grammaticalized (e.g. Heine et al., 1991: 2). Two of the elements at issue, *one* and *other*, were originally numerals, and have been the object of repeated grammaticalizations, acquiring various pronominal functions during the history of English' (227). As will be argued later, the development of *each other* and *one another* does not only concern the changing status of the component elements, but also the formation of new, complex expressions. Besides, it is not at all obvious in how far the relevant items really become 'more grammaticalized' (on *each other*, see Haas, 2007: 43).

11. The term 'secondary grammaticalization' is often used to describe further change of items that are already grammatical. In this case the relevant expression would become 'more grammatical'. If—as in the case of *each other*—it is not obvious if and to what degree the newly grammaticalized item is 'more grammatical' than its source, this begs the question.

12. Himmelmann does not include syntactic context expansion as a necessary condition for grammaticalization, thereby attributing more importance to semantic and pragmatic context expansion. In the following I will take both types as equally important.

13. Brinton and Traugott's (2005) view of lexicalization as opposed to grammaticalization does not seem to be easily applicable to the case of *each other*, given that the box metaphor of lexicon and grammar still plays an important role (see also Fischer, 2007: 316, n. 21).

14. I expect that an investigation into the phonetic properties of the reciprocal *each other*, as opposed to the non-reciprocal string *each other*, would support the view that the reciprocal is processed as a grammatical unit. A study of this type is beyond the scope of this book and has to be left to future research.

15. One might object here that there are two individuals in the set denoted by *other* if both possible relations are added up. This analysis would contradict the interpretation of *each*, however. To be sure, *each* is a universal quantifier. But in contrast to (one use of) *all*, for example, it quantifies universally by making reference to every participant individually, as witnessed by its incompatibility with plural nouns: **each children*. For this reason the number of participants has to be calculated for each relation individually.

16. This statement does not, of course, stand its ground when we look at earlier stages of English, i.e. OE and early ME, where many of the relations that are now expressed with the help of prepositions were instead expressed by case distinctions. Since the issue of univerbation arises only for those later stages in which the bipartite reciprocal strategy had established itself as the standard reciprocal strategy for ordinary transitive verbs, however, this change should not be a complication at this point. In fact, there is no significant

difference in frequency between *each other* following prepositions in FLOB in FROWN as opposed to the same structure in LOB, which is thirty years older than FLOB and FROWN.

17. Source: 'A Pleasant Dialogue Betwixt Honest John and Loving Kate. The Contrivance of their Marriage and Way how to Live', 1685, Lampeter Corpus.

18. Source: http://www.guardian.co.uk/society/2002/oct/30/volunteering.guardiansocietysupplement (accessed 5 March 2009).

19. Source: http://www.newtheatre.org.uk/autumn0708 (accessed 5 March 2009).

20. Source: http://my.telegraph.co.uk/diseverything/blog/2007/08/09/whats_happening_to_our_city_ (accessed 5 March 2009).

21. I remain neutral in regards to the synchronic analysis of floating quantifiers in PDE, especially with respect to the theory-internal issue of movement (for detailed discussion, see Brisson, 1998). As far as the diachrony of the phenomenon is concerned, Lightfoot (1979), closely following Carlson (1976, 1978), argues that the relevant expressions ('pre-quantifiers') basically had the same distributional freedom as PDE quantifiers, but should be analyzed as adjectives in OE. According to Lightfoot's and Carlson's scenarios, the category of quantifiers emerged only later and thus the syntactic similarity between today's quantifiers and their counterparts in OE is merely superficial. As shown by Fischer and van der Leek (1981: 311–317), however, the quantifiers in OE were already morphosyntactically distinct from adjectives.

22. One might object here that Japanese allows numeral quantifiers to float. There is an important difference between English and Japanese, though. Whereas the English floating quantifiers *each*, *all* and *both* interact with a definite noun phrase, this is not the case in Japanese. There, numerals are flexible as to their positioning in the clause, but semantically they do nothing more than quantify the noun (or nominal group) with which they interact.

23. Note also that Shakespeare uses intransitive *see* only in the sense of 'meet' and not in the sense of 'see each other'.

NOTES TO CHAPTER 4

1. Although Gleitman et al. (1996) do not explicitly subscribe to construction grammar, this is effectively a constructionist position.

2. In fact, the 'Extended Animacy Hierarchy' (cf. Croft, 2003: 130) commonly used in typological studies is often called 'empathy hierarchy' and is basically the same hierarchy that Kuno and Kaburaki (1977) describe. Typologists are more reluctant, however, to appeal to 'empathy' as the single explanatory factor behind the hierarchy.

3. It may objected that another option is a structure involving the preposition *with*, as in . . . *the lover of sex therapist Sara Dale, alias Miss Whiplash, with whom Courtney met when the pair became involved in the Life Shield Association*. Such a structure would not be compatible with the intended meaning, however. *Meet* followed by *with* has a relatively fixed meaning if both participants are human. It designates a meeting event that has been planned by the participants beforehand, a restriction that is not part of the situations expressed in (13).

4. As mentioned earlier, Kuno and Kaburaki (1977) discuss argument realization of the verb *meet* under the heading of 'empathy'. Kuno explicitly connects his empathy hierarchy to a hierarchy of topicality at one point (1987: 210) and does not really make clear why 'empathy' should not generally be reduced to topicality, at least in the case of symmetric predicates. In what

follows I will acknowledge that information structural factors such as the degree of topicality of a referent are conceptually different from 'empathy' (Fillmore's 1977 'perspective', Zubin's 1979 'focus of interest', DeLancey's 1981 'viewpoint' and the more widely used 'point of view' all refer to the same phenomenon), but it seems to me that in most cases the two coincide, at least as far as the argument realization of symmetric predicates in English is concerned.

5. In more recent work Goldberg puts greater emphasis on information structure (cf. Goldberg, 2004; 2006: 129–165).

6. Arguably, the phenomena that Hawkins (1994, 2004), Arnold et al. (2000), Wasow (2002) and others have examined have a different status from the 'symmetry alternations' we are interested in here. Thus, the ordering of prepositional phrases relative to each other, 'Heavy NP Shift' or the 'Dative Alternation', do not affect valency, whereas in the case of *meet* and similar verbs we are dealing with a transitivity alternation (cf. Levin and Rappaport Hovav, 2005: 189), i.e. an alternation between transitive and intransitive clauses. Yet, I take it that observations that have been made with respect to one type of alternation may well lead to insights into the nature of the other type.

7. The sentence is unacceptable in the intended reading that Rose came across the phenomenon.

NOTES TO CHAPTER 5

1. In many older treatments pairs of sentences of the type (1) a. versus (1) b. are taken to be related via a transformation deriving one variant from the other (cf. e.g. Gleitman, 1965; Stockwell et al., 1973: 299–311; Stuurman, 1990: 168–173). This suggests that there is no meaning difference. Note that syntactic transformations are traditionally assumed to be meaning-preserving in the generative-transformational framework (the 'Katz-Postal Hypothesis'). This assumption has not always been uncontroversial (see Newmeyer, 1980: 78–81), but at least in the older studies cited earlier (Gleitman, 1965; Lakoff and Peters, 1969; Dougherty, 1971, 1974; Wasow, 1977), the issue of meaning contrasts is not approached, and the underlying supposition seems therefore to have been that there is none. Similarly, descriptive treatments of English grammar do not normally mention any meaning contrast related to the presence or absence of the reciprocal expression. The most common explanation of the alternation is to say that the reciprocal relation is inherent in the verb meaning, its signalling through the reciprocal therefore being redundant and omissible (see, for example, Jespersen, 1924: 161). Haiman (1985a) also analyzes the intransitive variant in terms of omission resulting from predictability when he states that 'by and large, the reciprocal pronoun which specifically indicates symmetry may be rendered by zero in precisely those cases where symmetry is necessary or very likely' (169).

2. In fact, in many cases it is more adequate to consider the sequence of verb and light reciprocal marker/middle marker a lexicalized unit. Thus, there are verbs that cannot be used without the middle marker and in those cases in which the verb can occur alone the meaning of the one use does not seem to be regularly related to the other use.

3. Abbreviations: DU = Dual; NOM = Nominative; RDP = reduplication; MM = middle marker; NPST = nonpast; ERG = ergative; RECP = reciprocal; PST = past; PFV = perfective

4. See Bretherton (1995).

5. See Heath and Eaves (1985).

6. See Givón (2001: 15–22) on the relation between noun phrase conjunction and separateness of events. Givón shows that '[b]y conjoining two NPs as subject, object or oblique role in a single clause, one intends the clause to code a single event, within which those NPs participated together in the same capacity' (2001: 19). The same tendency towards a single-event interpretation holds of course for participants coded as a simple plural noun (see e.g. Fiengo and Lasnik, 1973: 451) and thus for all reciprocal sentences of the basic type. In sentences of the spell-out type this principle is then overridden by the overt indication of distributivity that the quantifier *each* provides for. Note also that the distinction is one of construal and not necessarily a truth-conditional one, as Fiengo and Lasnik (1973) already seem to indicate when they state that '[t]he requirement that the events referred to in reciprocal sentences occur in the same general time span seems to be the result of the fact that the events characterized by reciprocal sentences [of the basic type, FH] are *regarded* as one general event' (1973: 451; my emphasis). It would be hard to define exactly the borderline between single events and distinct events in truth-conditional terms, given that—strictly speaking—reciprocal sentences with what we analyze here as a single-event reading always involve subevents (e.g. John's staring at Bill and Bill's staring at John in [10] b.).

7. Source: http://www.literaryreview.co.uk/pryce-jones_03_06.html (accessed 1 August 2007).

8. Source: http://www.publications.parliament.uk/pa/cm200607/cmselect/cmfaff/55/701231-2.htm (accessed 1 August 2007).

9. 'X' stands for any property attributed to the object noun phrase, e.g. in the form of an adjective phrase.

10. Note that similar effects hold for the intransitive realization of other predicates that may be argued to be underlyingly transitive, e.g. predicates of bodily motion and grooming (cf. Kemmer, 1993b; König and Siemund, 1999). Again, the realization as a bare intransitive verb in English corresponds to overt middle marking in other languages.

11. Strictly speaking, in the context of certain narrower conceptions of the notion 'construction' it has therefore been inaccurate to call these structures 'reciprocal constructions' in the first place.

12. I include here complex-transitive structures involving prepositions like *They argued with each other.*

Primary Sources and Corpora

Ælfric's Catholic Homilies, Vols. I–II. Ed. Benjamin Thorpe. London: Ælfric Society, 1844/1846.
Ælfric's Lives of Saints. Ed. Walter W. Skeat. London: Early English Text Society, 1881.
Anglo-Saxon Chronicle, Ed. Benjamin Thorpe. London: Longman, Green, Longman & Roberts, 1861.
Beowulf: An Edition with Relevant Shorter Texts. Ed. Bruce Mitchell and Fred C. Robinson. Oxford: Blackwell, 1998.
The Guthlac Poems of the Exeter Book. Ed. Jane Roberts. Oxford: Clarendon Press, 1979.
King Alfred's Version of the Consolations of Boethius. Ed. Walter John Sedgefield. Oxford, 1900.
King Alfred's West Saxon Version of Gregory's Pastoral Care. Ed. H. Sweet. London: Early English Text Society, 1871.
Le Morte Darthur by Syr Thomas Malory. Ed. H. Oskar Sommer. Ann Arbor: University of Michigan Humanities Text Initiative, 1997.
The Norton Shakespeare. Ed. Stephen Greenblatt, Walter Cohen, Jean E. Howard and Katharina Eisaman Maus. New York/London: Norton, 1997.
The Old English Orosius. Ed. Janet Bately. Oxford: Early English Text Society, OUP, 1980.
The Riverside Chaucer. 3rd ed. Ed. Larry D. Benson. Boston: Houghton Mifflin Company, 1987.

Auster, Paul. (2004) *Oracle Night*. New York: Henry Holt and Company.
Bruce Dickinson: Anthology. DVD. Sanctuary Music, 2006.
Eugenides, Jeffrey. (2002) *Middlesex*. London: Bloomsbury.
Lodge, David. (1984) *Small World*. London: Penguin.
Lodge, David. (2001) *Thinks . . .* London: Penguin.
Lodge, David. (2004) *Author, Author*. London: Penguin.
McEwan, Ian. (2001) *Atonement*. London: Vintage.
McEwan, Ian. (2005) *Saturday*. London: Vintage.
Swift, Graham. (2003) *The Light of Day*. London: Penguin.
Updike, John. (2004) *Villages*. London: Penguin.

The British National Corpus, version 2 (BNC World). 2001. Distributed by Oxford University Computing Services on behalf of the BNC Consortium. URL: http://www.natcorp.ox.ac.uk/.
The Corpus of Contemporary American English. Available online at http://www.americancorpus.org.

The Diachronic Part of the Helsinki Corpus of English Texts. URL: http://khnt. hit.uib.no/icame/manuals/HC/INDEX.HTM.

The FLOB Corpus of British English. URL: http://khnt.hit.uib.no/icame/manuals/ flob/INDEX.HTM.

The Lampeter Corpus of Early Modern English Tracts. URL: http://khnt.hit.uib. no/icame/manuals/LAMPETER/LC-manual.pdf.

The LOB Corpus of British English. URL: http://khnt.hit.uib.no/icame/manuals/ lob/INDEX.HTM.

Bibliography

Allan, K. (1987) 'Hierarchies and the choice of left conjuncts (with particular attention to English)'. *Journal of Linguistics*, 23: 51–77.

Allen, C.L. (1995) *Case Marking and Reanalysis: Grammatical Relations from Old to Early Modern English*. Oxford: Oxford University Press.

Ariel, M. (1990) *Accessing Noun Phrase Antecedents*. London: Routledge.

———. (2006) 'The making of a construction: From reflexive marking to lower transitivity'. Unpublished manuscript, Tel Aviv University.

———. (2008) *Pragmatics and Grammar*. Cambridge: Cambridge University Press.

Arnold, J.E., T. Wasow, A. Losongco and R. Gingstrom. (2000) 'Heaviness vs. newness: The effects of structural complexity and discourse status on constituent ordering'. *Language*, 76: 28–55.

Asudeh, A. (1998) 'Anaphors and argument structure: Topics in the syntax and semantics of reflexives and reciprocals'. Unpublished master's thesis, University of Edinburgh.

Aitchison, J. (2001) *Language Change: Progress or Decay?* 3rd ed. Cambridge: Cambridge University Press.

Baker, C.F., and J. Ruppenhofer. (2002) 'FrameNet's frames vs. Levin's verb classes', in J. Larson and M. Paster (eds.), *Proceedings of the Twenty-Eighth Annual Meeting of the Berkeley Linguistics Society*. Berkeley, CA: Berkeley Linguistics Society, 27–38.

Baldi, P. (1975) 'Reciprocal verbs and symmetric predicates'. *Linguistische Berichte*, 36: 13–20.

Barðdal, J. (2003) 'Review of: L.A. Michaelis and J. Ruppenhofer, Beyond Alternations: A constructional model of the German applicative pattern. Stanford: CLSI Publications 2001'. *Studies in Language*, 27: 663–671.

Barðdal, J., and T. Eithórsson. (2005) 'Oblique subjects: A common Germanic inheritance'. *Language*, 81: 824–881.

Bates, E. (1998) 'Construction grammar and its implications for child language research'. *Journal of Child Language*, 25: 443–484.

Bates, E., and J.C. Goodman. (1997) 'On the inseparability of grammar and the lexicon: Evidence from acquisition, aphasia and real-time processing'. *Language and Cognitive Processes*, 12: 507–584.

Beck, S. (2000a) 'Exceptions in relational plurals'. *SALT*, 10: 1–16.

———. (2000b) 'Reciprocals and cumulation'. *SALT*, 9: 16–33.

———. (2001) 'Reciprocals are definites'. *Natural Language Semantics*, 9: 69–138.

Behrens, L. (2007) 'Backgrounding and suppression of reciprocal predicates: A cross-linguistic study'. *Studies in Language*, 31: 327–408.

Bhat, D.N.S. (1981) *Pronominalization*. Pune: Deccan College Research Institute.

———. (2004) *Pronouns*. Oxford: Oxford University Press.

Biber, D., S. Johansson, G. Leech, S. Conrad and E. Finegan. (1999) *Longman Grammar of Spoken and Written English*. London: Longman.

Birner, B.J., and G. Ward. (1998) *Information Status and Noncanonical Word Order in English*. Amsterdam: Benjamins.

Blake, N.F. (2002) *A Grammar of Shakespeare's Language*. Basingstoke: Palgrave.

Boas, H.U. (1984) *Formal versus Explanatory Generalizations in Generative Transformational Grammar: An Investigation into Generative Argumentation*. Tübingen: Niemeyer.

Bock, K., A. Cutler, K.M. Eberhard, S. Butterfield, J. Cooper Cutting and K.R. Humphreys. (2006) 'Number agreement in British and American English: Disagreeing to agree collectively'. *Language*, 82: 64–113.

Bolinger, D.D. (1986) *Intonation and its Parts: Melody in Spoken English*. Stanford: Stanford University Press.

———. (1987) '*Each other* and its friends', in D.D. Bolinger, J.K. Gundel and S. Cushing (eds.), *Another Indiana University Linguistics Club Twentieth Anniversary Volume*. Bloomington: Indiana University Linguistics Club, 1–36.

———. (1990) 'Remarking the English reciprocal: Commutation versus mutuality', in J.A. Edmondson, C. Feagin and P. Mühlhäusler (eds.), *Development and Diversity: language Variation across Space and Time*. Dallas: Summer Institute of Linguistics and University of Texas at Arlington, 265–272.

Bosque, I. (1985) 'Sobre las oraciones recíprocas en español'. *Revista Española de Lingüística*, 15: 59-96.

Bouchard, D. (1985) 'The Binding Theory and the notion of accessible SUBJECT'. *Linguistic Inquiry*, 16: 117–133.

Bretherton, I. (1995) 'A communication perspective on attachment relationships and internal working models'. *Monographs of the Society for Research in Child Development*, 60 (2/3), 310–329.

Bril, I. (2005) 'Semantic and functional diversification of middle prefixes in New Caledonian and other Austronesian languages'. *Linguistic Typology*, 9: 25–76.

Brinton, L. (2002) 'Grammaticalization versus lexicalization reconsidered: On the late use of temporal adverbs', in T. Fanego, M.J. López-Couso and J. Pérez-Guerra (eds.), *English Historical Syntax and Morphology: Selected Papers from 11 ICHL, Santiago de Compostela, 7–11 September 2000*. Amsterdam: Benjamins, 67–97.

Brinton, L., and E.C. Traugott. (2005) *Lexicalization and Language Change*. Cambridge: Cambridge University Press.

Brisson, C. (1998) 'Distributivity, maximality and floating quantifiers'. Doctoral dissertation, Rutgers University.

———. (2003) 'Plurals, all, and the nonuniformity of collective predication'. *Linguistics and Philosophy*, 26: 129-184.

Bruening, B. (2004) 'Verbal reciprocals and the interpretation of reciprocals'. Unpublished manuscript, University of Delaware.

Büring, D. (2005) *Binding Theory*. Cambridge: Cambridge University Press.

Bybee, J. (1985) *Morphology*. Amsterdam: Benjamins.

———. (1988) 'Semantic substance vs. contrast in the development of grammatical meaning'. *BLS*, 14: 247–264.

———. (2006) 'From usage to grammar: the mind's response to repetition'. *Language*, 82: 711–733.

Bybee, J., and Ö. Dahl. (1989) 'The creation of tense and aspect systems in the languages of the world'. *Studies in Language*, 13: 51–103.

Bybee, J., and P. Hopper (eds.). (2000) *Frequency and the Emergence of Linguistic Structure*. Amsterdam: Benjamins.

Bybee, J., and J.D. McClelland. (2005) 'Alternatives to the combinatorial paradigm of linguistic theory based on domain general principles of human cognition'. *Linguistic Review*, 22: 381–410.

Carlson, A.M. (1976) 'A diachronic treatment of English quantifiers'. Master's thesis, McGill University.

——. (1978) 'A diachronic treatment of English quantifiers'. *Lingua*, 46: 295–328.

Carlson, G. (1998) 'Thematic roles and the individuation of events', in S. Rothstein (ed.), *Events and Grammar*. Dordrecht: Kluwer, 35–51.

Clark, E. V. (2009) *First Language Acquisition*, 2nd ed. Cambridge: Cambridge University Press.

Croft, W. (1995) 'Autonomy and functionalist linguistics'. *Language*, 71: 490–532.

——. (2000) *Explaining Language Change: An Evolutionary Perspective*. London: Arnold.

——. (2001) *Radical Construction Grammar: Syntactic Theory in Typological Perspective*. Oxford: Oxford University Press.

——. (2003) *Typology and Universals*. Cambridge: Cambridge University Press.

——. (2004) 'Syntactic theories and syntactic methodology: A reply to Seuren'. *Journal of Linguistics*, 40: 637–654.

Croft, W., and D.A. Cruse. (2004) *Cognitive Linguistics*. Cambridge: Cambridge University Press.

Culicover, P.W. (1999) *Syntactic Nuts*. Oxford: Oxford University Press.

——. (2009) *Natural Language Syntax*. Oxford: Oxford University Press.

Culicover, P.W., and R. Jackendoff. (2005) *Simpler Syntax*. Oxford: Oxford University Press.

——. (2006) 'The simpler syntax hypothesis'. *Trends in Cognitive Sciences*, 10: 413–418.

Curme, G.O. (1935) *A Grammar of the English Language, Vol. II: Parts of Speech and Accidence*. Boston: Heath.

Dalrymple, M., M. Kazanawa, Y. Kim, S. Mchombo and S. Peters. (1998) 'Reciprocal expressions and the concept of reciprocity'. *Linguistics and Philosophy*, 21: 159–210.

Dalrymple, M., S.A. Mchombo and S. Peters. (1994) 'Semantic similarities and syntactic contrasts between Chicheŵa and English reciprocals'. *Linguistic Inquiry*, 25: 145–163.

Davies, W.D. (2000) 'Events in Madurese reciprocals', *Oceanic Linguistics*, 39: 123-143.

DeLancey, S. (1981) 'An interpretation of split ergativity and related patterns'. *Language*, 57: 626–657.

Dench, A. (1987) 'Kinship and collective activity in the Ngayarda languages of Australia'. *Language in Society*, 16: 321–339.

Denison, D. (1993) *English Historical Syntax: Verbal Constructions*. London: Longman.

Diessel, H. (2004) *The Acquisition of Complex Sentences*. Cambridge: Cambridge University Press.

Dik, S.C. (1968) *Coordination: Its Implications for the Theory of General Linguistics*. Amsterdam: North-Holland Publishing Company.

Dimitriadis, A. (2000) 'Beyond identity: Topics in reciprocal and pronominal anaphora'. Doctoral dissertation, University of Pennsylvania.

——. (2008a) 'The event structure of irreducibly symmetric reciprocals', in J. Dölling, T.H. Zybatow and M. Schäfer (eds.), *Event Structures in Linguistic Form and Interpretation*. Berlin: de Gruyter, 327–354.

————. (2008b) 'Irreducible symmetry in reciprocal constructions', in E. König and V. Gast (eds.), *Reciprocity and Reflexivity: Theoretical and Typological Explorations*. Berlin: de Gruyter, 375–409.

Dixon, R.M.W. (1988) *A Grammar of Boumaa Fijian*. Chicago: University of Chicago Press.

Donaldson, T. (1980) *Ngiyambaa: The Language of the Wangaaybuwan*. Cambridge: Cambridge University Press.

Dong, Q.P. (1970) 'A note on conjoined noun phrases', in A.E. Zwicky, P.H. Sallus, R.I. Binnik and A.L. Vanek (eds.), *Studies Out in Left Field: Studies Presented to James McCawley on the Occasion of his 33rd or 34th Birthday*. Edmonton: Linguistic Research Inc., 11–18.

Dougherty, R.C. (1970) 'A grammar of coordinate conjoined structures: I'. *Language*, 46: 850–598.

————. (1971) 'A grammar of coordinate conjoined structures: II'. *Language*, 47: 298–339.

————. (1974) 'The syntax and semantics of *each other*-constructions'. *Foundations of Language*, 12: 1–47.

Dowty, D.R. (1979) *Word Meaning and Montague Grammar*. Dordrecht: Reidel.

————. (1987) 'Collective predicates, distributive predicates, and *all*', in F. Marshall (ed.), *Proceedings of the 3rd ESCOL*. Columbus: Ohio State University, 97–115.

————. (1991) 'Thematic proto-roles and argument selection'. *Language*, 67: 547–619.

Dąbrowska, E. (2006) *Language, Mind and Brain: Some Psychological and Neurological Constraints on Theories of Grammar*. Georgetown: Edinburgh/Georgetown University Press.

Einenkel, E. (1903) 'Das englische Indefinitum'. *Anglia*, 26: 461–572.

————. (1916) *Geschichte der Englischen Sprache II: Historische Syntax*. Strassburg: Karl J. Trübner.

Erades, P.A. (1950) 'Points of Modern English syntax XII'. *English Studies*, 31: 153–157.

Evans, N. (2008) 'Reciprocal constructions: Towards a structural typology', in E. König and V. Gast (eds.), *Reciprocity and Reflexivity: Theoretical and Typological Explorations*. Berlin: de Gruyter, 33–103.

————. (forthcoming) 'Complex events, propositional overlay, and the special status of reciprocal clauses', in J. Newman and S. Rice (eds.), *Experimental and Empirical Methods in Cognitive/Functional Research*. Stanford: CSLI Press.

Evans, N., A. Gaby and R. Nordlinger. (2007) 'Valency mismatches and the coding of reciprocity in Australian languages'. *Linguistic Typology*, 11: 541–597.

Evans, N., A. Gaby, S. Levinson and A. Majid (eds.). (forthcoming) *Reciprocals across Languages*. Amsterdam: John Benjamins.

Everaert, M. (2000) 'Types of anaphoric expressions: Reflexives and reciprocals', in Z. Frajzyngier and T.S. Curl (eds.), *Reciprocals: Form and Function*. Amsterdam: Benjamins, 63–83.

Faiß, K. (1989) *Englische Sprachgeschichte*. Tübingen: Francke.

Faller, M. (2007) 'The ingredients of reciprocity in Cuzco Quechua'. *Journal of Semantics*, 24: 255–288.

Farmer, A.K. (1987) 'They held each other's breath and other puzzles for the Binding Theory'. *Linguistic Inquiry*, 18: 157–163.

Fiengo, R., and H. Lasnik. (1973) 'The logical structure of reciprocal sentences in English'. *Foundations of Language*, 9: 447–468.

Filip, H., and G. Carlson. (2001) 'Distributivity strengthens reciprocity, collectivity weakens it'. *Linguistics and Philosophy*, 24: 417–466.

Fillmore, C.J. (1972) 'Subjects, speakers and roles', in D. Davidson and G. Harman (eds.), *Semantics of Natural Languages*. Dordrecht: Reidel, 1–24.
———. (1977) 'Topics in lexical semantics', in R.W. Cole (ed.), *Current Issues in Linguistic Theory*. Bloomington: Indiana University Press, 76–138.
Fillmore, C.J., P. Kay and M. O'Connor. (1988) 'Regularity and idiomaticity in grammatical constructions'. *Language*, 64: 501–538.
Fischer, O. (2007) *Morphosyntactic Change: Formal and Functional Perspectives*. Oxford: Oxford University Press.
Fischer, O., and F. van der Leek. (1981) 'Optional vs. radical reanalysis: mechanisms of syntactic change'. *Lingua*, 55: 301–350.
Frajzyngier, Z., and T.S. Curl (eds.). (2000) *Reciprocals: Form and Function*. Amsterdam: Benjamins.
Franz, W. (1939) *Die Sprache Shakespeares in Vers und Prosa*. Halle an der Saale: Niemeyer.
Gaby, A. (2001) 'A typology of the reflexoid in Australian languages'. Master's thesis, University of Melbourne.
———. (2008) 'Distinguishing reciprocals from reflexives in Kuuk Thaayorre', E. König and V. Gast (eds.), *Reciprocity and Reflexivity: Theoretical and Typological Explorations*. Berlin: de Gruyter, 259–288.
Gast, V. (2006) *The Grammar of Identity: Intensifiers and Reflexives in Germanic Languages*. London: Routledge.
———. (2007) 'I gave it him—on the motivation of the "alternative double object construction" in varieties of English'. *Functions of Language*, 14: 31–56.
Gast, V., and F. Haas. (2008) 'On reflexive and reciprocal readings of anaphors in German and other European languages', in E. König and V. Gast (eds.), *Reciprocity and Reflexivity: Theoretical and Typological Explorations*. Berlin: de Gruyter, 307–346.
Givón, T. (1983) 'Topic continuity in discourse: an introduction', in T. Givón (ed.), *Topic Continuity in Discourse: A Quantitative Cross-Linguistic Study*. Amsterdam: Benjamins, 1–42.
———. (1993) *English Grammar: A Function-Based Introduction*, vol. II. Amsterdam: Benjamins.
———. (2001) *Syntax*, vol. II. Amsterdam: Benjamins.
Gleitman, L.R. (1965) 'Coordinating conjunctions in English'. *Language*, 41: 260–293.
Gleitman, L.R., H. Gleitman, C. Miller and R. Ostrin. (1996) 'Similar, and similar concepts'. *Cognition*, 58: 321–376.
Goldberg, A.E. (1995) *Constructions: A Construction Grammar Approach to Argument Structure*. Chicago: University of Chicago Press.
———. (2004) 'Pragmatics and argument structure', in L.R. Horn and G. Ward (eds.), *Handbook of Pragmatics*. Oxford: Blackwell, 427–441.
———. (2006) *Constructions at Work: The Nature of Generalization in Language*. Oxford: Oxford University Press.
Gries, S. Th., and A. Stefanowitsch (2004) 'Extending collostructional analysis: a corpus-based perspective on 'alternations''. *International Journal of Corpus Linguistics*, 9: 97–127.
Haas, F. (2007) 'The development of English *each other*—grammaticalization, lexicalization, or both?' *English Language and Linguistics*, 11: 31–50.
———. (2008) 'Symmetric verbs and constraints on passivization: An English–German comparison'. *Zeitschrift für Anglistik und Amerikanistik*, 56: 255–268.
Haegemann, L. (1994) *Introduction to Government and Binding Theory*, 2nd ed. Oxford: Blackwell.
Haegemann, L., and J. Gueron. (1998) *English Grammar: A Generative Perspective*. Oxford: Blackwell.

Haiman, J. (1985a) *Natural Syntax*. Cambridge: Cambridge University Press.

———. (1985b) 'Symmetry', in J. Haiman (ed.), *Iconicity in Syntax*. Amsterdam: Benjamins, 73–95.

Hanke, T. (in preparation) 'Bipartite reciprocal markers: A typological overview'. Doctoral dissertation, Friedrich-Schiller-Universität Jena.

Haspelmath, M. (2007) 'Further remarks on reciprocal constructions', in V.P. Nedjalkov (ed.), *Reciprocal Constructions*, Amsterdam: Benjamins, 2087–2115.

———. (2008a) 'Creating economical morphosyntactic patterns in language change', in J. Good (ed.), *Language Universals and Language Change*. Oxford: Oxford University Press, 185–214.

———. (2008b) 'Parametric versus functional explanations of syntactic universals', in T. Biberauer (ed.), *The Limits of Syntactic Variation*. Amsterdam: John Benjamins, 75–107.

Hawkins, J. (1994) *A Performance Theory of Order and Constituency*. Cambridge: Cambridge University Press.

———. (2004) *Efficiency and Complexity in Grammars*. Oxford: Oxford University Press.

Heath, A.C., and L.J. Eaves. (1985) 'Resolving the effects of phenotype and social background on mate selection'. *Behavior Genetics*, 15 (1), 15–30.

Heim, I., H. Lasnik and R. May. (1991) 'Reciprocity and plurality'. *Linguistic Inquiry*, 22: 63–101.

Heine, B., U. Claudi and F. Hünnemeyer. (1991) *Grammaticalization: A Conceptual Framework*. Chicago: University of Chicago Press.

Higginbotham, J. (1980) 'Reciprocal interpretation'. *Journal of Linguistic Research*, 1: 97–117.

———. (1985) 'On semantics'. *Linguistic Inquiry*, 16: 547–593.

Himmelmann, N. (2004) 'Lexicalization and grammaticalization: opposite or orthogonal?', in B. Wiemer, W. Bisang and N. Himmelmann (eds.), *What Makes Grammaticalization—A Look from Its Components and Its Fringes*. Berlin: de Gruyter, 21–42.

Hopper, P.J. (1991) 'On some principles of grammaticalization', in E.C. Traugott and B. Heine (eds.), *Approaches to Grammaticalization*. Amsterdam: Benjamins, 17–35.

Hopper, P.J., and S.A. Thompson. (1980) 'Transitivity in grammar and discourse'. *Language*, 56: 251–299.

Huang, C.T.J. (1983) 'A note on the Binding Theory'. *Linguistic Inquiry*, 14: 554–561.

Huddleston, R., and G.K. Pullum. (2002) *The Cambridge Grammar of the English Language*. Cambridge: Cambridge University Press.

Hudson, R. (1984) *Word Grammar*. Oxford: Blackwell.

Hüning, M. (2006) 'Reciprociteit in het Nederlands: de geschiedenis van *elkaar* en *mekaar*'. *Nederlandse Taalkunde*, 11: 185–217.

Hunston, S., and G. Francis. (2000) *Pattern Grammar*. Amsterdam: Benjamins.

Hurst, P., and R. Nordlinger. (forthcoming) 'Reciprocal constructions in English: *Each other* and beyond', in N. Evans, A. Gaby, S. Levinson and A. Majid (eds.).

Itkonen, E. (2005) *Analogy as Structure and Process*. Amsterdam: Benjamins.

Jackendoff, R. (1972) *Semantic Interpretation in Generative Grammar*. Cambridge, MA: MIT Press.

———. (1990) *Semantic Structures*. Cambridge, MA: MIT Press.

———. (2002) *Foundations of Language*. Oxford: Oxford University Press.

———. (2008) '*Construction after construction* and its theoretical challenges'. *Language*, 84: 8–28.

Jacobs, J. (2001) 'The dimensions of topic-comment'. *Linguistics*, 39: 641–681.

Jespersen, O. (1914) *A Modern English Grammar on Historical Principles, p. 2: Syntax*, vol. 1. Heidelberg: Carl Winter.
———. (1924) *The Philosophy of Grammar*. London: George Allen and Unwin Ltd.
———. (1927) *A Modern English Grammar on Historical Principles, p. 3: Syntax*, vol. 2. Heidelberg: Carl Winter.
———. (1931) *A Modern English Grammar on Historical Principles, p.4: Syntax*, vol. 3. Heidelberg: Carl Winter.
Jørgensen, E. (1985) 'Each other—one another'. *English Studies*, 66: 351–357.
Kahlas-Tarkka, L. (1987) *The Uses and Shades of Meaning of Words for Every and Each in Old English: With an Addendum on Early Middle English Developments*. Helsinki: Société Néophilologique.
———. (2004) 'A "two-way relationship in English" revisited: On reciprocal expressions in early English, with a digression into modern English uses'. *Studia Anglica Posnaniensia*, 40: 121–134.
Kaneko, T. (1972) 'Ist *ähneln* und *sind-ähnlich* ähnlich?', in K. Hyldegaard-Jensen (ed.) *Linguistik 1971: Referate des 6. Linguistischen Kolloquiums 11.-14. August in Kopenhagen*. Frankfurt: Athenäum, 118-149.
Kanskí, Z. (1987) 'Logical symmetry and natural language reciprocals', in I. Ruzsa and A. Szabolcsi (eds.), *Proceedings of the '87 Debrecen Symposium on Logic and Language*. Budapest: Akademiai Kiado, 49–68.
Keenan, E.L. (2002) 'Explaining the creation of reflexive pronouns in English', in D. Minkova and R. Stockwell (eds.), *Studies in the History of English*. Berlin: de Gruyter, 325–355.
Keenan, E.L., and J.P. Razafimamonjy. (2004) 'Reciprocals in Malagasy'. *Oceanic Linguistics*, 43: 177–207.
Kemmer, S. (1993a) 'Marking oppositions in verbal and nominal collectives'. *Faits de langues*, 2: 85–95.
———. (1993b) *The Middle Voice*. Amsterdam: Benjamins.
———. (1997) 'Collective and distributive marking, or: Where unity meets multiplicity', in A.K. Melby (ed.), *The Twenty-Third LACUS Forum 1996*. Chapel Hill, NC: Linguistics Association of Canada and the United States, 231–250.
Kjellmer, G. (1982) '*Each other* and *one another*: On the use of the English reciprocal pronouns'. *English Studies*, 63: 231–254.
Knjazev, J.P. (1998) 'Towards a typology of grammatical polysemy: Reflexive markers as markers of polysemy', in L. Kulikov and H. Vater (eds.), *Typology of Verbal Categories: Papers Presented to V. Nedjalkov on the Occasion of His 70th Birthday*. Tübingen: Niemeyer, 185–193.
König, E., and V. Gast. (2008a) 'Introduction', in E. König and V. Gast (eds.), *Reciprocity and Reflexivity: Theoretical and Typological Explorations*. Berlin: de Gruyter, 1–31.
———. (eds.). (2008b) *Reciprocity and Reflexivity: Theoretical and Typological Explorations*. Berlin: de Gruyter.
König, E., and S. Kokutani. (2006) 'Towards a typology of reciprocal constructions: Focus on German and Japanese'. *Linguistics*, 44: 271–302.
König, E., and C. Moyse-Faurie. (2009) 'Spatial reciprocity: Between grammar and lexis', in J. Helmbrecht, Y. Nishina, Y.-M. Shin, S. Skopeteas and E. Verhoeven (eds.), *Form and Function in Language Research: Papers in Honour of Christian Lehmann*. Berlin: de Gruyter, 57–68.
König, E., and P. Siemund. (1999) 'Intensifiers and reflexives: A typological perspective', in Z. Frajzyngier and T.S. Curl (eds.), *Reflexives: Form and Function*. Amsterdam: Benjamins, 41–74.
———. (2000) 'The development of complex reflexives and intensifiers in English'. *Diachronica*, 17: 39–84.

Koerner, E.F.K. (1994) 'The anatomy of a revolution in the social sciences: Chomsky in 1962'. *Dhumbadji*, 1: 3–17.

Krifka, M. (2007) 'Basic notions of information structure', in C. Féry, G. Fanselow and M. Krifka (eds.), *Working Papers of the SFB 632, Interdisciplinary Studies on Information Structure (ISIS)* 6. Potsdam: Universitätsverlag Potsdam, 13–56.

Krug, M. (2003) 'Frequency as a determinant of grammatical variation and change', in G. Rohdenburg and B. Mondorf (eds.), *Determinants of Grammatical Variation in English*. Berlin: de Gruyter, 7–67.

Kulikov, L., and H. Vater (eds.). (1998) *Typology of Verbal Categories: Papers Presented to V. Nedjalkov on the Occasion of His 70th Birthday*. Tübingen: Niemeyer.

Kuno, S. (1987) *Functional Syntax: Anaphora, Discourse and Empathy*. Chicago/London: University of Chicago Press.

Kuno, S., and E. Kaburaki. (1977) 'Empathy and syntax'. *Linguistic Inquiry*, 8: 627–672.

Lakoff, G. (1987) *Women, Fire and Dangerous Things: What Categories Reveal about the Mind*. Chicago: University of Chicago Press.

Lakoff, G., and S. Peters. (1969) 'Phrasal conjunction and symmetric predicates', in D.A. Reibel and S.A. Shane (eds.), *Modern Studies in English: Readings in Transformational Grammar*. Englewood Cliffs: Prentice Hall, 113–142.

Lambrecht, K. (1994) *Information Structure and Sentence Form*. Cambridge: Cambridge University Press.

Landau, I. (2000) *Elements of Control: Structure and Meaning of Infinitival Constructions*. Dordrecht: Kluwer.

Landman, F. (1989) 'Groups, I'. *Linguistics and Philosophy*, 12: 559–605.

———. (2000) *Events and Plurality: The Jerusalem Lectures*. Dortrecht: Kluwer.

Langacker, R.W. (1987) *Concept, Image, Symbol*. Amsterdam: Benjamins.

———. (1991) *Foundations of Cognitive Grammar*, vol. II: *Descriptive Application*. Amsterdam: Benjamins.

Lange, C. (2007) *Reflexivity and Intensification in English: A Study of Texts and Contexts*. Frankfurt am Main: Peter Lang.

Langendoen, D.T. (1978) 'The logic of reciprocity'. *Linguistic Inquiry*, 9: 177–197.

———. (1992) 'Symmetric relations', in D. Brentani, G. Larson and L.A. MacLeod (eds.), *The Joy of Grammar: A Festschrift in Honor of James D. McCawley*. Amsterdam: Benjamins, 199–211.

Langendoen, D.T., and J. Magloire. (2003) 'The logic of reflexivity and reciprocity', in A. Barss (ed.), *Anaphora: A Reference Guide*. Oxford: Blackwell, 237–263.

Lasersohn, P. (1990) 'Group action and spatio-temporal proximity'. *Linguistics and Philosophy*, 13: 179–206.

———. (1995) *Plurality, Conjunction and Events*. Dordrecht: Kluwer.

Latham, R.G. (1844) 'On the reciprocal pronouns and the reciprocal power of the reflective verb'. *Transactions of the Philological Society*, 1: 232–242.

Lebeaux, D. (1983) 'A distributional difference between reciprocals and reflexives'. *Linguistic Inquiry*, 14: 723–730.

Levin, B. (1993) *English Verb Classes and Alternations*. Chicago/London: University of Chicago Press.

Levin, B., and M. Rappaport Hovav. (2005) *Argument Realization*. Cambridge: Cambridge University Press.

Levin, M. (2006) 'Collective nouns and language change'. *English Language and Linguistics*, 10: 321–343.

Lichtenberk, F. (1985) 'Multiple uses of reciprocal constructions'. *Australian Journal of Linguistics*, 5: 19–41.

————. (2000) 'Reciprocals without reflexives', in Z. Frajzyngier and T.S. Curl (eds.), *Reciprocals: Form and Function*. Amsterdam: Benjamins, 31–62.

Lieberman, P. (2000) *Human Language and our Reptilian Brain: The Subcortical Bases of Speech, Syntax and Thought*. Cambridge, MA: Harvard University Press.

————. (2005) 'The pied piper of Cambridge'. *Linguistic Review*, 22: 289–301.

Lightfoot, D.W. (1979) *Principles of Diachronic Syntax*. Cambridge: Cambridge University Press.

Lindstroem, T. (2005) 'The history of the concept of grammaticalization'. Doctoral dissertation, University of Sheffield.

Lødrup, H. (2007) 'Norwegian anaphors without visible binders'. *Journal of Germanic Linguistics*, 19: 1–22.

Lüdeling, A., S. Evert and M. Baroni. (2007) 'Using web data for linguistic purposes', in M. Hundt, C. Biewer and N. Nesselhauf (eds.), *Corpus Linguistics and the Web*. Amsterdam: Rodopi, 7–24.

MacKay, C., and F.R. Trechsel. (2003) 'Reciprocal /laa-/ in Totonacan'. *International Journal of American Linguistics*, 69: 275–306.

Malamud, S.A. (2006) '(Non)maximality and distributivity: A Decision Theory approach', in M. Gibson and J. Howell (eds.), *SALT XVI*. Ithaca, NY: Cornell University, 120–137.

Mari, A. (2006) 'Linearizing sets: *Each other*', in O. Bonami and P. Cabredo Hofherr (eds.), *Empirical Issues in Syntax and Semantics 6*. Paris: CSSP, 249–283.

Maslova, E. (2008) 'Reflexive encoding of reciprocity: Cross-linguistic and language-internal variation', in E. König and V. Gast (eds.), *Reciprocity and Reflexivity: Theoretical and Typological Explorations*. Berlin: de Gruyter, 225–257.

Maslova, E., and V. Nedjalkov. (2005) 'Reciprocal constructions', in M. Haspelmath, M. Dryer, D. Gil and B. Comrie (eds.), *The World Atlas of Language Structures*. Oxford: Oxford University Press, 430–433.

McCawley, J.D. (1970) 'Similar in that S'. *Linguistic Inquiry*, 1: 556–559.

————. (1977) 'Lexicographic notes on English quantifiers'. *CLS*, 13: 372–383.

————. (1988) *The Syntactic Phenomena of English*, vol. I. Chicago/London: University of Chicago Press.

Mchombo, S.A., and R. Ngalande. (1980) 'Reciprocal verbs in Chicheŵa: A case for lexical derivation'. *Bulletin of the School of Oriental and African Studies*, 43: 570–575.

Mchombo, S.A., and A.S.A. Ngunga. (1994) 'The syntax and semantics of the reciprocal construction in Ciyao'. *Linguistic Analysis*, 24: 3–31.

Michaelis, L.A. (2003) 'Word meaning, sentence meaning, and syntactic meaning', in H. Cuyckens, R. Dirven and J.R. Taylor (eds.), *Cognitive Perspectives on Lexical Semantics*. Amsterdam: Mouton de Gruyter, 163–210.

Milroy, J., and L. Milroy. (1985) 'Linguistic change, social network and speaker innovation'. *Journal of Linguistics*, 21: 339–384.

Mitchell, B. (1985) *Old English Syntax, vol. 1: Concord, the Parts of Speech, and the Sentence*. Oxford: Clarendon Press.

Moltmann, F. (1992) 'Reciprocals and *same/different*: Towards a semantic analysis'. *Linguistics and Philosophy*, 15: 411–462.

Mohanan, K.P., and T. Mohanan (1998) 'Strong and weak projection: lexical reflexives and reciprocals', in M. Butt and W. Geuder (eds) *The Projection of Arguments: Lexical and Compositional Factors*. Stanford: CLSI Press, 165-194.

Moravcsik, E. (2006) *An Introduction to Syntactic Theory*. London: Continuum.

Mustanoja, T.F. (1960) *A Middle English Syntax*. Helsinki: Société Néophilologique.

Næss, Å. (2007) *Prototypical Transitivity*. Amsterdam: Benjamins.

Nedjalkov, V.P. (ed.). (2007a) 'Encoding of the reciprocal meaning', in V.P. Nedjalkov (ed.), *Reciprocal Constructions*. Amsterdam: Benjamins, 147–207.

——. (2007b) 'Polysemy of reciprocal markers', in V.P. Nedjalkov (ed.), *Reciprocal Constructions*. Amsterdam: Benjamins, 231–333.

——. (2007c) *Reciprocal Constructions*. Amsterdam: Benjamins.

Nevalainen, T., and I. Tieken-Boon van Ostade. (2006) 'Standardisation', in R.M. Hogg and D. Denison (eds.), *A History of the English Language*. Cambridge: Cambridge University Press, 271–311.

Newmeyer, F.J. (1980) *Linguistic Theory in America: The First Quarter Century of Transformational Generative Grammar*. New York: Academic Press.

——. (1983) *Grammatical Theory: Its Limits and Possibilities*. Chicago/London: University of Chicago Press.

——. (2005) *Possible and Probable Languages: A Generative Perspective on Linguistic Typology*. Oxford: Oxford University Press.

Ohlander, U. (1943) 'Omission of the object in English'. *Studia Neophilologica*, 16: 115–127.

Partee, B.H., A. Ter Meulen and R.E. Wall. (1993) *Mathematical Methods in Linguistics*. Dordrecht: Kluwer.

Partridge, E. (1957) *Usage and Abusage*, 5th ed. London: Hamish Hamilton.

Payne, John R. (1985) 'Complex phrases and complex sentences', in T. Shopen (ed.), *Language Typology and Syntactic Description, vol. 1: Clause Structure*. Cambridge: Cambridge University Press, 3–41.

Plank, F. (2006) 'The regular and the extended reciprocal construction, illustrated from German', in T. Tsunoda and T. Kageyama (eds.), *Voice and Grammatical Relations: In Honor of Masayoshi Shibatani*. Amsterdam: Benjamins, 247–270.

——. (2008) 'Thoughts on the origin, progress, and pro status of reciprocal forms in Germanic, occasioned by those of Bavarian', in E. König and V. Gast (eds.), *Reciprocity and Reflexivity: Theoretical and Typological Explorations*. Berlin: de Gruyter, 347–373.

Polinsky, M. (1996) 'Situation perspective: On the relations of thematic roles, discourse categories, and grammatical relations to Figure and Ground', in A. Goldberg (ed.), *Conceptual Structure, Discourse and Language*. Stanford: CLSI Publications, 401–419.

Potter, S. (1953) 'The expression of reciprocity'. *English Studies*, 34: 252–257.

Poutsma, H. (1926) *A Grammar of Late Modern English, Part II: The Parts of Speech*. Groningen: Noordhoff.

Pullum, G.K., and B. Scholz. (2002) 'Empirical investigation of stimulus poverty arguments'. *The Linguistic Review*, 19: 9–50.

Quirk, R., S. Greenbaum, G. Leech and S. Svartvik. (1985) *A Comprehensive Grammar of the English Language*. London: Longman.

Raumolin-Brunberg, H. (1997) 'Reciprocal pronouns: from discontinuity to unity'. *Studia Anglica Posnaniensia*, 31: 227–236.

Rice, S. (1987) 'Towards a transitive prototype: Evidence from atypical English passives'. *BLS*, 13: 422–434.

Rissanen, M. (1967) *The Uses of One in Old and Early Middle English*. Helsinki: Société Néophilologique.

Ritter, N.A. (2005) 'On the status of linguistics as a cognitive science'. *Linguistic Review*, 22: 117–133.

Roberts, C. (1991) 'Distributivity and reciprocal distributivity'. *Semantics and Linguistic Theory*, 1: 209–229.

Rydén, M., and S. Brorström. (1987) *The Be/Have Variation with Intransitives in English: With Special Reference to the Early Modern English Period*. Stockholm: Almqvist and Wiksell International.

Saeed, J.I. (2003) *Semantics*, 2nd ed. Oxford: Blackwell.
Safir, K. (2004) *The Syntax of Anaphora*. Oxford: Oxford University Press.
Sauerland, U. (1994) 'The representation of reciprocals in grammar', in J. Fuller, H. Han and D. Parkinson (eds.), *Proceedings of the Eastern States Conference on Linguistics (ESCOL '94)*. Ithaca, NY: DMLL Publications, Cornell University, 270–281.
———. (1998) 'Plurals, derived predicates, and reciprocals', in J. Fuller, H. Han and D. Parkinson (eds.), *The Interpretive Tract*. Cambridge, MA: MIT Press (MIT Working Papers in Linguistics), 177–204.
Scha, R., and D. Stallard. (1988) 'Multi-level plurals and distributivity', in *Proceedings of the 26th Annual Meeting of the Association for Computational Linguistics*. Morristown, NJ: Association for Computational Linguistics, 17–24.
Schein, B. (2003) 'Adverbial, descriptive reciprocals'. *Philosophical Perspectives*, 17: 333–367.
Schmidt, A. (1875) *Shakespeare-Lexikon*. Berlin: Reimer.
Schwarzschild, R. (1996) *Pluralities*. Dordrecht: Kluwer.
Seidl, A., and A. Dimitriadis (2003) 'Statives and reciprocal morphology in Swahili', in P. Sauzet and A. Zribi-Hertz (eds.), *Typologie des langues d'afrique et universaux de la grammaire*. Paris: L'Harmattan, 239–284.
Sheen, D.-T. (1988) *The Historical Development of Reciprocal Pronouns in Middle English with Selected Early Modern English Comparisons*. Muncie, IN: Ball State University.
Siemund, P. (forthcoming) 'Grammaticalization, lexicalization and intensification. English *itself* as a marker of middle situation types'. *Linguistics*.
Spies, H. (1897) *Studien zur Geschichte des englischen Pronomens im XV. und XVI. Jahrhundert*. Halle: Niemeyer.
Sternefeld, W. (1998) 'Reciprocity and cumulative predication'. *Natural Language Semantics*, 6: 303–337.
Stockwell, R.P., P. Schachter and B.H. Partee. (1973) *The Major Syntactic Structures of English*. New York: Holt, Rinehart and Winston, Inc.
Stuurman, F. (1987) 'Each other-one another: "There will always prove to be a difference"'. *English Studies*, 68: 353–360.
———. (1989) 'Each other-one another: To reciprocate'. *English Studies*, 70: 356–359.
———. (1990) *Two Grammatical Models of English: The Old and the New from A to Z*. London: Routledge.
Talmy, L. (1978) 'Figure and ground in complex sentences', in J. Greenberg, C. Ferguson and E. Moravcsik (eds.), *Universals of Human Language*, vol. IV. Stanford: Stanford University Press, 625–649.
———. (2000) *Towards a Cognitive Semantics, vol. I: Concept Structuring Systems*. Cambridge, MA: MIT Press.
Thielmann, P. (1892) 'Der Ersatz des Reciprocums im Lateinischen'. *Archiv für Lateinische Lexikographie und Grammatik*, 7: 342–388.
Tomasello, M. (2003) *Constructing a Language: A Usage-Based Theory of Language Acquisition*. Cambridge, MA: Harvard University Press.
———. (2005) 'Beyond formalities: The case of language acquisition'. *Linguistic Review*, 22: 183–196.
Trousdale, G. (2008) 'A constructional approach to lexicalization processes in the history of English: Evidence from possessive constructions'. *Word Structure*, 1: 156–177.
van der Kerke, S. (1998) 'Verb formation in Leko: Causatives, reflexives and reciprocals', in L. Kulikov and H. Vater (eds.), *Typology of Verbal Categories: Papers Presented to V. Nedjalkov on the Occasion of His 70th Birthday*. Tübingen: Niemeyer, 195–203.

van Gelderen, E. (2000) *A History of English Reflexive Pronouns*. Amsterdam: Benjamins.

Van Valin, R.D. (2005) *The Syntax-Semantics Interface: An Introduction to Role and Reference Grammar*. Cambridge: Cambridge University Press.

Van Valin, R.D., and R.J. LaPolla. (1997) *Syntax: Structure, Meaning and Function*. Cambridge: Cambridge University Press.

Visser, F.T. (1963) *An Historical Syntax of the English Language, Part 1: Syntactical Units with One Verb*. Leiden: Brill.

Wandruzska, U. (1973) 'Zur Syntax der symmetrischen Prädikate'. *Papiere zur Linguistik*, 5: 1–31.

Ward, G., B. Birner and R. Huddleston. (2002) 'Information packaging', in R. Huddleston and G.K. Pullum (eds.), *The Cambridge Grammar of the English Language*. Cambridge: Cambridge University Press, 1363–1474.

Wasow, T. (1977) 'Transformations and the lexicon', in P.W. Culicover, T. Wasow and A. Akmajian (eds.), *Formal Syntax*. New York: Academic Press, 327–360.

———. (2002) *Postverbal Behavior*. Stanford: CLSI Publications.

Wierzbicka, A. (1980) *Lingua Mentalis*. Sydney: Academic Press.

———. (2009) '"Reciprocity": An NSM approach to linguistic typology and social universals'. *Studies in Language*, 33: 103–174.

Williams, E. (1991) 'Reciprocal scope'. *Linguistic Inquiry*, 22: 159–173.

Winter, Y. (2001) 'Plural predication and the Strongest Meaning Hypothesis', *Journal of Semantics*, 18: 333–356.

Wischer, I. (2000) 'Grammaticalization versus lexicalization: Methinks there is some confusion', in O. Fischer, A. Rosenbach and D. Stein (eds.), *Pathways of Change: Grammaticalization in English*. Amsterdam: Benjamins, 355–370.

Zubin, D.A. (1979) 'Discourse function in morphology: The focus system of German', in T. Givón (ed.), *Syntax and Semantics*, vol. 12. New York: Academic Press, 469–504.

Index

For Product Safety Concerns and Information please contact our EU representative GPSR@taylorandfrancis.com Taylor & Francis Verlag GmbH, Kaufingerstraße 24, 80331 München, Germany

Batch number: 08153776

Printed by Printforce, the Netherlands